An Officer and a Lady

An Officer and a Lady

The World War II Letters of Lt. Col. Betty Bandel, Women's Army Corps

EDITED BY Sylvia J. Bugbee

WITH AN INTRODUCTION BY Lorry M. Fenner

University Press of New England

HANOVER AND LONDON

in Association with the Military Women's Press of the Women In Military Service For America Memorial Foundation, Arlington, Virginia

Published by University Press of New England, One Court Street, Lebanon, NH 03766
In association with the Military Women's Press of the Women In Military Service For America
Memorial Foundation
www.upne.com
© 2004 by Sylvia J. Bugbee
Printed in the United States of America
5 4 3 2 1

Library of Congress Cataloging-in-Publication Data
Bandel, Betty, 1912–
An officer and a lady : the World War II letters of Lt. Col. Betty Bandel, Women's Army Corps /
edited by Sylvia J. Bugbee ; with an introduction by Lorry M. Fenner.
    p.   cm.
Includes bibliographical references and index.
ISBN 1–58465–377–9 (alk. paper)
1. Bandel, Betty, 1912—Correspondence.   2. United States. Army. Women's Army Corps.
3. United States. Army—Women—Correspondence.   4. United States. Army—Officers—
Correspondence.   5. Women soldiers—United States—Correspondence.   6. World War,
1939–1945—Personal narratives, American.   7. World War, 1939–1945—Participation,
Female.   8. World War, 1939–1945—United States.   I. Bugbee, Sylvia J. II. Title.
D769.39.B36 2004
940.54′1273′082—dc22   2004007174

Permission to print Betty Bandel, Emma Frederick Bandel, and Bert and Helen Frederick's letters
is granted by Betty Bandel.
Permission to print David Brinegar's letters is granted by Becky Gill.
Permission to print Emily Brown's letters is granted by Christopher McGuire.
Permission to print Anne Dragonette's letter is granted by Anne Dragonette Lind.
Permission to print Marie Padgett Hamilton's letter is granted by Peggy Boliek, Emmie Padgett
Hileman, Martha Willis, and Dorothy W. Wittman.
Permission to print Fred Finney's letters is granted by Fred Finney, Jr.
Permission to print Jean Melin's letter is granted by Gordon J. Schmarzo.
Permission to print Dorothy Muni's letter is granted by Steven Muni.
Permission to print Mattie E. Treadwell's letters is granted by Mattie E. Treadwell.
Permission to print Janet C. Varn's letters is granted by Janet Varn Loadholtes.
Permission to print Anna Wilson's letter is granted by Margaret A. Byroads.

All letters are in the Betty Bandel Papers, Special Collections, Bailey-Howe Library, University of
Vermont, Burlington, Vermont.

CONTENTS

ACKNOWLEDGMENTS

Preparation of the letters for publication was supported in part by the generous support of Lilian Baker Carlisle, Sarah Dopp, and the University of Vermont Women's Studies Program; and by Betty Bandel.

I wish to thank Fiona Gagnon for her invaluable aid in transcription and proofreading, and for her research on biographical notes; also Linda Witt, Judy Bellafaire, Pat Jernigan, and Lois Beck of the Women In Military Service For America Memorial Foundation; and especially Betty Bandel and Sarah Dopp, for their indefatigable editing advice during the preparation of this book. I would also like to thank Connell Gallagher, Director for Research Collections at the Bailey/Howe Library, University of Vermont, for his support in obtaining funding for this project and in facilitating its preparation.

I am also indebted to Dr. Mark Stoler of the University of Vermont Department of History for his advice on sources for military history and on publishers; and to Edie Hinton and Charlotte Phillips, Women's Army Corps veterans and members of the U.S. Army Women Veterans' Association, for directing me to that organization and to the Women's Memorial Foundation, a journey that led to the publication of this book. I would like to thank the following people for advice and help on bibliographic and biographical sources: Colonel Lorry Fenner, USAF; Judy Bellafaire; Lieutenant Colonel Verb Washington, Ph.D., Engineers Combat Studies Institute, Army Command and General Staff School; Dr. Christopher Gabel, CGSC; and many others whom I contacted through their Web sites on military history.

Finally, I thank Betty Bandel for affording me the opportunity to enter the world of the Women's Army Corps in World War II. It opened my eyes to the importance of their contribution to the advancement of women in the twentieth century, a story that needs to be told.

Sylvia J. Bugbee

EDITOR'S NOTE

The letters in this book have been excerpted from the very long originals. Due to the extensive editing of some of the letters, ellipses to indicate deleted text have been omitted as they would have distracted the reader without contributing to the narrative.

After the first few letters from Bandel to her family, most salutations and signatures from such correspondence have been left out, as being redundant, and are understood to be the same as in the first letters. Likewise, since most of Bandel's letters were written from Washington, D.C., after the first few letters from there, the address is omitted and is understood to be Washington unless otherwise noted.

BIOGRAPHICAL SKETCH

Betty Bandel was born in Washington, D.C., in 1912 to middle-class, well-educated parents. The family moved to Tucson, Arizona, in 1918. One of two girls in a closely knit family, Bandel was especially close to her mother, Emma Frederick Bandel, a former actress, who not only supported her joining the army when it sought women to serve but was also clearly thrilled with her daughter's success in the Women's Army Auxiliary Corps (WAAC), which became the Women's Army Corps (WAC) in 1943 (*see illustration 2*).

Bandel graduated from the University of Arizona in 1933 with a degree in music and worked as a newspaperwoman for the *Arizona Daily Star* prior to joining the WAAC. Selected in June of 1942 to be one of the first, elite group of women to train at the Officer Candidate School at Fort Des Moines, Iowa, she served in the WAAC/WAC from 1942 to 1945. She was assigned to WAAC headquarters in Washington, D.C., having graduated second in her class at Fort Des Moines. Soon after, WAAC director Oveta Culp Hobby chose Bandel to serve as her aide. Serving at times as acting deputy director as well, Bandel rose quickly through the ranks, becoming a captain by late 1942 and a major in the spring of the following year. She was put in charge of the WAC Division of the Army Air Forces in 1943. She attained the rank of Lieutenant Colonel in January 1944 and received the Legion of Merit award for exceptionally meritorious service at the end of the war.

One of the most influential officers in the WAC during its early years, Bandel was often the mind behind planning and policy decisions effected by Director Hobby and the army command structure. Yet her avowed style was to remain outside the limelight. It was not uncertainty about her own value to the Corps that kept her behind the scenes; her letters prove that. It was just that planning, not administration, was what she felt most comfortable doing.

After the war, Bandel entered graduate school in English at Columbia University, attaining her Ph.D. in 1951. Her dissertation, "Shakespeare's Treatment of the Social Position of Women," argued that women prior to the early modern period in England had considerable autonomy and personal freedom within a certain sphere, a stance that has begun to receive more attention recently in the field of women's history. She was recruited from Columbia to teach English at the University of Vermont in 1947, where she became an inspiring teacher of English literature, retiring in 1975. Her many students still recall her rigorous but exhilarating classes in expository writing and in Shakespeare.

Since that time, true to the philosophy that served her so well in the WAC of never resting on her laurels, Bandel has published numerous books and articles on Vermont history, early New England music, and Shakespeare. In 2001, she was honored by her colleagues and friends for her long service to the university and to the Vermont historical community. One of her former English Department colleagues offered perhaps the most cogent statement about Bandel's life, and about her very essence. Gender, she said, was irrelevant to Betty. A person's worth is not defined by her sex but by her abilities and her utilization of those abilities, and Bandel expected that she would be judged accordingly. It is the principle upon which she has lived her long, very rich, and admirable life.

INTRODUCTION TO THE LETTERS

Lorry M. Fenner

For many today the face of women in the modern American military is that of Jessica Lynch or Lori Piestewa or Shoshana Johnson—a racially diverse group of young enlisted army women, close to the fight, injured, killed, or taken captive. The American public has seen these and other brave military women, officer and enlisted, most recently in Afghanistan and Iraq—air force, navy, Marine Corps, army, and Coast Guard as well as the reserves, National Guard, and merchant marine. We started seeing more and more media coverage of women in the armed forces from the Panama intervention to Gulf War I to the USS *Cole* bombing. Their presence, injuries, and deaths have become so commonplace that, if they warrant it at all, they do not hold our attention long—as happened with air force Lieutenant Tamara Archuleta, the young helicopter copilot who died March 23, 2003, flying a humanitarian mission in Afghanistan while all eyes were on the invasion of Iraq.

Still, many Americans have been asking, how did so many women come to be in the military? How did military women come to be so close to the "front lines?" If we have another draft, will women be included? Most of those who are asking have very little sense of the history of women in the American military, or the history of women in war more generally. Ideas that women have not been a part of war are based predominantly on a visceral, cultural ideology about "women's place." People know that women do serve and have served in leadership positions in business, sports, religion, academe, and politics, but something about that ideology gives them pause when women are too high in the hierarchy or, more specifically, in what is believed to be an arena dominated by men. Military women still surprise us.

Betty Bandel and her compatriots were not the first women to support the nation in wartime or to serve with the military. Women's military service has a long evolution in America. Female colonists took up arms and stood beside men to carve out places in their new land and to defend it against other settlers, as well as against the Native Americans who tried to reclaim it. During the Revolutionary War, legendary figures such as Molly Pitcher and the real Deborah Sampson represented the tradition of women actively participating in conflict. Women served in support roles, some joining the nascent medical corps as nurses or matrons, and some dressing as and fighting alongside men in the Continental army and the militia. Women were essential to that war effort.

This eighteenth-century Revolutionary War experience, based on practical

needs arising from the merging of home front and battlefield, was largely repeated in our nineteenth-century Civil War. Women served as soldiers, scouts,
saboteurs, and spies. Many more joined relief associations on both sides of the
conflict. In this first industrialized war, with machinery improving the lethality
and range of weapons, and casualties and disease continuing to hamper military efficiency, women's medical contributions were most significant. But despite their contributions, after the Civil War all female doctors and nurses were
dismissed. During the Spanish-American War the surgeon general contracted
civilian nurses to serve overseas and on the hospital ship USS *Relief.* The effectiveness of the nurses' service, as well as the army's desire for more control
over them, led to the founding of the Army Nurse Corps in 1901; the Navy
Nurse Corps followed in 1908. Military and civilian leaders' concerns about
limiting the possibilities of women commanding male soldiers and officers led
to the nurse corps being established but not being an official part of the services; these women served without formal military rank and did not receive
benefits equal to those of male veterans; and female doctors were not accepted
for service at all.

In the early twentieth century, these military nurses led the way in altering
public and military perceptions of women's capabilities. During the First World
War over 21,000 army and 1,400 navy nurses served, and many were decorated
for valor. Almost 10,000 women served overseas and, as in earlier and subsequent conflicts, some were wounded, some were taken prisoner, and some gave
their lives. In recognition of their substantive contributions the commander of
the American Expeditionary Forces, General "Black Jack" Pershing, and military medical officers supported "relative rank" for female nurses in 1920; they
could wear "officer rank" but were not afforded commensurate pay, privileges,
or command responsibilities.

Beyond the medical arena, manpower was critical to the armed forces in
World War I but often in short supply. Secretary of the Navy Josephus Daniels
led the way to a solution by enlisting women as clerical personnel under the
designation Yeomen (F). Joining a few in the Coast Guard, over 11,000 women
served in the naval reserves and another 300 enlisted in the marine reserves.
Most served in administrative billets, but several were designated draftsmen,
recruiters, camouflage designers, translators, and messengers.

In contrast to the navy's approach, the army civilian leaders wanted nothing
to do with women during World War I even while military officers in the field
demanded their help. When General Pershing finally requested civilian French
speakers for his Signal Corps, some 200 women were sent to Europe. Nearly
5,000 other American women joined them as volunteers with various civilian
agencies to serve his troops. Benefits, while better for women in the Marine
Corps, were still not equal, and all these women were discharged after the war.
Women won the vote in 1920, partly in recognition of their service and other

contributions in World War I, but that did not constitute a broad expansion of political and economic roles for them.

Very little was done during the interwar years to actually organize women for the next emergency, despite the recognition that industrialized warfare required vast armies and the associated administration and infrastructure to maintain them—areas where women could be, and were previously, used effectively. Congresswoman Edith Nourse Rogers (Massachusetts, Republican), in her attempts to gain recognition and benefits for American women who had served overseas during World War I, furthered some thinking on future and further integration.

While the War Department killed legislative attempts to form a women's corps, in 1925 the army appointed Major Martin Hughes to study the formation of such a corps in case of a future emergency. In her letters Betty Bandel mentions meeting Martin Hughes later and recognizing that he had actually come up with a plan. In fact there were two such plans. Anita Phipps, whom the secretary of war had appointed to the War Department as Director of Women's Relations in 1920, had been tasked with combating American women's "growing pacifism." She resigned in frustration in 1930 but left behind her own plan as well. If Colonel Oveta Culp Hobby, the first director of the WAAC, had seen these plans, some of the initial mistakes in the organization and utilization of the army women might have been prevented. Typical of military bureaucracy even today, the earlier plans were ignored until after the fact.

As World War II began in Asia and Europe, the debate about women's appropriate place in society grew louder. Despite a lot of support for women contributing to the waging of this "total war," some opposition against their crossing the boundaries of cultural ideology resurfaced. Yet World War II was probably the most significant war in U.S. history in setting the foundations for the contemporary utilization of women by our military. It was the first American war in which large numbers of women served "in" the armed forces rather than as volunteers "with" the services. During the 1940s, military women's duties went beyond nursing and other traditional functions to a greater extent than in previous conflicts. And since it was the first time that women were formally incorporated into the nation's military, it took a great deal of planning, guesswork, policy formulation, and effort for these almost 300,000 women to make an effective contribution in that great national endeavor. Beginning in World War II, the military found ways to effectively use a large number of women—first segregated into a separate organization (WAAC), then integrated into the army in a separate women's corps (WAC), and finally fully integrated in the 1980s. But this was a long process.

As in earlier periods, before and during World War II Americans could and did look to the example of foreign women involved in the conflict overseas. Chinese women were fighting, British women were mobilized as civilians and in the military, all over Europe women had joined resistance organizations—and many of them, including eventually thousands of Russian women, would make the ultimate sacrifice as part of militaries resisting Nazi invasion and occupation. American women and the larger public had a clear view of what these women were doing from accounts in the contemporary media.[1] In addition, women in the 1930s were making great strides in sports, business, and aviation, as well as in academe. Achievements in all these areas helped women transition into the military.

At home, as war loomed, American women both argued for inclusion in the armed forces and formed their own preparedness organizations to lend a hand. From the late 1930s until the WAAC and WAVES (navy: Women Accepted for Voluntary Emergency Service), as well as the civilian Women's Air Ferry Service (WAFS) and Women Air Service Pilots (WASP) were formed, numerous organizations benefited from the contributions of those mostly upper-middle-class white women who could afford the time and expense of participating.

In the period immediately preceding U.S. entry into the war, Franklin Roosevelt called for rearmament and in September 1939 announced a "limited national emergency" that included moral and logistical support for England and France. With the start of America's first peacetime draft in September of 1940, the public stepped up home front preparations for possible involvement more than a year before the attack on Pearl Harbor. Women were no strangers to these preparations, and some of their involvement was decidedly martial as they joined veterans' and preparedness units.

Despite our historical memory to the contrary, many women worked outside the home during the 1930s and early 1940s. Most did so out of necessity either as single women or because their husbands did not earn wages enough to support the family. Increasing industrialization to aid U.S. allies and increased defense industry production created better-paying jobs for many women (and minority men) as more men were called to arms. White middle-class women worked in the service sector and professions, and their opportunities increased too as that sector expanded in the 1930s and 1940s and as more men were drafted. Some working women found time to volunteer outside the home, but more women of means increasingly volunteered for community service in organizations like air-raid warning units, firefighting brigades, and ambulance and hospital groups. Members of these organizations frequently created and wore uniforms. The Molly Pitcher Brigade, Inc., trained women in marksmanship, ambulance driving, air-raid safety, and first aid. The Daughters of the American Revolution (DAR) called on members to be ready for the defense of their communities, and the Daughters of the Defenders of the Republic held weekly "drills" for first aid and ambulance training, physical fitness, and discipline. The Women Defense Cadets of America (part of the American Women's Association) drilled under an army officer's supervision; this group emphasized exercise, first aid, mechanics, and "heavy driving." The United States

Women's Defense Corps, started in July 1940, boasted 3,000 members at its inception. In addition, the Green Guards trained members in shooting, marching, driving, and air-raid service. The National Federation of Business and Professional Women and the American Association of University Women not only supported these volunteers for emergency service but started taking steps to pass legislation to create a women's corps like the Yeomen (F) of World War I or the British auxiliaries. Colonel Julius Ochs Adler, retired civilian aide to Secretary of War Henry Stimson, even told women they might be drafted for emergency defensive service. A contemporary Gallup poll reflected that the public felt that women had an equal military responsibility to defend the nation in "total war" and that a statement like "women's place is in the home . . . sounds too much like Hitler."[2]

Administration, military, and legislative efforts to militarize women gained momentum just before, and immediately after, the attack on Pearl Harbor and would finally succeed in 1942 with women in the army, navy, Coast Guard, and marines joining military nurses serving either "with" or "in" the services.[3] Despite the example of British and other women pilots, American female pilots first joined the WAFS and then the WASP as civilian war workers. Later, female pilots served in the Army Air Forces and Marine Corps as flight and link trainer instructors. All the nonmedical women would be temporary, and reserve members and the terms of their service differed in each branch as to pay, benefits, whether they could be married at all or married to military men, and whether they could have children or other dependents.

Congresswoman Edith Nourse Rogers had continued to fight for veterans' benefits for the American women who had served overseas during World War I, and by 1940 she had proposed several plans to enlist women in preparation for another war. She wanted to make sure that they were adequately trained and that pay equity and benefits would be arranged in advance to prevent further unjust treatment after the fact. Before the end of 1941, military leaders joined her call for the enlistment of women. General Emmons asked the government to induct 25,000 women for air-raid work, saying they should be promised commissions, equitable pay, and attractive uniforms. He wanted women in the army, as in the British example, in order to facilitate better discipline than was possible in civilian auxiliaries or volunteer organizations.

Immediately after the Japanese attack, the War Department led the way as Secretary Stimson lent his support when Rogers reintroduced her bill to the House Military Affairs Committee at the end of December, as did Secretary of the Navy Frank Knox and Army Chief of Staff George Marshall, in January 1942. Some maintain that the War Department supported Rogers only because the military chiefs wanted to shape the bill and control the form the women's services took, since they thought passage was inevitable. Whether this was true or not, the bill would give female volunteers, age twenty-one through forty-five, noncombat duties under women officers; Mrs. Roosevelt endorsed it as well. Throughout January, February, and March women tried to enlist even before the bill was passed. But because there was still some opposition in committee it took General Marshall's public comments of support to get the measure to a vote in the full House by mid-February.[4]

As the debate raged in the House, Representative Rogers read letters on the floor from women in forty-six states, Hawaii, and the District of Columbia who were anxious to join. Despite some opposition, the bill made the front page of the *New York Times* when it passed the House 249 to 86 on March 17, 1942.

In the meantime, Alabama's Senator Hill had introduced a companion measure in the Senate in February to which there appeared to be no concrete opposition into March. At the same time both the Senate and House were acting on a bill to bring women into the navy, creating an issue for the army's bill, which called for women only to serve "with" that service as auxiliaries. When General Marshall told the Senate that he really wanted women "in" the army as well, the army bill was sent back for a rewrite. The Senate, however, declined a formal request by the army to this effect even though it passed the navy's similar measure.[5]

By May an impatient army was ready to accept whatever it could get from Congress, and the Senate passed the women's auxiliary measure 38 to 27 on May 12, 1942, without an amendment to restrict their service to the continental United States as the WAVES initially were. Franklin Roosevelt signed the Rogers bill into law on May 15, 1942, and named Oveta Culp Hobby as director of the WAAC. At the same time Marshall announced that he and she had been working on plans for the organization since September of 1941.

Despite this prior planning, after passage of the law the army had to ask volunteers to wait two weeks so that it could make preparations for testing and in-processing. Women rushed to 440 recruiting stations, with the first to enlist being Mrs. Jayne House. Her husband, also a volunteer, and her eight-year-old daughter were completely supportive. The latter said she intended to sign up as soon as she was able. In fact, recruiting was front-page news as 13,208 women applied for the first 440 officer slots.[6] As we find out in her letters, Bandel was one of the few accepted to train as an officer so that enlisted women could be recruited by women and put under female leadership.

Arizona newspaperwoman Betty Bandel served in the leadership of the WAAC and Women's Army Corps (WAC) at this critical moment in our nation's history and at a significant time of women's progress socially, economically, and politically. Through her letters we learn a great deal about wartime America, cultural understandings of "women's place," society's view of women in this nontraditional realm of the military, and about the rapidly expanding national capital—wartime Washington, D.C. Like memoirs and oral histories, Bandel's firsthand accounts of and keen insight into current events, and her descriptions of famous and not-so-famous people, bring this period vividly to life.

Beyond the war effort, what was important to the nation and to women during the three years of these personal letters, 1942 to 1945, was the expansion of women's roles in the political realm and social and economic arenas. For many women, their confidence increased with their horizons. A world of new possibilities for their future was opened, not just in the military, but in work, politics, government administration, academe, and community service, far beyond the disappointments of the 1920s and 1930s that had followed the suffrage victory of the Nineteenth Amendment. This view of the expansion of opportunities for women should not be diminished by the fact that many women who took on new roles during the war years returned to more traditional pursuits after the war. The blinders had come off, the windows had been opened, and the doors pushed ajar. Even if numerous boundaries (and ceilings) were left intact or rebuilt after 1945, more women, and men, had come to believe that women could overcome them. This new optimism and belief would make all the difference to those who fought for broader inclusion in the 1960s and 1970s and who continue the struggle even today.

Military women, in particular, benefited from the efforts of Bandel and her contemporaries. While Bandel and other female wartime leaders were focused on supporting the armed services in their war efforts and did not set out to generally improve the lot of women, their examples of efficiency and effective contributions, and the administrative groundwork they laid, formed the foundations from which many would work when the postwar permanent women's service components were formed. Despite some of the detractors' arguments against women in the services before, during, and after the war, or even today, congressmen, servicemen, and male officers would not be able to dismiss the success of military women during World War II, nor the respect that these women had earned from the American people and military leadership.

Bandel's letters are very personal and practical and reflect her intelligence and wit. One can enjoy her references to her home and friends in Arizona, her explanations and entreaties to her mother to visit her in basic training and Washington, and her obvious love for her newspaper work before the war. Readers will marvel at the way she enters the service with a keen eye for the bureaucratic and military necessities that might seem silly to the uninitiated. She is absolutely unflappable and keeps good humor in the face of stressors to which others might have responded with frustration, irritation, and anger. She is a shrewd judge of character, and charitable but savvy in describing the relative strengths and weaknesses of her peers and superiors, male and female.

Bandel's writings address many of the difficulties military women faced: the challenges of starting a huge organization of military women from scratch; negative reactions to female military service from some military leaders and male soldiers; and the military's frequent misuse of women's education and skills. On the public's reaction to the 1943 WAC "Scandal" or "Whispering Campaign," she writes: "The rumors—about wholesale immorality and stuff—

are utterly without foundations. If I weren't in uniform, and having to be respectable, I would punch the noses of a couple of reporters in this town—their disregard of standard newspaper ethics in regard to checking the accuracy of what they write is shocking." But she also revels in the things the government and military do right, including visiting and working with the British and Canadian military women; designing a recruiting effort that responds to the difficulties of the too rapid initial growth of the WAAC; developing military, specialty, and management schools for army women; persuading the Pentagon bureaucracy to more fully and appropriately utilize women; and implementing an effective demobilization campaign at the end of the war.

We do not learn much from Bandel's letters about women in the other services or about minority women in the military or in society at the time, but her offhand references to race and religion as well as "regionalism" can be revealing and a starting point for other researchers. Bandel clearly has a soft spot for southerners; she invariably describes southern female officers as well mannered, soft and sweet in appearance, and wonderfully well spoken. Although we know that segregation in the Corps was the rule, Bandel does not discuss it at all. She also does not talk much about the war itself, perhaps due to her knowledge of the censors' sensitivities and her position as removed from the actual fighting. Bandel's personal evaluations of women she meets in her short military career, their various professions and educational backgrounds and their status as wives and mothers, are also revealing.

First and foremost we learn, through her letters, about the many women who are working long, tedious hours over days and months to lead, manage, and administer all women who are joining the military to support the war effort. As Bandel describes it, "[We] work at such a pitch that I try to conduct my business something like a newspaper city room, with enough breaks from concentration and enough laughter to keep us from losing our balance—and work, work, work as I swear no other two stenographers in the Pentagon work." Bandel also discusses the difficult conditions sometimes faced by these women in wartime Washington and at training centers and bases around the country. And we do get a sense of the importance of the fight overseas and their efforts to support it. We also learn a bit about those women who are working even harder under more challenging conditions overseas, from North Africa to Latin America to the South Pacific to the Far East. Some of these women, she tells us, were rescued from torpedoed troop transports, and some gave their lives in service to the nation.

Bandel's letters and her oral testimony are unselfconscious. It is obvious she is amazed and amused at the times and situations in which she finds herself. She is determined to do the best job she can and live up to the surprising (to her) regard in which she is held by the senior leadership of the women's services and military. We are lucky that she could type, that she took the time to write many letters, that many survived, and that she had a newswoman's eye for detail and a good story.

Bandel's lack of self-conscious feminism does not detract from her accomplishments nor from our views of other women leaders that come to us in her writing. On the one hand, the definitive book on Oveta Culp Hobby has yet to be written. Our glimpse of her from Bandel's letters shows how much that needs to be done. On the other hand, while we have exhaustive treatments of Eleanor Roosevelt, we can still learn more about her through these letters. Bandel alludes more than once to Mrs. Roosevelt's indefatigable energy. She also recalls a moving vignette of the first lady's visit to a military base in England, where she was to inspect a group of men and women soldiers. It was pouring rain, and the enlisted were soaked. Mrs. Roosevelt got out of her limousine, pushed aside the umbrella offered by someone from the State Department, and walked down the entire row of soldiers, talking to each one. Elsewhere, Bandel introduces other leaders who are less well known but were essential to establishing the future of women in the military services, including Westray Battle Boyce, who directed the WAC in North Africa and later followed Hobby as director of the WAC, and Jessie Rice, who established and led the first WAC management school at Purdue University.

Even this researcher, who has studied military women extensively, learned much from Bandel's letters about the first WAC officers' attendance at the army's Command and General Staff School at Leavenworth and about the organization of the Wacs at their headquarters in Washington. Most importantly, I came to know many of the women who have been identified in secondary sources (and others never mentioned in current historical narratives) as real persons. These letters are most amazing in their ability to paint such portraits.

Although Bandel does not refer much to race in her letters, press accounts of the formation and beginning of the Corps do. During the debates over the army and navy bills race was a major concern. Director of the National Negro Council Edgar G. Brown urged that the army accept women of all races, and the House's acting chairman of the Military Affairs Committee, Ewing Thompson, agreed. Senator McNary's proposed racial nondiscrimination amendment to the WAAC bill passed unanimously, but it was not included in the navy version. Black men in the navy at that time were segregated and given menial jobs. There were no black naval officers in 1942.[7] But by May, McNary's amendment was omitted, and the *New York Times* reported that Eleanor Roosevelt, despite her support for most antidiscrimination measures, did not think this one necessary since "the Constitution protected all people from discrimination." The army promised that omitting the amendment would not affect its plans to include black women and that it would not discriminate against them. This did not mean the army would not segregate. Black leaders were not only unhappy that the McNary amendment was not included in the final WAAC legislation.

They also opposed the appointment of a southerner, Oveta Hobby, as director. Not attacking her directly, they complained of the "lily white traditions and Jim Crow practices" of her home state, Texas. To compensate they asked that President of the National Council on Negro Women Mary McLeod Bethune (mentioned in Bandel's letters) be appointed assistant director of the WAAC. Although Bethune was not appointed, Hobby gained some support when she announced that forty black women would be accepted for officer training to provide leadership for two black companies and that black auxiliaries would be recruited in proportion to their numbers in the population. While African-American women were included, they were not integrated with white women. Moreover, although the army protested that the rumor was not true, the press reported that at least some people believed that black Waacs were being enlisted so that black soldiers would have social outlets overseas. In contrast, Native American and Japanese-American women recruits were treated differently by the press, as their enlistment served great propaganda value; and they were not segregated. The official WAC policy on segregation was to follow army practice—army official policy was to follow "local customs" for the area in which troops were stationed. In reality, the army never followed its "official policy" but rather segregated black soldiers through the duration of the war.[8]

As only obliquely referred to in Bandel's letters, opposition to creating women's military services revolved around three arguments: women would hurt military effectiveness because they would not be able to handle the physical or emotional stress; their participation would harm their femininity; and their participation would destroy the home and our American culture. Early in 1942 opponents to legislation allowing women into the armed forces believed that women had enough to do in the war industries and at home, and that other legislation was more important. Critics claimed that while civilian nurses and clerks helped the military, the idea of women in the military, including the World War I yeomen (F), was just silly. Congressmen Hoffman (Michigan), Somers (New York), Randolph (West Virginia) and Hare (South Carolina) opposed the bill, arguing that women's place was at home and enlisting them would be a poor reflection on American men.

Through their service, military men who actually served with women were soon converted, realizing that women could do some jobs better than men could and other jobs just as well. Military leaders came to realize that their manpower problem could best be solved by tapping into this pool of willing (while men were being conscripted) and usually better-educated volunteers. The army was reportedly eager to get its first female soldiers and requested 80,000 to start. Military leaders were even more impressed as they witnessed those first women excel in training at Fort Des Moines with their only fault (as Bandel confirms) being that some of them worked too hard. In addition, foreign examples showed that women were taking on more and more roles and responsibilities in countries that were in far more dire straits in the war, and that these women were performing magnificently.[9]

The American public was divided on the issue despite what seemed a clear majority in favor of women serving in the armed forces. Catholic leadership, in particular, was outspoken in opposing "another threat to the sanctity of the home" and to the foundations "of a true Christian and democratic country." Massachusetts Bishop James Cassidy went so far as to ask Catholic women not to join the WAAC, claiming it was contrary to the teachings and principles of the church. Others argued that our national soul would be lost even if the war was won.[10]

In addition to public opposition, some press treatment belittled and trivialized the idea of military women and emphasized congressional opposition, citing concerns about morals and the possible breakdown of the American family. *Newsweek,* in particular, focused on the free girdle to be issued each army recruit with headlines like "New Women's Army Will Girdle 25,000 for War." And *Time* must have scared many a parent and husband or fiancé when it reported that Margaret Sanger had suggested that the army should give all Waacs contraceptive information, as it did for men.[11]

Although Bandel does not discuss military nurses much in her letters, the debate about the WAAC is informed by their presence. Nurses had served, and were serving, overseas and in harm's way. On the one hand, knowing that these women were in danger made people aware that enlisting more women might make the danger greater. On the other hand, nurses were proving that women could stand up to deprivation, danger, combat, and prison. By 1942 the media were reporting on the military nurses on Bataan and Corregidor who had been captured by the Japanese. These women, and others who survived the attack on Pearl Harbor and assisted its male defenders, received military decorations for bravery and for their injuries. Military nurses arrived in North Africa in December 1942, and Waacs followed close behind.[12]

After the bill authorizing navy servicewomen finally became law in late summer, it highlighted the difference between the army auxiliaries and the WAVES. The Senate then started to consider equalizing the women's pay because WAAC recruiting was suffering by comparison. The pay bill easily passed both houses by late October of 1942, but in November Representative Rogers introduced legislation to solve the larger problem by transforming the WAAC into the Women's Army Corps, as General Marshall had originally wanted.

At the same time that the army was prepared to ask for many more women, opposition continued. It soon erupted in the 1943 "rumor campaign" of WAAC immorality, which would hurt WAC recruiting. (In some ways similar opposition persists today.) Despite earlier opposition and other issues that had impeded recruiting, later in the war women were criticized for *not* joining; men were criticized for not wanting wives and daughters to join; and the public was reassured that women would return home immediately after the war, and that female veterans would be better wives and mothers for the experience.

In the face of such opposition before and during the war, Bandel and her contemporaries showed us the way as competent women. But they were never "on a mission" to do anything but serve the nation, manage the WAC efficiently to support the war effort, and take care of the members of the WAC as people and as resources. In doing so they performed brilliantly and laid the groundwork on which military women's efforts and achievements still rest today. In fact, advances in many areas in the years between 1960 and today owe much to these women who served during World War II. Many of them returned to academe or the professions after the war, and others utilized their GI Bill benefits and other veterans' programs, belatedly bestowed, to go beyond what they might have thought possible before their life-altering wartime experience. Others returned to home and family but kept the dreams of additional possibilities alive for their daughters and granddaughters.

Waacs and Wacs of the World War II era and later have said in interviews that they thought the disbanding of the WAC as a separate entity in 1978 and the integration of women into regular army units was not a good thing for women. While this integration may have been necessary for women to gain greater parity, what many modern researchers fail to grasp is that for the past two decades army women have no longer learned of women's past experiences in the military. Prior to the integration, part of WAC training included presentations on the creation and role of the WAC during previous American wars. This information and knowledge, including the role of Wacs during World War II, has been lost to young female soldiers today. They no longer "meet" these women—Betty Bandel and thousands of others—who faced the challenges to become an absolutely essential part of the American military during the Second World War. These older stories and also contemporary stories that garner a bit of the media's and public's attention should be incorporated into today's training of recruits.

Policy makers, social and political historians, and both male and female military members can truly enjoy and learn from these unmediated letters home from a truly remarkable military woman. Because of Betty Bandel, all of us can better appreciate how Jessica, Lori, and Shoshana came to represent the face of American women in our first twenty-first-century war.

An Officer and a Lady

CHAPTER I

Basic Training

In the late spring of 1942, the war in Europe and Africa is not going well for the Allies. Hitler has overrun much of western Europe, and Rommel's panzers are advancing in North Africa against the British. The United States, having entered the war after the Japanese attack on Pearl Harbor on December 7, 1941, is frantically building up its armed forces in preparation for joining the Allies in Europe and the Far East. The newly formed Women's Army Auxiliary Corps (WAAC) is gearing up to become a part of that effort when newspaperwoman Betty Bandel, at work at the *Arizona Daily Star* in Tucson, hears the word: the WAAC is calling for women to enroll. Remembering her decision to join, Bandel says, "I was sitting at my desk, and Emily Brown was in the [newspaper] morgue getting some stories out, and she called to me and she said, 'Hey Bandel, they're organizing a women's army.' I said, 'Who is?' And she said, 'The United States.' And I said 'Well, let's join.' So we walked down the street and did." When asked what had prompted her to do so, she replied, "That's a funny question. What else would there have been for an unmarried woman except to be in the service one way or another? Everybody was in something. And so you naturally went in."[1]

For Bandel, joining the army was both an obligation and a joyous adventure. From the moment of her decision to join and throughout all of her career in the Women's Army Corps, her zest for the military life and her intense dedication to helping win the war are made vividly apparent in her letters home to her family in Tucson. But equally, these letters document her transformation from a fresh enrollee and greenhorn officer, awestruck in the presence of the famous people she meets while serving as aide to Director Oveta Culp Hobby, to a confident, mature woman, aware of her own worth, and one of the highest-ranking woman officers in the army. This is the story of her time in the Women's Army Corps, in her own words. Interspersed among her own letters are those from family, friends, and fellow Wacs. Bandel's colleague Emily Brown, who persuaded her to join the WAAC, appears often on these pages in counterpoint to Bandel's story. The tale of Brown's checkered career as she flunks out of Officer Candidate School, re-ups as an auxiliary, and trains to be a radio operator, eventually to achieve success as an officer in public relations, tells a story of the enlisted Wac.[2]

How do Bandel's family, friends, and the public view her success, and what do they think about women joining the military? Clearly, her family is behind her 100 percent. And throughout this and subsequent chapters, Bandel hears from friends and colleagues who not only applaud her success but are also thoroughly in favor of the WAAC idea. Some of them encounter goodwill toward Waacs both from military men and from civilians. As one army friend from Tucson puts it, "I think the feeling that [Waacs] are fellow soldiers is very general."[3] Even the governor of Arizona writes, "We are all proud, in Arizona, of the fine type of women and the good showing being made by our representatives in the WAAC."[4] That there are naysayers and those adamantly against women being in the military will also become apparent, but Bandel's friends and many of the people of Tucson are not among them.

Here, Bandel begins her epic adventure—on a train en route to Salt Lake City with other applicants for Officer Candidate School. After her interview in Salt Lake City, she will be one of only 440 selected from 10,000 women to be the first group of officers trained at Fort Des Moines in Iowa. This chapter relates her often hilarious, invariably enthusiastic account of basic training.

1.   *Betty Bandel to her family;*

She is en route to Salt Lake City.

June 20, 1942 [Phoenix]

Dear Family—

Please pardon stationery—I am at one hotel, & my stationery is at another. We are having an uproarious time—the army is paying our way, on the usual "recruit basis." That is to say, we go in flocks, have a meal ticket for the whole bunch cashable at the "Busy Bee" café, a room ticket cashable at the Portland Hotel—room with wash-stand, 75 cents. Emily [Brown] signed the tickets, & thus if the 5 of us from Tucson want to eat, we have to find her. The motherly old soul who presides at the Portland let out a whoop when she heard we were on an army pass. "Well, you're the first ones anything like you we've had," says she. The finance sergeant assured us the hotel was clean and "had no women— you know what I mean." Emily said she wanted to answer, "Well, it will have tonight, & you know what *I* mean." Tomorrow the whole pack of us—13 for the entire state—will entrain at 9 a.m. again on a group pass. This time we will get $1 per meal, plus Pullman accommodations. It broke Emily's heart that I ate only 40¢ of my 60¢ lunch ticket, & she figures if she has to eat a whole dollar's worth every meal from here to Salt Lake, to get her money's worth, she will be overweight again. We may stay right on the post at Fort Douglas if there is a hostess' house. Of the 13 going, we have Pat Peters, Emily, me, Edna Floyd (bookkeeper & ex-Florida schoolteacher), & Gwen Watson (physical ed. teacher at Safford) from Tucson.

The other 8 are all Phoenix—1 lawyer, 1 teacher, the rest office workers & housewives. Of the 3 housewives (all prominent Legion women)[5] 1 has 4 children (including a baby of $3\frac{1}{2}$), & one is an ex-physiotherapist & World War I veteran. She & the little redhead brainbox are the only 2 Phoenicians I would bet on.

Everybody looks at us as at a circus sideshow when they find out our mission. Personally, I shall consider this a first-rate vacation, no matter what happens. I am being very lazy, & am being led around whenever a sergeant or anybody yells "Fall in!"

Tell Anne my four-leaf clover is right with me.[6]

Love, Betty

2. *Betty Bandel to Mrs. Bandel*

A Western Union telegram.

June 24, 1942
[Salt Lake City]

SURVIVED INTERVIEW. FEAR BOARD MOST INTRIGUED BY TRUMPET BACKGROUND. WURRA WURRA. HOME EARLY FRIDAY. SALT LAKE WONDERFUL.[7] LOVE BETTY.

3. *Uncle Bert and Aunt Helen Frederick to Betty Bandel*

The Fredericks write to Bandel upon her selection for Officer Candidate School. They live in Pittsburgh, Pennsylvania.

July 17, 1942.

Dear Betty:

We are thrilled—thrilled and more thrilled. Congratulations on your accomplishment. We know you have worked hard and it must take what you have to have you make the grade.

I believe you will find this even better than you had hoped for from the Navy, and if you don't become a General by Sept. 1st, I'll be disappointed. This is going to be a wonderful experience for you—something you probably will only go through once in a lifetime—and I hope you find real pleasure and enjoyment in it. This takes me back 25 years and I just wonder what it will mean to all you women. I mean just how you will handle it and how it will affect you. Your leaving is going to be a blow to Mater—but her pride in your achievement and her determination will carry her through.

If you can wear my old Sam Brown belt—or my should[er] bars, which are out of style, I think—you are welcome to them.[8]

Love and good wishes to you from us both, Lieutenant.

4.   *Betty Bandel to her family*

She is en route to Fort Des Moines, Iowa, to commence officer training. Bracketed text in this letter is in the original.

July 18, 1942

Dear Family—

Ten minutes into El Paso—on time, after making up 50 minutes! All fun so far—one amazing spectacle (peculiar red hair, gap-toothed, practical nurse, was once connysoor of good foods when she had money ["before the crash"]) and 22 other very nice people. I like the three truck drivers best—one a former phys. ed teacher, one a doctor's assistant, one an honest-to-goodness truck driver.[9] One cook—she really a housewife & former nutrition expert. We have both dressing rooms—one at each end of car—& can smoke. The soldiers can't come in & spend the day.

I think this is going to be a lazy life, for me. I seem to have no urge to do 18 things at once—I just sit back & let people wait on me & read the time table & my book. As a matter of fact, the last week has been a rest, despite the hectic pace—I wonder if I'll ever see the inside of a newspaper office again? More anon.

5.   *Betty Bandel to Mrs. Bandel*

She is still en route to Fort Des Moines.

July 19, 1942

[Imitating a news release] WITH THE WAAC, USA, SOMEWHERE IN THE NEW MEXICAN DESERT, JULY 19—(AP)—The Rock Island [Railroad], bless its little heart, believes in the old saw about an army travelling on its stomach. For breakfast this morning we had tomato juice, oatmeal, two eggs, four slices of bacon, two pieces of toast, strawberry jam, butter, and coffee. Also the very observing steward, who took Helen Harris' meal check for 19 and mine for two, noticed that Helen was travelling with 18 Waac's, but that I was travelling with "one enlisted man."[10] He liked that. The train crews all think we are great fun—

the fatherly old conductor salutes whenever he sees us. It is fun to have the whole car to ourselves—I have always wanted to use a men's dressing room, because of all the extra space they seem to have. Except for this one red-headed woman, who will probably get tossed out on her ear as soon as the army gets hold of her—everybody on the car seems a nice sort, very earnest about the army business, and what I would call good material. There is a cute little Mexican girl from Willcox, signed on as a truck driver, whom I like particularly, never got beyond grade school, and has been a maid, among other things, but is bright as they come.

Everybody is settled into his particular amusement. Mrs. Reilly is reading the manual of infantry drill (which she let me study a bit yesterday) and an imposing book on the organization of the army. Bessie is typing on the other side of the table from me. Last night I taught Bessie and Helen Harris the round about "A Southerly Wind"—it works beautifully.[11]

You will all be glad to know I got my hair up this morning. Gwen was full of tall promises last night to do it, but this morning (as always with her) I had to beat a tattoo on her two or three times before she would become even half conscious. Maw, you should have come with me. Susan Faherty's mother, a lady in her eighties, came with Susan. Susan had to get a special dispensation to get her on the car with us, and the two of them are occupying the drawing room at the end of the car.

The El Paso paper says we are to be met at the train, and that the enlisted men made up our beds for us—for the first and last time. The auxiliaries and officer candidates are to be housed together in the old post barracks until new barracks can be built for the auxiliaries. I am getting anxious to begin work— I betcha it will be fun. We get in at about 7 tomorrow morning.

Well, that is about all so far. Everything is going smoothly—too smoothly —I keep thinking something must be about to break loose. More when I hit the fort.

Love—Betty

Tell Anne there are no other nieces that I can discover in the outfit—at least none that wants to be a little Wack.

6. Betty Bandel to Mrs. Bandel

July 20, 1942
Co. 3, 1st WAAC Trng. Regt.
[Fort Des Moines]

Well, for Lord's sake, here I am! I am perched on an army foot locker, at the head of my bed, with my folding chair between my knees, and my typewriter on my folding chair. [*see illustration 1*]. As usual, I have misplaced my luggage; so, until they find the missing bag, I am at leisure." I have just finished reading a 20-page manuscript on the organization and function of the WAAC, and am increasingly aware of how much book larnin' we will have in the next six weeks. Six weeks, because the last two weeks will be devoted to organization of the companies which we will officer and later take out into the field. By a little fast maneuvering, Gwen, Shadow (Mrs. Reilly), Susan, and I all managed to get not only into the same company but even in the same platoon, so that we are quartered right here together. We are, by a stroke of luck, in two small rooms, rather than in the general barracks. The entire upstairs of our company barracks is devoted to two large dormitory-like rooms, and these two small rooms that were left over. Each small room has three beds in it, with three foot lockers (quite roomy—bigger than my little trunk) at the head of each bed, and with three upright wall lockers against one wall, for clothes that hang, etc. The floors are hardwood, everything is immaculate. Down on the first floor there are more dormitories, the offices of the company, etc. In the basement are the roomy shower and bath rooms, a laundry room, and a recreation hall with desks, lounging chairs, ping pong table, etc., in it. Everything here has been scrubbed and cleaned in preparation for our coming, and some of the things are not yet ready—ash trays and waste-baskets, for instance, which our grinning company commander assures will be forthcoming in a few days. [Describes training grounds].

Bessie and Helen Harris got separated from us, but managed to stay together—in Company 1, Rgt. 3. When I saw Bessie at lunch, she was so excited over getting her uniform this afternoon that she couldn't swallow—and that is something for Bessie, who can consume the most amazing amount of food for a little girl of anything I have ever seen.

The place is filled with grinning sergeants, corporals, and privates, who are more or less in charge of us. I asked one sergeant about my bags, and he said, "Yes sir, ma'am, I'll check up on that."

Well, I might just as well start at the beginning. I got up this morning at 5, in order to prepare for an early departure from the train and breakfast. We had been in Kansas City last night, fooling around in the big station (Gwen had never seen the eternal flame that burns outside the station there), and didn't get to bed until after 12. The train turned out not to have a diner, and we landed at Des Moines at 7 o'clock, breakfastless. We started off the train, only to be met by a captain and several enlisted men. The captain told us to stay aboard, while they shifted the car around. We did, and a nice chap from the Tribune came aboard and got some "human interest" stuff from us. This is the biggest story Des Moines has had since the end of the Indian Wars—the whole post is being turned over to the women, and 7000 will be here in a few weeks. Every paper and magazine in the country had a representative here this morning—I have never seen so many cameras and harassed newspapermen and women in my life [*see illustration 3*]. The army was herding them around, letting them take this and that, before tomorrow, when no more stories will be released for a two-week period (or until we get used to our uniforms and don't look so silly). The Tribune had pictures and stories all over this morning—I'll try to get you a copy.

Anyway, when they got the car shifted back into the yards, they piled us all out, lined us up, shoved us in army trucks, and drove us to the fort. There we were herded into the induction center (all very efficiently and smoothly—the thinking has all been done ahead of time). While we were waiting to be signed up, a nice woman strolled up and talked to us who turned out to be Mrs. Putnam, dean of women of this joint. Two gals who are to be physical education instructors also showed up—nice ones—and Mrs. Van Renssaeller [sic], in charge of the physical training program, blew in in the blue fatigue uniform (which in my opinion is far prettier than the khaki garrison uniform—same style exactly but a nice blue color). The place was lousy with officers, all assigned to teach us—nice fellows, very earnest, for the most part. While we were being given our first instructions, the press blew in, herded by a girl who is evidently a WAAC public relations officer. They took one look at Gwen, and used her as their principal model, shooting her with the captain who was enrolling us, etc., while the rest of us made up the background—so Arizona may get its face in the papers. Then they filed us by the captain's desk, and we pretended to give our names, while some newsreel men took movies. Later doctors looked down our throats, to be sure we hadn't contracted chicken pox since our last examination, or some similar ailment, and we went outside the building into the hands of our grinning sergeant.

I am amazed to find I don't mind all these females about me—I just type my little typewriter, and don't know they are here. Incidentally, the two others in this room (Gwen, Shadow, and Sue are in the next room) both type—they are nice Chicago Jewesses. We get along well. All these people look the earnest small professional type—schoolteachers, etc. No glamour girls, I can assure you. Some bright, some bossy. I am really having a wonderful time—I haven't felt so free, so in a sense irresponsible, since I was five. Everything is thought out for you. All you have to do is do it—and often it is things which seem laughably childish to me, like standing in a line, or marching across a field. This will be both a rest and a change for me, and I expect it will put me in tiptop physical condition. Still, I will get enough free time to do some work on my own account. I want you to come up here before it is all over, Maw—for graduation, or sometime soon thereafter. It is a sight to behold. We are really the ones who are getting off easily. Those who stay at home, and have to do the same old job, and eight or ten extras because of the war, and can't have vacations, and have to save enough money for bonds and taxes, are the ones who are getting it in the neck. Theirs the work, and ours the glory, the uniforms, the change.

7. *Betty Bandel to Mrs. Bandel*

Telegram.

July 20, 1942

HAPPILY AND AMAZINGLY IN ARMY AFTER ONE SHORT DAY EATING, MARCHING, LISTENING. LOVE BETTY

8. *Alice Tildesley to Betty Bandel*[12]

Hollywood, Calif.
July 20, 1942

Dear Officer Betty:

I don't wonder that the army chose you above any other candidates. So would I. I know the sort of competition you were up against for the girls from here were all very special and only 7 out of 42 were taken after Salt Lake City. Mary Beaton Robertson, the one we knew best, had given over 700 hours to the interceptor command that gives air raid warnings here—and she failed to get in.

Buck privates get $50 a month O whadda they mean paying the Doe privates $21?[13]

Wardens still have no tin hats or gas masks, although every speaker warns us that gas attacks are near. No wonder Hitler scoffs at us. When you gals get going, there may be a different story.

I hear that the officer in charge of you gals is a bachelor—wonder if one of you will pick him off? Or would so many women all at once sour him on matrimony? Must be a story idea there somewhere—or a play. Charles Boyer says the day of indifference is past—that is, a man or woman who used difference as a sex attraction would be out of luck now.[14]

As ever, Alice

9. *Betty Bandel to Mrs. Bandel*

July 22, 1942

Dear Maw & Tribe:

I knew it. For two long days I have been trying to find 5 minutes to get a letter started. Just when I think I have it, the trumpeter blows first call, & that means I have just about 5 minutes before retreat.

What makes me mad is, so many wonderful & screamingly funny things are happening every minute, I am afraid I will forget them unless I get a chance to put them down as they happen. Here I am sitting policed up to within an inch of my life—shoes shined, new uniform on for the first time, seams of my cotton stockings straight, hat on straight, hair rolled up right, face washed—waiting for the retreat ceremony. The officers—who are doing a lot of head work on this business, & burning a lot of midnight oil—have decided we are to salute during the playing of the National Anthem, despite the fact that troops in formation never salute—only the officers do. But the reason for that is that they (the troops) have weapons, & it has suddenly occurred to the army that we will never have weapons in any way, shape, or form, & that therefore we ought to do something to correspond to the "present, arms!" So when they yell "present" we salute, & when they yell "order, arms!" we return to attention.

I am back after dinner, & am much more comfortable: to wit, I am perched on my foot locker, with my writing materials on my folding chair, the #12 can which we are allowed to use for an ash tray beside me, my hat off, my tie pulled loose, my sleeves unbuttoned, & my bedroom slippers (government issue, or "G.I.") on. The reason I am writing with pen is that my arm is full of typhoid, anti-tetanus, & smallpox shots, & is stiff as all get-out.

This is a most amazing organization & experience. Can you imagine 800 women wearing cotton stockings, & thinking it funny? Already that peculiar, indescribable thing called "esprit de corps" is beginning to show up. Quietly & sometimes subtly the officers encourage it. This morning an officer, lecturing on military courtesy, said "never let any company in the WAAC or the army outdo you in courtesy," & you could just see the women determining to outdo each other, & jump on anyone who got out of line. Then in the marching—even though we have only been at it one or two days, when we pass another barrack, we straighten up our lines & march for dear life, because of the women of another company who are watching us from the porches. The "military courtesy & discipline," already in effect although we know nothing about them, are creating some wonderful situations. Last evening Shadow, Gwen, & I were walking back from the post exchange (PX) in our new play uniforms (a cross between a house dress & a reform school costume), when four officers passed us & saluted! We had not been instructed in the salute, altho other companies had. Of course it was a gross breach of etiquette on our part—but nobody had told us, & after they saluted there was nothing to do but go on, since it would have looked even worse for us to acknowledge their salute. They seemed to think it funny, & could not resist smiling.

Another funny thing is the frantic way we try to get ready for things—15 min. to get dressed & make our beds! Lights out at 9:30—& beginning tomorrow study hour every evening, so that free time will practically vanish from the horizon except for the week-ends. Today we were talking about whether we should lock our foot lockers or not, & Gwen says, "If anybody has the time for any thieving, I'd like to know how they work it in."

I have just taken time out to try to teach a very funny woman named Evelyn Porter—who has the horrible job of being our first student "company leader" (same as first sergeant) for the next 3 days—how to breathe from the diaphragm. She says, "It was never like this in the 'Y! We used to say, 'Now, girls, lay your hankerchiefs on the stage, and form a circle'." She can now scream out

"Companeeee—'ten-shun!" quite creditably. Poor Sue Faherty, in the next room, is groaning over her sore arm, sore muscles, & sore brain. She says in all her years of managing a staff of social workers, she never thought she would come to the place at which her every desire & energy would be devoted to triumphing over the problem of making a bed without wrinkles. She is to be company 2nd officer tomorrow, & she suggests that we get her a wheelchair & a nice blue uniform of Civil War vintage, & wheel her out in front tomorrow, so that the officers will mistake her for an honored guest & leave her alone. She just yelled out, "But I *don't* wish I were home! And that's something." I asked her what exercise she has had in the past five years, & she said she hasn't even picked a flower. So far, I haven't a sore muscle—but our first setting up exercises are tomorrow.

Yesterday they blew First Call at 5:45, & I was getting my hair brushed out at its wildest when Reveille went at 6 a.m., & the 1st sergeant downstairs yelled "Everybody out! Fall out in front!" Well, Shadow pinned up my hair in one horrible mess, & we rushed down to fall in. As Shadow says, I have gone to 5 meals without having a chance to wash my hands. They always catch me off guard.

Then we rushed back upstairs, made our beds & dusted (you should see me with a broom) & rushed down again at mess call. In the morning we were classified by psychologists, etc., who asked us all about our hobbies, etc. I don't know what they thought of me, except that they uncovered the inevitable trumpet. We also had our first drill. The company got so mixed up that a young lieutenant, unable to swear in our presence, reached down & pulled up handfuls of grass. In the afternoon we got our uniforms—actually two, a summer garrison uniform of khacki [*sic*] & a light play dress of seersucker, brown & white striped. I got 1 girdle, 2 bras (both pink), 3 prs. pants, 3 slips (all khacki—very funny). My play suit includes dress & bloomers under it of the same material; tennis shoes; khacki socks; & a pull-down khacki fatigue hat. I also get a raincoat & galoshes; pink seersucker pyjamas; blue seersucker bathrobes (the corporals almost died when they heard these last were "government issue.") I never had so many new clothes in my life. Incidentally, a big store in Des Moines had the job of fitting us, & turned an army of women loose in one big warehouse out there to fit us. They acted like salesmen in a French (Parisian) store, ushering one in with smiles & bows, & saying, "Miss Blank, this is Miss Bandel. Would you be kind enough to try the coat on her?" and thus you got shot down the line from one to the other. They took especial care with the shoes.

Last night the first sergeant himself—looking like a frightened deer—made bed inspection. We will have our room "charge of quarters" soon.

Today we got shots, drilled twice (a nice Lt. Muff drilled us, & said "Miss Bandel, you have a good attention position."). Then we had a lecture & movie on military discipline & courtesy (in the post theatre). Then we learned—or began to learn—to salute. We have to salute all the officers—you should see us. I practiced (as did the others) marching across the field, saluting Lt. Muff,

& saying, "Sir, Miss Bandel has the first sergeant's permission to report to the company commander."

I saw Bessie fleetingly after dinner, & she is getting very snappy on her salute. She loves it—as we all do. We have to take our hats off in mess, & in barrack. I said to Lt. Muff, "Sir, do you want us to take them off in church?" and he said, "Gosh, I don't know. I'll ask somebody."

10.   Betty Bandel to Mrs. Bandel

July 24, 1942

Please don't think I am neglecting you—there just isn't such a thing as time around here. It looks now as if I will wedge one letter in a week (week-ends) & perhaps one note in mid-week.

Yesterday it rained, & we sloshed to mess (in formation) in galoshes & rain-coats. Gwen said she hadn't had so many clothes on, counting her girdle, even when she went bear-hunting in New Mexico. I cleaned my brown shoes 3 times during the day, & my galoshes once. If you could see me frantically wielding a broom in the morning, trying to get the last speck of dust off the sloping tops of our wall lockers or out from under the beds, you would laugh yourselves sick. Mrs. Reilly & I are going to have a horrible laundry bill—neither one of us can wear a skirt longer than two days. Last night they sprang the news that we would have regimental inspection this morning, & the place went mad. Such a policing of quarters, polishing of shoes, cleaning of lockers you never saw. Col. Faith passed down the lines of the entire 440 of us, & what I mean [is that] he examined every shoe lace.[15] Nobody wavered, & he complimented Capt. Jarman on the appearance of the company.[16] He then examined the barracks. Our foot lockers were open, with the tray up & back so that both trays were visible. Our wall lockers were also open. You should have seen us—we even figured out whether to push the catches on our lockers up or down, so as to get them uniform. We don't get to look at the Colonel, because our eyes have to be fixed in the middle distance, about five miles away. But he called us into an informal circle yesterday, to the horror of his 2nd lieutenants, & talked most charmingly about how we mustn't take things so seriously that we work ourselves into nervous inefficiency—there is a terrific competitive spirit, since he announced that only about half would receive commissions right away. He said he had never seen such a spirit in a group. He also advised using caution in dating enlisted men—or rather in forming "romantic attachments" for them —since it might cause embarrassment if we become officers a few weeks from now. Someone said, "How about if they are our husbands?" And he smiled and said, "Your husband is your husband. I have a son who is an enlisted man, & if he ever gets a furlough & comes home to visit, you can be sure I won't send him down to the enlisted men's barracks to sleep." In the same way he said that women could wear their hats in church, after all the 2nd lieutenants had said we couldn't, because "the flag of the United States bows to the flag of the church—and only to that flag."

You should see my salute. I forgot to salute our first lieutenant (very swell fellow named Muff) when I wanted to ask him a question yesterday, got started on my question, remembered the salute, made him snap to attention to acknowledge it when his mouth was half open to answer—& he valiantly refrained from going into hysterics.

Things are beginning to settle down so that the routine becomes apparent. We rise at 5:45, are dressed & out by 6 for Reveille & roll call, return to clean up our barrack, go to breakfast at 6:30. At 7:30 classes begin, with drill then, formal classes at 8, 9, & 10. We lunch at 12, & have classes at 1, 2, & (if the commanding officers wish) 3. We drill again at 4, & at 4:45 stand Retreat, going immediately to mess at 5, & ending our day with study hour at 6. From 7 to 9:30 we are theoretically free—but we need the time for study, or will by this [time] next week, when classes in company administration, mess management (me & the vitamins), etc., begin. At 9:30 lights go out, & if you are not ready for bed you go down to the day room in the basement, where lights are on until 10:40, when the "charge of quarters" conducts bed check. Incidentally, being a "B," I inherit "charge of quarters" Monday. That means that from noon Monday to noon Tuesday I am a kind of female officer of the day: I sleep beside the telephone, turn the company out in case of fire, call an officer in case of emergency, check leaking faucets & fire extinguishers between taps (at 11) & midnight, make bed check, etc. Or perhaps the better term would be a high class upstairs maid.

We must fix it so you can see this place, Maw. Dotty, you would cringe at this place—all 440 women have given up nail polish—it takes too long to put on.[17]

11. Betty Bandel to Mrs. Bandel

July 30, 1942

There is wonderful material for plays around here. I also celebrated my birthday by taking a tour of duty as "charge of quarters." While the men are here, during the day, you have little to do, but after 6 p.m. the whole place is your responsibility. I got about $3\frac{1}{2}$ hours sleep. Oh, & I stoked my first furnace! At 12 midnight you go down to the little hot water furnace & throw in 3 shovelfuls of coal. And you make bed checks at 10:45 to be sure everyone is in bed, & turn lights out at 9:30. And the questions the dames can think up to ask you! One came in & wanted to know if I thought it would be all right for her to consult a civilian doctor. You really have to exercise diplomacy in keeping them quiet after "lights out."

Col. Faith, who is a perfect lamb, called a special meeting of the company a couple days ago & said we were working too hard—said he was ashamed of grown women for not having more sense than to go to bed late when they have to get up at 5:45. He said we were too tense & too competitive. This didn't apply to me, because from 5:45 am to 7 pm is plenty for me. If I can't get the stuff in that time, it's just too bad—we are getting into hard stuff now—company administration, & property accountability (practically a statistician's course).

Lt. Muff, commanding officer of our platoon, is interviewing us all, & got around to me the other night. He gave us a real workout in drill yesterday, & when we came back to form in front of our barrack, two girls fainted (typhoid shots) & another walked into the barrack. I lifted my sleeve to wipe the sweat from my brow, & 3 guys grabbed me—they thought I was going too.

12. This song in a November 1942 letter was composed by an unknown member of Bandel's platoon.

The Third Platoon
We Like Us
To the Tune of "Over There."

Sing a tune, to our Platoon,
To 3rd Company, 1st regiment, a boon,
If you like 'em brainy, or just plain zany,
You'll find the tops in Third platoon.
Got a Test? We'll rate best,
Work or play, we're just that way, we live with zest.
With brains we cow 'em,
In Drill we wow 'em,
We're that HUT-2 – 3 – 4 Struttin' Third Platoon

13. Betty Bandel to Mrs. Bandel

August 1, 1942

Well, we had our first review this morning—band out, Col. Faith the reviewing officer, the whole two regiments passing in review, the colors leading the line of march, a scattering of officers' wives in the grandstand, everybody marching along with heads in line, eyes on a point "five miles in front," as our lieutenant says, feet brushing through the still slightly dewy grass. I think a slight chill ran up and down the whole line when the adjutant bellowed out, "Pass in review!" We had had only one practice—yesterday, and it was all kind of sudden and exciting. They got us out on the company street yesterday morning, and Capt. Jarman himself took command, instead of the student company commander. I sensed something coming up, and when I saw the fourth company move up behind us, and the first and second form ahead of us, I knew we were going to have some kind of a show. We have not yet worked out the way to turn left or right when we are marching in column. Thus when the command "column right, or left" is given, the three women at the head of the company must turn in the direction indicated, and each successive three must turn when they get to the same spot. It sounds simple, but they have a cute little way of turning that corner, with the corner man turning squarely and the two on the outside turning obliquely, which can simply leave you wondering if you're standing in Iowa or Arizona, by the time they finish the turn. Well, our platoon could at least execute a wavering "column left, or right," thanks to some extra drill under Lt. Muff, but only Thursday did we have our first taste of "by the left flank, march." It was the first time we had had music to march to, so naturally our marching improved a hundred percent right away. The men have been trying to teach these women a 30-inch step, 120 steps to the minute, when the average woman speeds up her walking by taking shorter, faster steps. They have gone nuts trying to get us down to 120 cadence, and have had to prance along beside us while we were doing about 145 or 150. I suggested to Lt. Muff that they ought to detail a drummer to go with each company until the women get the swing of the thing. So yesterday, when for the first time everybody who was trying to march could hear the beat of one good bass-drum, the women delightedly stepped out in time, and looked good. The only hitch was, poor Sue Faherty was standing in front of me as no. 1 man in the squad, and she can't hear music— not even rhythm—and consequently cannot march in time at all.[18] Well, we got lined up and started, when Lt. Muff, walking alongside, saw Sue faltering along, and realized she could gum up the whole platoon, so he jumped over beside us and said out of the corner of his mouth, "Miss Bandel and Miss Faherty, change places quick!" Sue didn't hear him, so I grabbed her and shoved her back and jumped into her place, trying to do it in one movement so it wouldn't look too bad across the field. We got up to our corner, and executed our left flank not too badly, and were nicely straightened up by the time we passed Col. Faith. In fact, we were swinging along fairly creditably, for raw recruits. The flag, the music, the uniforms, our first review—we all got a thrill out of it, I think, and performed accordingly. One girl said it was a good thing Col. Faith didn't examine us too closely, because the tears were streaming down her face.

Then today, when it was time for the real thing, we really got policed up. Our hair is still very hard to make neat—ends fly out from under our hats, with all the permanents around here. We went through the same performance, with the addition of an inspection of the regiment by the colonel just after we lined up. As he and his staff reached our company, Capt. Jarman gave "eyes right," and we all turned our heads right and followed Col. Faith as he passed us until our heads were straight forward again, holding them in that position. He whipped down both regiments (officer candidate and auxiliary—the auxiliaries march much better than we, having concentrated on it more, while we have been wrestling with company management, etc.), and came up the back, while every woman was wondering whether the seams in her stockings were straight, and what the back of her head looked like. Then he went back out to the reviewing stand, and his adjutant yelled "Pass in review!" At the last moment some idiot jumped up to our company and said, "Squad leaders, as you pass the reviewing stand, execute 'eyes right,' just as every other woman in the squad will do." The idea of having the squad leader continue to look straight ahead is to have somebody guide the bunch on by the stand while the rest are executing the "eyes right" courtesy. Well, the two girls ahead of me and I all obediently "eyes righted," and found ourselves staring at Col. Faith and not having the faintest idea how to keep a straight line forward. We simply couldn't see, because we were all looking across the field to the right. We compared notes afterwards, and discovered that we all did the same thing—looked out there, realized our plight, held our heads in that direction but screwed our eyes back around as near front as possible, so we wouldn't lead our squads plumb out of the regiment. Col. Faith later sent his commendation to each company. Now next Saturday we have our first public review, and there will be newsreel cameras, Des Moines citizens, and all the rest of it to watch.

Now to get down to really important things. Maw, your cake arrived yesterday and was an A Number 1 success, with a capital "S." Lillian Reilly had a wedding anniversary (21st, I think), Wednesday, the day after my birthday (her husband wired her a dozen red roses, and we all went into hysterics, because she not only couldn't wear any of them but also couldn't keep them in our barrack—she gave them to our nice, Irish, young first sergeant, who took them home to his wife). So we made it a double celebration last night, and had a party. Last night we did a "Drink To Me Only with Thine Eyes" that was simply gorgeous. We ate that whole blamed cake, except for some crumbs.

Tell John one of the women here said, after drill the other day, she didn't realize a private had to be a genius.[19] Today Lt. Muff gave us some extra coaching in voice work on the field, after chow—Col. Faith was still wandering around, and he came up and told us about diaphragmatic breathing and bouncing out the commands—an old story to us voice majors, but it takes plenty of practice on the drill field. I let my voice rise on the command of execution (the actual explosion), but anyway they can sho' hear me, which they can't do with some of the gals.

We have a very bright young lieutenant, Christiansen, teaching us property accountability—he looks like a Phi Beta Kappa who has been teaching in a crack boys' school. He goes so fast he has the women's heads swimming—it's really a course in book-keeping, and thus far I think I'm even with him. Company administration is taught by a nice, conscientious harried Jew named

Lt. Woolf, who helps us work out our practical exercises, because he doesn't think the schedule has allowed us time enough to do them ourselves—which it hasn't. Mess management is taught by a wonderful old hard-boiled captain who, I suspect, was a mess sergeant for about 25 years before the war broke out, and was then commissioned. He says "ain't" and "I seen," he can't figure out any of the charts we are supposed to use himself, but I'll bet you he can take a squint at how many men he has to feed and what money he is allowed to spend and turn out the best meal that would be possible under the existing conditions. One woman with a pronounced Boston accent got into discussion with him, asking how you arrived at proper calorie content when you only had so much money to spend, and he said, "Lady, de first day you feeds 'em calories; de second day you find out you gotta dig down in your jeans for 15 bucks you spent yestiday you shouldn't of; de third day you trows dem calories out de window." I thought I would have hysterics. Somebody asked how they could prepare the excellent meals we have here on 55 cents a day per woman. He said, "Well, today you get hamburger loaf—it's on the menu. Yestiday you had pork. Maybe some of that pork got kind of left over. Now where do you figure that pork ended up?"

14. Betty Bandel to Mrs. Bandel

August 4, 1942

Answers [to questions in family letters]: Shots not bad—second worse than first, with slight fever all day. The hair is OK—I do it up at night, put a net over it, and never even comb it in the morning—just stick the cockeyed hat on over it that I have to wear whenever I stick my nose out the door. No, ma'am, I certainly haven't lost. I haven't been near a scale, but I'll bet you I've gained five pounds—we get fed three big meals a day. I feel fine—better than I have in years, in fact—nerves steady, digestion good.

I got a grand letter from Uncle Albert—he seems quite thrilled about my being here. He has been practicing the "about face" the way I told him we do it now.

Sunday evening Gwen, Bessie, and I put on our jackets, and went into town—for the first time for me. Des Moines is far, far different from a tourist center—despite its several hundred thousand inhabitants, it has no dine-and-dance place, no music with meals. We finally ate a not too good meal (but a steak, which we were hungry for—and a good one) at one of the better hotels, and wandered down to look at the Des Moines river. A fellow was fishing, and let us watch him. He was a nice working man, who liked Wacks. Some of the people don't—one old bum followed me along for a half a block, and said, "Blank blank you, why don't you go home where you belong?" Please do not pass this information on to anybody—or any other of a critical nature. They are very fussy here about giving out "military information"—anything that might reflect upon the army. Also see to it that no snapshots get out in any way that might make it possible for them to be published—we would really be in the soup if a picture or story of us was published without the official OK of the public relations officer here—none can be released before Aug. 8, when the camp will again be opened to the general press. And we can write nothing which would be in competition to what the established news agencies might write—in other words, no straight news about the camp, only anecdotal stuff. He asked me if I'd like to go into publications, and I said I would, er, like to try my hand at straight administration. That doesn't mean they'll let me, of course—they'll stick me where they think I'll be most useful. We were having a special drill yesterday, and I got my first shot at giving commands to the squad (12 women)—voice audible but too high, commands on the right foot and easy to understand, I was told. Not a bad beginning.

The jaunt to Des Moines was fun, just for a change, though I doubt if I'll go in often. The parade ground and trees are so lovely here, and there is plenty of relaxation if you want it right on the post. The service club has ping pong tables, the PX soft drinks and a bowling alley.

15. Betty Bandel to Mrs. Bandel

August 6, 1942

Just a note—I am as busy as busy. Everything happens to me at once. Last night I glanced at the bulletin board casually, & was brought up short by the notice that I was to be first sergeant of the company for this half-week. The student officers change every half-week, & we all are supposed to be in some position of command twice during our six-week training. However, the 3 jobs that have to do with the company as a whole, rather than with one of its platoons or squads—first officer (captain), second officer (1st lieutenant), and first leader (first sergeant)—can only get around to about $\frac{1}{3}$ of the 110 women, so I feel very fortunate to have hit one of them. It is a real chore, tho, since the 1st serg't. is responsible for the assembling of the company at all formations, classes, etc.—in other words, you have to harass 110 women into getting in line about a thousand times a day. Lt. Muff is worried by our slowness, so I got hold of my platoon sergts. last night, & passed along the word, & we really herded the gals into line today. I have a whistle which makes a frightful amount of noise—it belongs to our real 1st serg't, Sgt. Kellihan—as Irish as Irish. One of my jobs, incidentally, is to polish the silly whistle daily during my 3 days of office.

My 3rd chore of the day was having to give the day's 3-minute talk in Company administration, given always at the beginning of the class as a summary of the last day's study. I was so het up over my sergeancy that I took the speech

in stride, & the kids said I was at least coherent. Lt. Woolf didn't say anything—he never does, of course—but he didn't look displeased. It was on an
easy subject—the Personal Service Record kept for every man & woman in
military service.

The 4th excitement of the day was Pay! We had our 1st payday. Lt. Muff had
me line them all up alphabetically, & we filed into the captain's office, hat in
hand, saluted, received our pay, walked out, paid the amount due the collection
sheet (laundry, etc.), & filed out. All very formal, with officers sitting all
around—& very cute. I got $35 for the part of a month I have been in, less
$2.94 for laundry & our identification pictures.

Saturday we have our review—I jump back into the squad leader position
for that. Must run now—have to polish my whistle.

Maw, you must come here at graduation.

Cannot believe our basic training is $\frac{1}{2}$ over!

16. Betty Bandel to Mrs. Bandel

August 8, 1942

After two and one-half days as a first sergeant for the company, I feel as if I
had been in the army for a year—either there, or in a hog-calling contest. You
may not believe this, but they get me to bellow when they can't hear the student
company commander—me, who was always accused of not being able to get
my voice out. I have Oscar Colcaire to thank for my sergeancy, I think—and
also for instruction which I have passed along to several gals who had no more
idea how to bounce a tone out from the diaphragm than they did how to fly to
Mars.[20] I wouldn't go so far as to say it is a musical tone I produce—but, boy,
they hear it.

Everything has gone along quite smoothly. We have speeded up the company on its falling-in technique, and Hannah Ashby, who has been my company
commander, worked out a way to march the company out on the parade ground
for physical drill which simplified the procedure and won the approbation of
the officers. Hannah is too much of a lady to yell loudly enough for the front
rank to hear her when she stands (as required here) at the rear of the company—
but otherwise she is a fine captain. This morning, before our big inspection and
first parade (with Mrs. Hobby present), our swell Lt. Muff advised me to get
a "blitz" cloth (all the sergeants use them as polish rags) and really give the
whistle the works.[21]

We arose at five this morning, and tip-toed around getting ready for the
blamed inspection. I put up my hair just right, got on clean underthings, and my
second-day shirt and skirt, in order to avoid the hazard of spilling breakfast on
my clean Saturday-go-to-parade clothes (as we have named them). I went
below, whistled the women out, got them on the line, took the roll report, and
turned the company over to Hannah, who marched us to chow. Then we rushed
back to the barracks to get everything policed up before inspection at 8. I dusted

out and lined up everything in my wall and footlockers, made my bed with its clean linen so that you could measure its every fold with a ruler, lined up my shoes on top of my bed, soles down, dusted out every corner of the floor with a big broom, while Ruth Spivak dusted the lockers, beds, floor boards, and window sills, and Bee Rosenburg cussed her unmakeable bed.

Then I doffed my dirty shirt and skirt, washed my face in the drinking fountain in the hall (I had had to rush down and turn the girls out, at a bellow from Sgt. Kellihan—whenever there is a job to be done, they yell for the first sergeant), and put on my clean shirt and skirt. I tied my tie beautifully, fastened my name plate at the precise spot over my pocket, powdered my face, had Lillian Reilly re-fix a couple of bobby pins so they wouldn't be so noticeable, and went downstairs for orders. Lt. Muff, who is a love, crinkled up his blue eyes when he saw me and said, "Well, all policed up for inspection, I see." You get so you are afraid to let yourself be seen by whoever is guide officer, when you are first sergeant, because one of your jobs is to dog the guide officer's steps and be always there when he decides it is time to form the company, so that you can whistle them into place. The result is you trot around like a St. Bernard puppy at their heels, and you are sure they are ready to die at the sight of you— but you do have to do it. Poor old Muff was guide officer this week, so he was the one who had to bear with me. Capt. Jarman came out, looked at me owl fashion through his spectacles, and said in his deep, slow voice, "Miss Bandel, prepare the company for inspection at 8 o'clock. You will accompany us, following Miss Ashby, during the inspection. At 9:22 you will give a warning whistle, and at 9:24 you will form the company for the review. At 9:25 you will see to it that we are ready to pass onto the field." I said, "Yes, sir," and proceeded up the stairs three at a time to inform the women that Sister Hobby was not going to call on our company in barracks, and that we were going to be inspected right away indoors, and for pete's sake to take their hats off and lay them on their pillows.

At 8 precisely we started our little rounds, me first, to yell "Ten-hut!" in each room (it is a non-commissioned, rather than a commissioned, officer's job to do the vulgar yelling under such circumstance), then Capt. Jarman, then Lt. Muff, then Lt. Herndon (a pompous Junior Chamber of Commerce type who is overawed at finding himself in the army, with a commission), and then Lt. Grimball, a sweet southern boy who is still scared when ladies salute him, and then Hannah Ashby. After I got 'em at attention, Capt. Jarman would call "at ease!" and inspect—and I do mean inspect—he ran his fingers along the springs of one cot, to see if they had been dusted. I had a little notebook in hand, but Capt. Jarman did not ask me to make any entries. We ended up down in the latrine, poking around to see if the orderlies had thoroughly washed up the bowls, etc. Well, we barely got through before it was time for the review. Sister Hobby was hopping from one place to another, trying gallantly to fit herself into army procedure—she really has a terrific job there, with no background in the field. She had to inspect the two regiments, and when she got alongside us, the colors company for the review, I heard Col. Faith mutter to her out of the corner of his mouth, "The flag! The flag!" Evidently nobody had thought to tell her that she had to salute, along with the regular army officers. She managed to get her hand up to her hat quite creditably, however, and to trot along at Col. Faith's side very nicely. She takes it all very seriously. I like her, even from a distance—she has magnetism, charm, sincerity. Nobody had warned the photographers that they could not come out on the field, and they were swarming around us when Faith and Hobby came by—Faith called out to them so that two companies could hear, "Please leave the formation! This is most irregular!" And a mess of privates swarmed out and picked up their cameras and hurried them off the field.

Well, I got the company formed, turned it over to Capt. Jarman, and took my place back in my own platoon, as leader of the third squad. As colors company, we stood while they brought the flag out in front of us, and saluted when Capt. Jarman called "Present, arms!" Then the band struck up, and the four companies of the first regiment, followed by the three of the second, marched swinging onto the parade ground, lining up facing the reviewing stand. They had the big garrison flag flying, and it seemed to cover half the sky, up at the east end of the parade ground [*see illustration 4*]. After Hobby and Faith galloped by to inspect us, and got back to the reviewing stand, the adjutant bellowed "pass in review!" and we all went round the field in front of them. I think we were all trying a little too hard, because our lines were not as straight as they have been in practice. However, we got through it without falling on our faces, had one more formation to go to lunch, and then Hannah and the rest of us student officers heaved a sigh of relief and realized we were through. From Saturday noon to Monday reveille, there are no formations. Bessie, Gwen, and I went into town this afternoon, for a little dimestore shopping. I also found a funny little old book store, with some swell old books in it.

The enclosed tintype is an enlargement of the one on my pass—I shall employ it to scare small children.

There goes tattoo—nine o'clock, and I have been up since five. Hasta la vista.

17. *Betty Bandel to Mrs. Bandel*

August 14, 1942

Well, well, well, here it is the end of another week, with just two more to go! I am waiting anxiously for some definite word as to whether there is to be an actual graduation. I would love you to see this place. From what they told us today, however, it looks as if we will probably be here for some time—almost all of us will be kept to work into the new companies as they are formed and trained, to teach, or to get specialist training. The embryo officers will be assigned to companies, and will learn with them, under the supervision of regu-

lar army officers, until they are ready to take the field—and they don't expect
to send any companies out until about Nov. 1. We had a lecture on organization
of the WAAC today, and from what I can see, they expect to bring auxiliaries
in here, beginning late this month, at a constantly increasing rate until they are
training around six thousand women at a time on the post. As each small unit
is trained, it will be sent out. The standard company, for use at the big posts,
will consist of 3 officers to act as administrators (see that the women are
clothed, housed, fed; handle disciplinary and morale problems; etc.) and about
147 auxiliaries and "leaders" (non-commissioned officers). There will be about
three platoons in each company—one clerical, one communications, and one
motor transport, with a "leader" in charge of each. This, of course, is merely the
tentative set-up for the standard service companies which are to serve in the big
posts of the country; special companies, for service with the signal corps, etc.,
will receive different training and be organized in a different manner. The lieutenant who made the speech said there seemed little chance for foreign service—but our officers feel differently—I haven't much hope of that, however.
Don't spread these figures around—they are not yet official. The normal army
organization is one commissioned officer for each platoon, and as you can see
we will have only non-commissioned officers with the platoons, while all officers assigned to each company will merely act as administrators for the entire
organization. There is considerable sense in this plan: ordinary army companies are all performing one job—infantry rifle companies, for instance. Each
platoon officer acts as administrator, under that plan, for a group of men doing
one specific job which he knows and which they know; the company officers
(captain and one executive officer, usually) act as administrators for the entire
group when it is doing its specific job as a unit, and also for the group in matters of housing, feeding, etc. Our companies, however, will have all kinds of
jobs to do, and there is no reason to wait and train commissioned officers to run
each of these specific jobs, when there are plenty of good specialists in the sten-
ographic and similar fields who can jump right in as non-commissioned officers and do the actual supervision of the jobs. All we need officers for is to see
to housing, feeding, discipline, etc. (deans of women, as you see), and so we
can get along with a smaller number of officers per company.[22]

I'm not surprised that you don't understand the marching—I don't understand it myself, and I have to take a test on it Monday. As a matter of fact, they
have found out that adult women—fairly bright ones, that is—get the idea right
away, but can't make their feet and hands do what their brains tell them to do.
Lt. Muff was telling us that was the big surprise to the officers when they first
began to drill us. Ordinary recruits stand and stare at them when a new maneu-
ver is explained and demonstrated, and simply don't get the idea; once they get
the idea, however, they execute it almost faultlessly. We, on the other hand, get
the idea the first time, and execute the movement in such a straggly manner that
we end up scattered all over the parade ground. That isn't quite true, because

the officers told us at mess today that our parade this morning looked like the
sort of parade recruits do after five months of training—but of course we are
supposed to be a picked group. It is funny about this picked group business—
I find them a pretty average bunch as far as intellect goes. They are the type you
meet in all the "A" classes in school—quick, earnest people who absorb everything teacher says, but have few original ideas and little of that important stub-
bornness which you find in the "B" sections, where the real scholars fall. Of
course there are exceptions to this generalization—Danovsky, a big, round-
eyed Slavic girl who is a teacher and social service worker, a Ph.D. I believe,
and a linguist, besides being a very individual type; Spangenburg, who is nuts
and formerly headed the accounting division of some big unit for Montgomery
Ward—she is really a case. The other night she got me to do column left and
column right movements with her across the tops of the cots in the big squad
room up here on the second floor. We simply marched one behind the other
across the beds (pretty long steps between), trying to avoid trampling people in
the beds which were occupied, and she would sing out "by the left flank," or
"column left," or whatever she wanted, and we would execute the movement,
usually ending up with one foot on a bed and the other on the floor. It's funny,
but some of the gals accused us of having imbibed spirituous liquors.

I sent the *Star* a story, on which Capt. Kennedy gave me an unconditional
"OK," plus a nice compliment for its form and substance. He asked me if I
would like to go into public relations when I received my commission, and I
sidestepped clumsily, saying, well, er, I didn't know, er. He said to come and
see him occasionally, anyway—he wanted to keep me in mind. I said, "Yes,
sir," but I probably won't, because I don't think I want to get stuck in public relations—I know that field, and there are plenty others to learn. The poor public relations outfit here is worked to death. The whole nation want news of the
Wacks, and they have two officers and two non-coms to get it out.

Bessie's outfit finished its initial training today. She and Helen Harris are
being transferred to the second regiment (first regiment, officer candidates; second, specialists; third, auxiliaries) for specialist training. They are being moved
into new companies, and into new barracks—stables which have been converted, and which are fixed up very nicely. The girls say they are nicer inside
than our regular barracks; foot lockers have been built-in in such a way as to
half shut off each four beds, so that each four girls have a kind of half-private
room, within the whole long barrack. Plumbing, etc., is more modern than ours,
although ours is perfectly adequate and always immaculately clean. All these
big old barracks will be used for incoming officer candidates. New barracks,
now under construction, will be used by the incoming auxiliaries, as they are
given their pre-specialist basic training. We are getting intensive study of company administration and leadership in the army generally, with less drill. We are
supposed to know every form a company officer has to fill out to keep his company going—morning report, telling the day-by-day history of the company;

ration and mess accounts; individual service records of the people in the company; sick reports; duty rosters; and the Lord only knows what else. I now talk about WD QMC Form 424 (War Department, Quartermaster Corps Form 424—stock record account) as glibly as I once did about a galley of type, or a trio in the dominant key. The trouble is we haven't time to work it all out as practical exercises; we must simply have the theory jammed down our throats, and trust to Heaven we can actually do the various things we should do when the time comes.

Bessie and the other auxiliaries eat in another mess, but I see them quite often. Bessie took us to a movie last night—first since I have been here—because, when we are commissioned, she can no longer play around with us in quite the same way. No officer can play favorites among the enlisted personnel, and that of course means no social intercourse with one that couldn't be shared with all. I think both Bessie and Helen will have a chance for officer candidate classes, as soon as we begin to expand—they are both too bright to be passed over. Several of the Arizona women have already been assigned to the mess, and are in there in immaculate white uniforms and caps learning army methods of preparing food. Capt. Steinbaugh says they seem handier at cutting vegetables, etc., than men; he says the only trouble will be the lifting of heavy pots and vessels.

Mrs. Lt. Muff isn't here—he was just sent up from Fort Riley before this all began, and I suppose she is wherever their home is. I inclose a picture of him, which Midge took and peddled to all the gals in the platoon—we are all of the opinion he is the best officer in the regiment, except maybe our own captain, Capt. Jarman. Stick it away with my stuff someplace, when you get through admiring it.

Steinbaugh said they were behind 400 dollars in our mess here one day last week, and didn't consider it anything unusual, for so large a mess. They went over by serving us milk three times a day, when one 8-oz. glass a day is the ration allowance. But they can usually do it for us, because they make money on portions of meat and vegetables—we don't eat as much as men. They can also afford to feed us more oranges than they would men (which we yell for, and the men don't), for the same reason.

Tell Anne if I don't get some "things" on my collar and shoulders, I'll certainly get some on my sleeves. Tell her not to mind my being away—think of all the things she will learn while I am gone, and have to show me she can do when I get back.

No, they don't inspect our underwear—not yet, at least. This morning, while I was standing stiffly at inspection beside my open foot locker, little Lt. Grimball, peering in, remarked in his southern drawl, "I wondah wheah all those boxes of candy are, I heah so much about." Capt. Jarman said, "They probably saw you coming."

We had a test in mess management yesterday—a farce—questions like

"Should a cook keep his hair trimmed neatly, and wear a hat?" Next week we get all our important tests, and the last week mostly reviews. The army believes in following examinations with further detailed discussion—they think you get more out of the exams. I shall have to spend tomorrow really boning up on my Punitive Articles of War, WAAC regulations, military courtesy and discipline, military sanitation, organization of the army, company administration, and property accountability. We have short courses (just a few lectures) still to begin in map reading, defense against chemical and aerial warfare, and leadership.

I had a chance to drill the platoon some this past week, during special practices, and enjoyed it. I like this Saturday-go-to-parade feeling, too. We get so blamed cleaned up, Saturday morning. Then you feel all set for the week-end. Mrs. Holbrook led the platoon this morning during parade, made a couple of mistakes, and all these ex-school teachers jumped her—largely because she is generally right, and they loved catching her in a boner. She has a way of being pretty positive about her rightness, too, so I suppose she partially brought it on herself; but it made me mad to see them so ready to criticize her for errors they would make themselves. They don't realize what it feels like to be out in front there all alone and see your outfit bearing down on a tree, before you have time to figure out how or where to turn them. This week-end we have the unpleasant job of rating all the other members of our squads, and saying whether we think they should receive commissions—what a responsibility! I think I'll give all mine commissions—I'm feeling generous today.

Do you know Tillie the Toiler, in the funny papers?[23] She has joined the WAAC! Her creator is here, drawing a series of strips about her life in the WAAC.

Helen Harris has been assigned to the administrative school (for statistician's training), & Bessie to the clothing depot as a typist. I have seen their new barracks—it still suggests the stable.

[Added at the top of page one]: Flash! Graduation exercises Saturday morning, August 29! No way of knowing whether we will have time to do more than turn around & go right back to work, but come on, Maw!

18. Alice Tildesley to Betty Bandel

August 15, 1942
[Hollywood, California]

Dear Betty the Brave:

Glad to have your card and know that the WAACs are fun. All the news reels we've seen show a grand looking crowd of girls. I picture you in the band—or do you sound the bugle at 6 a.m.?

Do picture stars visit you and entertain the gals? I am trying to track down Bob Hope to do a series of twelve stories on camps with him, but up to now he doesn't want to do them. I would write them for him, and his p.a. wants to send me around to the camps with him, but he thinks it will be too hard.[24]

My editor thinks families need reassuring. Does yours? He gets letters by the dozens worrying about conditions in camp, etc. Please let me hear about what worries you?

Do you gals put on shows there? Or does duty fill each shining minute?

19. Betty Bandel to Mrs. Bandel

August 18, 1942

Monday we had a class in "field cooking," & had our noon dinner out on the grounds, with the mess detail preparing a delicious stew on an "army field range no. 3." Some of the auxiliaries, who have just been assigned to the cooks' & bakers' school, after their month's Basic training, rode over in an army truck & served the food, & were tickled to get the assignment to the "picnic" instead of to the mess hall for that day. We found out how to manage stew, tomatoes, bread, butter, ice cream, & coffee in our mess kits & canteen cups—& then how to string them all, plus our knives & forks & spoons, on the handle of the mess kit & sluice the whole business up & down in the boiling water the army uses to clean utensils with. Great fun—Col. Faith ate with us.

The big excitement of this week came Monday, when we marched home for our last class of the day—physical drill—Cap't Jarman came out & said, "Everybody whose last name begins with 'A' or 'B' see me on the porch. Don't change to your fatigue clothes." We clustered around, & he informed us that the commanding officer—Col. Faith—would see us for 5 minutes apiece beginning in 10 minutes. (He is personally interviewing all the 440 officer candidates.) We died, & rushed into clean shirts & shined shoes (over the day's dirt), & went panting up to the 1st training regiment headquarters. There, as the last woman before me came out of the door, I walked into the office, succeeded in refraining from falling on my face, saluted, said, "Sir, Miss Bandel reports to the Commandant as ordered." He—a small, quiet man, old army style, with the sharpest eyes you ever saw—relaxed from the stiff attention, waved me to a seat, offered a cigarette (I refused—my hand would have wobbled a foot from side to side), looked at my card, smiled, & said, "Well! I'll bet you'll like to get your hands on the band!" I said, "I've been out of music for ten years, Sir—in the newspaper business." He said, "Oh, yes! I remember from your record." He went on to explain that the band officer does no music, only runs the band company—housing, feeding, etc.—which I already knew. I also knew it to be a dull job, so I said I was really more interested in straight administration, with a standard WAAC company, & he said that would be where the greatest need would come, particularly at first. He asked if I was interested in public relations, & I said not as a first choice. He asked if I had any questions, & I asked about the possible establishment of Signal Corps companies (telegraphy, etc.); he said it would depend on future requests from the Signal Corps, & said anybody who had some training, like me, would very likely have a chance to transfer, under such circumstances. He asked if there were any other questions, & I said, "What chance is there for foreign service." He grinned & said, "That's the reporter coming out in you. I don't blame you for asking, but I'm not going to answer. I declare I think all you women want to get on a boat & go someplace." Then he rose, & I rose & saluted & about faced & departed—so relieved at having remembered everything that I was supposed to remember that I let the screened door slam as I left. He is an old fox—I never talked to anyone for 5 minutes before & knew so little what he thought of me at the end. But I like him, & respect him immensely—he is doing an amazing job here.

All the gals are worried by the tests this week (our biggest ones are tomorrow), & by the fact that not all the class will be commissioned right away. I'm not—I like the army & the Wacks, & I'll serve wherever they put me.

20. *Mildred Leven to Betty Bandel* [25]

Hollywood, California
September 8, 1942

Dear Betty—

Gee, I'm proud to know a real W.A.A.C. & a real lady officer—Congratulations! Guess this is the first time I've ever envied any one. Itch to do even a little.

Now 'member that I expect you to be a *General* before you get thru'. Any one with your ability & personality should reach the top quickly. I hope the women will show up the men & are rewarded for ability & not pull & politics. Of course if you marry a General that will please me even more for you would have a delightful home.

Have to think of this whole situation as a tremendous, exciting game with the highest stakes ever played for in order to keep my balance. Wish I were a part of it.

Love Mildred

CHAPTER 2

Aide to the "Little Colonel"

Bandel is one of eighteen newly graduated officers to be assigned to WAAC headquarters in Washington, D.C. She is quickly singled out by Director Oveta Culp Hobby to be her first aide [*see illustration 12*]. Bandel would speculate later, with characteristic modesty, that Hobby chose her because of her background as a newspaperwoman.[1] In truth, Hobby quickly recognizes Bandel's intelligence and leadership abilities after her arrival in Washington. Bandel's admiration for her "Little Colonel" is equally enthusiastic. Likewise, Betty is well loved by her fellow Waacs, who take great delight in her ongoing triumphs on the job. At the same time, they seem to feel that she needs assistance in keeping herself organized. They make her arrangements, move her in and out of living quarters, shepherd her around protectively, lend her garments, and put her hairdo right as she prepares to leave on her many journeys: "aides to the aide," as Bandel puts it. Even Director Hobby finds herself sewing a button on Bandel's uniform, at which point, jokingly, she points a finger at Bandel and screams, "You're fired!"[2]

In her capacity as aide, Bandel accompanies Hobby to England with Eleanor Roosevelt in late October on an observation tour of British women's military services. Bandel, an Anglophile to the core, has the trip of a lifetime in wartime Britain. The trip is kept secret for security reasons until they have landed in England, but Bandel cannot resist hinting at what is about to happen in a letter to her mother: "Please send my black suit the quickest way you can. I may need it for a little special occasion which may be in the offing. This little party is so nebulous I don't even know whether I'll need civilian dress for it, but I may."[3]

Bandel recalls a moving vignette of Roosevelt in England: "On one occasion, we were meeting at a given base to see a great number of 'other ranks,' as they call them in England, men and women soldiers all drawn up to be seen by the wife of the President of the United States. It's been raining as it can only rain in England, and they're all standing out there with the rain coming down over their caps and everything. And Mrs. Roosevelt got out of her limousine, and some State Department guy starts an umbrella up over her head. She pushes him to one side, and she goes down this entire row with the rain coming right down her flowers, speaking to everybody, talking to each one. I thought very highly of her" [*see illustration 7*].[4]

Family letters from Bandel often hold tidbits of secret WAAC operations and internal gossip. Clearly, she considered such news to be safe from enemy agents when confided to her family and friends. Censorship of wartime letters from the home front in the WAAC, or at least of these letters, seems to have been remarkably lenient—perhaps too much so: "Things are getting tighter on censorship," she writes. "From now on don't spread anything of my activities, except what I specifically say is O.K."[5]

In November, in recognition of the great need for Waacs to take over critical noncombatant jobs in the army, Secretary of War Henry L. Stimson petitions the president to increase the number of WAAC recruits to 150,000. The G-3 Division of the Army (Army Ground Forces) sets a goal of 1.5 million recruits by 1946.[6] It is at this time that Bandel's significant contribution to the development of WAAC administrative policies begins. On her trip to England, she and Hobby meet with General Everett S. Hughes, whose prewar plan for a women's corps to be fully integrated into the army was ignored when the WAAC was established.[7] Bandel builds upon his ideas and is instrumental in the development of policies and procedures in WAAC headquarters.[8]

A second WAAC training facility is established at Daytona Beach, Florida. But a chronic difficulty in obtaining adequate supplies for trainees becomes a central concern at WAAC headquarters, and is a common theme throughout this chapter. Colonel Faith, commandant of the WAAC training school at Fort Des Moines, complains that Waacs are being refused essential equipment and even uniforms by the Services of Supply, because they are not regular army. An early cold snap in Iowa compounds the serious problems that the army is having with supplying trainees with even such basic necessities as warm clothing and uniforms. After seeing the plight of the women at Fort Des Moines, Hobby contacts army headquarters in Washington and manages to obtain men's winter coats, which the trainees are forced to wear all winter.[9] At a meeting shortly after her return from England, Hobby stated that if the commandants of the training schools were not getting supplies, then she should hear of it, and "it was my job to fight for it."[10]

1. *Betty Bandel to her family*

Sept. 18 I think
1942 I'm pretty sure

Dear Family—

Good gawsh, what a beautiful life! You may believe this or not as you see fit, but I am taking my ease in the Hotel President, Kansas City, Mo., U.S.A.

Colonel Hobby is taking her ease in Room 1030 of the same establishment. Yesterday I was in Omaha, Nebr., at 1:30 p.m., Kansas City at 5 p.m.—oh, yes, & Washington, D.C., at 5 a.m. How come? Don't ask me—I only know it happened—& is continuing to happen. To start at the beginning—& this is an under cover story, so the dommed Citizen won't get hold of it, & make it look as if I were boasting (of course you can tell Alexander or Binda anything you like):[11]

I got to Pittsburgh Tuesday morning, was met by an enthusiastic Uncle Albert & Aunt Helen. Was the 8th wonder of the world, in Pittsburgh—Uncle A. had fun introducing me to his office force. I left, arriving Washington Wednesday a.m. & going to Hotel Raleigh with Gretchen Thorp, my public relations sidekick.[12] I had strained my back slightly picking up a trunk in Des Moines Monday, so I went to an osteopath in Washington, while the others house-hunted. And what did they find but a nice old girls' school which can't open this fall & had just decided to rent itself out. We took 17 rooms, for the whole bunch of us—7 (including me) will be in a modern apartment, the rest in rooms in the main dormitory next door. Now this is the laugh: the school is *Gunston Hall.* Why is that a laugh? Because *Emily Brown* went there in the 3rd grade, during the last war! The minute the girls told me what they had taken, I began to laugh like an idiot, & they couldn't figure out what was the matter with me. What a cycle! If Emily hadn't gone to Gunston & to Panama & to Fort Sill & to Tucson I would probably not have gone to the army to Des Moines to Washington to Gunston. Please call her up & tell her. I think the deal—including linens & maid service—will cost us $25 to $30 apiece a month. Not bad, eh? The look of blank astonishment that came over WAAC headquarters' faces the next day when we calmly told them we were taken care of, was a scream—some of them have been looking for houses for months.

Thursday we reported, spic & span, at Temporary M (WAAC & several war department division headquarters) at Constitution & 26th. You show a pass every time you go in or out—despite uniform. Nice Capt. Clark, the adjutant, took us to our classroom, where for 2 weeks we will be instructed in duties of the various staff officers. Then for 3 weeks we will observe our staff chiefs, & for 4 more work under their guidance, before we are turned loose to do any damage on our own hook. More school—but we all welcome the opportunity. Col. Macy, assistant director who has as one of his hundred chores the job of public relations officer, will supervise Gretchen & me.[13]

Then we were trotted over to the munitions building to be fingerprinted & photographed, fed, & taken back to Temporary M to make out pay vouchers. While we were sitting around there, a sergeant came out in the hall & asked for Lt. Bandel. I said, "Yes," & he said, "Where shall I pick you up in the morning, ma'am?" I said, "Are you picking me up in the morning?" and he said, "Hadn't you heard? At 5 o'clock you're going with Col. Hobby to Omaha

& Kansas City—flying, you know." Well, when they brought me to, I went into the Colonel's outer office & nice Miss Smith, a secretary, handed me the Colonel's & my orders, & I gradually soaked up the idea that Smith couldn't go along, because it was a military transport plane, so I was doubling in brass for Smith, carrying briefcase, seeing that uniforms were pressed, & generally acting as a cross between a secretary, valet, & aide. They asked me if I minded flying, & you can imagine what my answer was. A little later Col. Hobby had us in her office, welcomed us, & as we left, said to me, "See you in the morning, lieutenant." She is, up close, what she seems from afar—simple, intense, sincere, intelligent, womanly. Why me? God knows, unless she wants to break us public relations people in on her press interviews.

Oh, & the Saturday just after you left, Maw, we were called in for 5-minute interviews with the lady, & then, just before we left for Washington, Capt. Kennedy (public relations) said to me out of the corner of his mouth, "The boss-lady was favorably impressed—believe all will be well in Washington."[14]

Well, anyway, when the gals found out about it, & found out I was supposed to kind of police her clothes, they let out one concerted scream & said, "But who's going to police Bandel?" They've all been taking over the job which somebody always seems to take over around me—that of watching over my clothes & things. Then they scattered like quail, & one went to the Station & got my foot locker while another lent me her Pallas Athenas & another pressed my shirts & another lent me her overnight case & another went out to get me an alarm clock.[15] You would have thought *they* were going. Aren't people nice? And the nicest thing was what Jess Rice, a grand, competent southerner said, when I said, "Well, if I don't get Sister Hobby back in one piece, it won't be your fault."[16] She said, "What we care about, is for Sister Hobby to bring *you* back in one piece." All this time I was being moved into the Hall, but I didn't see much of it, because I only had time to get myself ready & go to bed in preparation for a 4 a.m. start. At 5 a.m. Friday Capt. Yost, of our staff, called for me. We went for the colonel, & thence to the airport, where a captain wise in the ways of big planes gave us a most delicious ride to Omaha—where the hell is Omaha? The main street we were whisked down on our way to the luncheon at the Fontenelle hotel looks just like the main street of Des Moines, or Kansas City. Is the whole middle west one ugly main street? Anyway, the plane ride was *above* pink clouds, & I was entranced. For two mortal days I have been tagging around behind enough brass to make a cannon—colonels, majors, a general. I remain at my colonel's left, ready to take her bag, or dig something out of her briefcase (which I carry). Well, in Omaha she talked before a women's group at lunch, & I sat & ate & let the motherly souls ask me questions & compare me with their daughters. Then Capt. Yost, the colonel, & I hopped off for Kansas City, where today the colonel spoke at the American Legion Auxiliary National Convention. Last night was devoted to getting the colonel policed (you should see what a good lady's maid I am—at least when it comes to pinning on eagles), and getting my own things pressed. I got her off to dinner with friends, made phone calls for her, etc. This morning I sat by during an interview. Then the colonel decided we needed an extra cup of coffee, over which we got into a fine discussion of books & philosophy & things—she's all right, as you may have gathered. Last night she called up her kids in Houston, & tried vainly to locate "the governor," who was between two towns.[17] Then there was the speech this afternoon, & flying weather wasn't right, so we stay until Sunday at 9 a.m. Gawsh, amighty, it's really me that all these houses are falling on! I am so swamped by the trip itself that I can't remember many meaty details to give you.

Well, how's that? Remember not to spread the story. How are you all?

2. *Betty Bandel to Mrs. Bandel*

Sept. 23, 1942
Washington, D.C.

Just 2 hours ago, at the office, they calmly informed me that I am again spending the week-end gallivanting around the country with Her Ladyship. We are going to Des Moines by plane. We leave Friday, & I don't know how long she will be away, since she has a couple more places to go after Des Moines. I will wire you from Des Moines, so you will know I negotiated the plane trip successfully. There is no doubt of that, however—we have a very special plane, & a very special pilot.[18]

I, personally, am quite beyond being surprised at anything anymore. Life is moving too fast. If they say to me tomorrow, "Lt. Bandel, you will escort Franklin Delano Roosevelt on an inspection of this headquarters," I won't even bat an eyelash. When I got the news this afternoon, I sailed out, dumped my coat at a cleaner's & told them it was a matter of life & death for me to get it by tomorrow night, grabbed a bite to eat, & came here to have my hair done.

I am tickled pink over the chance to go to Des Moines again—can't you see the kids' faces? And right now our studying here is pretty routine, so the trip will make a nice break. All this is, of course, only added to the privilege of being with the Little Colonel, & observing her remarkable way with the press, etc.[19]

My Lord, I was almost forgetting the big news! Jack Walsh of the Samuel French office in New York wrote me saying that Miss Mayorga wanted to include my *Viva Mexico* in her volume of one acts, that they liked it, & that they would like to buy it for $25.[20] I didn't expect to get any money out of the deal, & I rather hate to let go of the title even to such a little script, but that is their usual proposition on one-acts, so I said "Yes." His letter was waiting for me when I got home from my last jaunt with the Little Colonel, but so much had happened I hardly got excited over the added surprise.

Gawd, what a life! And do I love it. Haven't had time to take a look at Wash. yet.

Love, Betty

3.   *Betty Bandel to Mrs. Bandel*

Sept. 27 [1942] I think

B & O Station, Chicago, I'm sure

By now you know that I have been to Fort Des Moines again—with the Little Colonel. Once more, the kids had to move just as I was pulling out—into the apartment next to Gunston Hall proper, where 7 of us will live (myself, Arthyeta Van Dalsam [nice Texan], & Virginia Beeler in one large room). Thorp says if I go on one more trip, she'll resign—claims she spends all her time getting me policed to go joy-riding. And Van Dalsam wouldn't trust me to get my hair combed right for a trip with the Colonel, & staggered out of bed at 4:30 Friday morning to put it up for me. I have Van Dalsam's suitcase & summer coat (cleaners ruined mine), hers & Gates' Pallas Athenas to wear on my collar, Thorp's gloves—oh, yes, & the Colonel's utility coat (she knew I didn't have a coat, & brought it along for me).

This time, I had a very definite usefulness, other than the general secretarial sort of thing. Last trip I shot off my big mouth about some ideas I had for a speech, & the Colonel asked me to submit them to her. Well, I was embarrassed, because we are not officially at work yet, & for me actually to submit anything to Col. Macy before he called for it would be presumptuous. Everything is, however, supposed to go through "the channels of command" in the army. I decided it was just as if she had asked me to do her any little personal favor, & so wrote up my ideas informally & gave them to Miss Smith to slip on the Colonel's desk—trusting they would die there, or, if she wanted to use any of them, she would dictate them for incorporation in speeches the public relations department might be working up. But it was not to be. The Colonel called me into her office the day before our trip, & said she liked my approach (naturally much more personal than that used by Mrs. Knight, with no WAAC experience) & wanted me to put Mrs. Knight's & my speeches together, on the plane going out to Des Moines.[21] (This speech is to be given before the Southern Newspaper Publishers' Association, & she had an idea for a lead of her own which she also wanted to work in.) Well, poor Mrs. Knight had spent the day slaving to get the speech out, & she is to start teaching Thorp & me this next week—so I had a vision of how she would feel when an entirely different speech was given to the press from the one she prepared. I murmured something about clearance with the War Department Bureau of Public Relations, & she picked up a phone, called Col. Macy in, asked him if he had seen my script, & he said he had. I felt like two cents, but he didn't seem annoyed, & she asked if it would be all right to put the two speeches together without clearing the finished manuscript, since they were both routine re-hashings of the WAAC story. He called the BPR, & got a verbal clearance for this one time. So when we boarded the plane next morning at 6, Bandel started to work. Her lead & my conclusion, plus a few figures from Mrs. Knight's speech, went into the thing. However, the Colonel never sticks to her manuscript, so what she actually says Monday may be quite different.

Well, as to the trip itself, & the fun. I wish I could give you a real idea of what the Colonel is like. She is much loved—whenever she meets someone who has known her in the past, he or she usually lets out a yell of delight & starts pumping her hand up & down, or grabbing her in an enthusiastic embrace. Jackie Martin, the crazy photographer we have had at the post, jumped for her & almost knocked her down, yelling, "Boss lady!" Jackie is a clown, wears pants constantly, calls everybody by a first name, & is a nationally known photographer.[22] She called me "Betty" all over the place, until the Colonel, in a moment of stress, said, "Betty, get your notebook—I mean lieutenant, get your notebook." I have never known anyone with a deeper sense of responsibility than the Colonel has—she says she only acquired it when her children were born. It shows up in little ways—remembering to bring her utility coat, because I wouldn't have one, for instance, & telling me to wear my winter uniform, because of the cold. When we got to Des Moines, it was snowing! As soon as I hit the post, I realized winter uniforms had not yet been issued—new companies did not even have their complete summer outfits! And mud & slush was a foot deep. Col. Morgan said my classmates, when they found I was coming out, had plotted to put me up in a cold barrack, but had finally relented & put up a bed for me in Quarters #2. The kids greeted me with open arms—little Gwen [Watson] came shivering into post headquarters to bury her snow-cold little muzzle in my collar. Then I discovered there was *no heat* in many barracks—shortage in metal pipes made it impossible for the plumbers to install radiators. Col. Morgan was tearing up the countryside looking for old pot-bellied stoves, & was installing them as fast as he could get them—but the mills had fallen down on the clothing deal, & it was impossible to outfit all the kids with winter uniforms. Incidentally, this is the first time in 67 years snow has fallen in Des Moines in September—it's usually hotter than anything. Well, Friday night Muni & Nicholson & I got together, & they said they thought there were enough pieces of clothing in the warehouses to wrap something around each girl, if you paid no attention to sizes.[23] Saturday morning I reported that to the Colonel, giving her a picture of what I had seen out in the slush of "Boom Town," & she, with a gleam in her eye, sailed up to Col. Morgan & asked for an order issuing every piece of warm clothing, no matter what the fit or anything, on a temporary, emergency basis. Even enlisted men's coats, if there were any, were to be issued. By mid-afternoon the kids were getting a coat here, a raincoat there, a sweater the next place. In a few days it will all have to be taken in again, when the uniforms come in—but in the meantime, that is a sample of how the Little Colonel works. This is another story *not* to pass on. Similar shortages are cropping up many places—but we can't be the first to talk of them. The kids have been such good sports it would make you cry. They wear pyjamas & winter underwear under their clothes. One girl tied her feet into her barracks bag before going to bed. In the two short weeks since I left, the fledgling officers have begun to perform actually as officers, & the auxiliaries here accepted them as *their* officers (not just as temporary teachers, as they consider the men), & take the durndest pride in them. Gwen was leading her platoon someplace, & they said it was too cold for her—she should go back. They seem eager to salute all women officers, & smile as they do. For one thing, when the girls' companies were activated, they themselves set up the 150 beds, foot lockers, mattresses, etc., in preparation for the auxiliaries—& the auxiliaries know it. No men were available at the time, & the women officers, rather than have their companies come in unprepared for, pitched in & did the heavy work themselves.

Saturday morning, before reporting to the Colonel at the Officers' Club, I called her up & asked if she wanted to wear wool or khaki. She said, "What is your thought, lieutenant? That if most of the women don't have wool, we shouldn't wear it?" I said, "Well-er—." She said, "Correct. Summer uniform." In summer stuff, & the regular light raincoat, she inspected barracks & mess halls in Boom Town—& one hour later it was all over the post that she had done so, & the girls were eating out of her hand. She spoke at graduation in the big old riding hall—in summer uniform—& personally presented diplomas. At noon she flew south, & I returned to the post for some wonderful talks with the old gang. Gwen & Reilly took me to dinner—& half the old platoon came along.

4. Betty Bandel to Mrs. Bandel

Sept. 29, 1942
Washington or bust

Hello, dear family, you pretty people, gawsh amighty how are you? I gather from your so kind letters, all waiting for me when I got home Monday, that you are all flourishing. Drag sounds too busy to live—how are he and Ginger Rogers getting on by now? And how does Anne like second grade? And how does Anthony like the world? And, Maw, are you still flourishing? And is Dotty?[24]

As to me, I don't know which century I'm living in. I think the Fates said, along about 1912, "Well, we'll give Bandel 30 years to vegetate, and then all hell will pop loose." I got home Monday morning, train a half-hour late, rushed to the office, and found a laconic order in my desk, dated last Friday, "Effective this date, Third Officer Betty Bandel is relieved from duty in the Office of Technical Information and is assigned to duty in the Office of the Director." In other words, my friends, I am now the handy man to the Little Colonel, just as Muni is to Col. Faith—a job which makes me feel like a fish out of water, since the Lord knows I am the last person to dance around being an agreeable, socially acceptable aide, but which I am still thrilled to get, because of what I can learn from that most diplomatic of diplomats, and most forceful of leaders, Director Oveta Culp Hobby. I have a feeling the assignment is just to have me learn all I can about a number of things, and will not constitute the end and aim of my army career—though the Lord only knows what it may lead to. However, I have ceased to worry about such details—in their own good time they will tell me what they want me to do next. At the moment, many of the other gals are doing much more responsible things, since they are already assigned in departments like personnel and training and operations, where they are actually getting their teeth into some of the work. I still feel very much an apprentice, particularly since the Little Colonel is out of town this week, and all there is for me to do at the moment is soak myself in all the background and information about the WAAC and the office and the Little Colonel that I can find. I am wondering if she thought I knew about the order before we left here Friday, and, if so, what kind of a three-toed eohippus she thinks I am for not saying anything about the new assignment—but she must have realized right away that I didn't know, although I believe she told Col. Morgan, out at Des Moines, since he said, "Next time you come, check the weather at least three days ahead," and I said, "Oh, I probably won't be coming along again, sir." Someone suggested that one reason she might have picked me for the job was because I am nearer her size than anybody else—I am surrounded by Amazons, I might add, who would look definitely strange trotting along three paces behind and one to the left in a review. But also I suppose I did all right on the trips, or she wouldn't have made the change. I think she also wants to use me for part-time public relations, perhaps working on her speeches—the last one ended with me doing the whole thing over, and she seemed to be satisfied with it in its final form. Well, there's nothing like change, I always say—and there's no danger of being bored in this army. I'm kind of tickled—she's a grand person, and it's good to know I have thus far performed to suit her. Col. Macy grinned at my obvious amazement when I got my orders, and then let me sit down and tell him all about the Des Moines trip, and some little public relations tidbits I picked up there.

A nice Sgt. Simms—George Washington graduate in business administration—is breaking me in in the Director's office. There is also a nice Mrs. Gruber, who is a kind of personal secretary (she is the wife of a high-ranking army officer, incidentally); and Miss Smith, Radcliffe graduate and secretary to the Director.[25] Then there is Mrs. Hill, a crazy kid who is a stenographer. We are the bunch "up front." In adjoining offices are Col. Tasker, executive officer, and Col. Macy, assistant director—with Her Ladyship, the "Big Three."[26]

Go easy on radio or papers about us WAACs—*every* mention of us is sup-

posed to be cleared through public relations channels there or at Des Moines—
still should like to have heard your contribution.

I just got nice letters from Binda & Pat, & from Alexander. Binda would
like it better if I would have a grand passion—tell her I might, at that—I
wouldn't put anything past this year.

5. *Betty Bandel to Mrs. Bandel*

Sept. 30, 1942
Washington, D.C.

Tonight Van Dalsam and I were walking home, and a lovely Englishman—
a group captain in the RAF [Royal Air Force]—came up and chatted with us,
and asked us to come down to his office and meet his WAAFs [Women's Auxiliary Air Force]—"your counterpart, you know," all attached to his office here,
and "doing frightfully secret work, you know."[27] We are going to take him up
on the invitation, if we can figure out a way to get over to his office. Our hours
are from 8:15 to 5, and as long after as it takes to get done, with 45 minutes as
the outside limit for lunch.

Yesterday I walked up town to meet the kids from Temporary M, got in F
street, ran into the White House, began to walk around it, and ran onto the sen-
tries who patrol it nowadays.[28] The first boy presented arms—the sentry
salute—when he saw me, and I think the others did it just for a lark. Anyway,
I went along being saluted and saluting every 50 paces, with much slapping of
guns and they came to the "Present," and much staring of passers-by. These uniforms are the ninth wonder of the world here, and we have some difficulty in
getting down the street without stopping every two steps to answer questions.
Also, we salute everything from Dutch generals to doormen.

I am living, now, at 1904 Florida. We are in an old section, very quiet, full
of big, square, three-storied houses and apartments. The two big rooms on one
side of the hall are bedrooms for three apiece (Beeler—big, dark, vivid, about
to get married; Van Dalsam—smaller, dark, southern, a Texan and married to a
Texan who is in the air corps; Bandel—the dope, all in the second room back).
We bought a steam iron between the seven of us, and now can press our winter
uniforms, as well as our summers. The kitchen has seven little gas stoves, such
as we used to use in home economics classes. It didn't occur to me there was
anything strange about that until tonight, when I mentioned it, and the rest all
howled. "Bandel, nobody but you could have gone on this long and not noticed." It was a girls' school, you know, and they taught them cooking in there.
We have a cot and two single beds in here, plus two closets and two chiffoniers.

As to my office, it is a long, low building of paper and wood and a little
metal—definitely not decorative, but full of busy people. There is a riding
stable just across the street, on the banks of the Potomac, and I intend to go over
and talk to the horses soon.

6. Betty Bandel to her family

October 11, 1942
The Deah Old Capital

Well, my friends, get ready for chapter fourteen in this tale of Aladdin and his wondrous lamp. If I ever wished for anything in my life, it was to have you all, Alexander, and Binda here this week-end, so I could come home each night, flop down in a big chair, kick off my shoes, wiggle my toes, and tell you everything that had happened during the day, minute by minute, and excitement by excitement.

We were getting set to receive Chief Controller Jean Knox here this weekend.[29] I have had not only a ringside seat but, in my own peculiar way, a bit of a hand in the festivities. Knox runs the biggest uniformed women's service in England [the Auxiliary Territorial Service, ATS], and is the equivalent of a major general. Plans were that Lt. Woods was to be Knox's aide for the WAACs, during her stay here; Subaltern Grayrigge (the head ATS stationed here) was to be her aide representing the British forces in Washington; Maj. Margaret Eaton, who accompanied her here from Canada, was to represent the Canadian forces; Chief Commander Gowers (same thing as a lieutenant colonel), her own aide from England, was to represent the home front; and Bandel was to tag along, as usual, as the tail to the comet (with a capital "C").[30]

Early in the week they got around to telling me (you find out things piecemeal up in the head office—nobody has time to sit down and draw you a diagram) that the WAAC officers were being entertained by Col. Hobby Sunday evening, to meet Gen. Knox. I knew Hobby was also giving a lunch for her Sunday afternoon, at which she planned to have only her divisional heads. Mrs. Gruber said the arrangements for Sunday's two shindigs were in Lt. Woods' hands, but during the week more and more little details fell her way—things like getting the new curtains and rugs for the Colonel's apartment, etc. Then all of a sudden it developed I was supposed to be in on the deal, when the Colonel turned to me one morning and said, "What wine would you suggest for luncheon, lieutenant?" So I got her some nice Chablis, & gradually inherited a number of other jobs, like seeing that invitations actually went out, & remembering the Navy Nurse Corps, which everybody else had forgotten. Then it developed we were all to attend a White House tea for the General Saturday afternoon. When we all came to, we said, Yes, we thought we could work it in, & it then became my job to see that everybody had all the insignia (I had to borrow the Colonel's for two gals). We had to go in O.D. skirts, since some of the girls have no pinks (actually gray) as yet.[31]

Well, dawned Saturday. The Little Colonel came sailing in, & said, "Lieutenant, be sure to order the car in time for us to reach the station to greet Chief Controller Knox." That was the 1st time I had heard I was to go along on that detail, & it gradually dawned on me that I was to really act like an aide, & that probably Woodsie had failed to tell me, perhaps out of a little bit of ruffled-feathers feeling—she was, in her old civilian days at WAAC hq, a big shot in some ways, & I believe it grates on her to serve even a few months as a lowly shavetail.[32] So I got the car, & managed to pry the Director out of the conference room & away from some 2-star generals in time to make the train. We arrived just as the White House car got there, & followed them into the east end of the station, right up to the tracks. We were early, so we went in & had coffee & donuts, & came out again to find the Station Master looking for us, & saying 3 British officers & a lady officer had gone on down to track 15. We trotted after, & came on enough brass to build a battleship. The train pulled in, & out stepped General Knox, followed by Chief Commander Gower & 2 Canadian majors—one male & one female. I was so entranced by all the funny insignia that I almost forgot to salute as I was introduced. She is a charming, intense, typically clipped-British-speech type of human dynamo, with all the brains in the world, & far more feminine appeal than her pictures would lead you to believe—the Colonel wondered where she found time to keep her hair so perfectly done, etc. The British can always make you feel your shoes aren't shined, when they are in uniform. Well, we all trailed out of the station, Woods & I bringing up the rear, with the baggage, & the brass hats piled into the White House car. I followed in our military car, with Major Sykes & Woods. We rolled merrily up to the White House, were identified, & drove up to the front door, me feeling as if I had stepped through Alice's Looking Glass. Woods joined the bunch in front, I instructed the car to wait, & when I turned around Major Sykes & I were alone, faced by flocks of dignified old colored men in white tie & white gloves & tails, ushers, police, soldiers, etc.—& the massive pillars & doorway of the White House. Major Sykes said, "Shall we step inside?" & we did—just like that. Then the others had gone on ahead, & I said I thought I'd better wait right there for the Colonel, & he said, no, it looked like a female party, & I should join them. Just then the First Lady came sailing out, with white orchids & a nice smile on, & a flock of aides in her wake, & said, "I'm *so* sorry not to be able to stay with my guests, but the train was *so* late, wasn't it?"—& shook hands with the Major & me, & busted on out the door. He said that was a bit of a surprise, wasn't it, & I said it was. He called an usher, & said, "Look here, we're frightfully embarrassed, you know—we've been left behind. Will you take Lt. Bandel to Gen'l Knox's party, & I'll push on?" I was ushered into the red room, where I sat & stared at pictures of Cleveland & Taft, & wanted to run my hand over the walls. One of the old colored men took me up in the elevator, & there were Knox & Hobby & Gowers & Woods sitting around on the lovely spreads of the White House beds, smoking & talking & generally letting their hair down. After all the formality at the station, it was funny. So I sat down, too, & listened to some very swell talk between the Colonel & the Chief Controller as to ATS & WAACs & their problems. Hobby & I left, after a bit, with me gently reminding her to ask Knox to speak at Des Moines graduation Wednesday. You know what I was thinking about, all the time I was in the White House? How I rolled eggs there, in 1917.

We barely had an hour at the office—with 400 frantic things to do—before I had to start prying her loose to return to the White House for tea, where the Colonel greeted Lady Halifax, Mrs. Morganthau & Mrs. Wallace, & presented me to them.[33] Then the aide took us into the state dining room. Mrs. Roosevelt was a typical, average, cordial, well-bred American hostess, with nothing to distinguish her from 400 women who have entertained me in Tucson—just as nice, & just as average. She came over to a cluster of us, after the line broke up, & started talking about "This Is the Army," the current legitimate show in town, & talked as you or I would, after seeing an average movie. Despite the splendor of many uniforms—WAACs, WAVES, ATS, WRENs [Women's Royal Naval Service], WAAFs [Women's Auxiliary Air Force], etc.—my eye was immediately caught by that magnificent portrait of Lincoln as a young man, which hangs on the west wall over the fireplace. I couldn't get away from it, so finally I sidled up to the woman at the coffee urn, & asked her. She turned out to be Mrs. Helm, White House standbye (secretary, I believe) of many years' standing, & she was so tickled that I had noticed her favorite painting in the house that we got into a regular old gab-fest.[34] She told me how it had been the favorite with Lincoln's son, & I told her about the WAACs, & finally she said she hoped she would see me again, because "I like Betty Bandel." We hopped back to the office, worked until 7, & went on home.

Today I reported at 11:30 at her apartment, phoned Col. Flikke of the Army Nurse Corps & Lt. Cmndr. Dauser of the Navy Nurse Corps to ask them if they would receive tonight, & stood by as the Colonel greeted her guests.[35] Ten sat around a lovely oval table in the dining room & five (Jere Knight, Woods, Bandel, Maj. Powell, & Maj. Gifford) had a small table in the living room. Mrs. Gruber got to telling a story about how some fool women in Pennsylvania sent greeting to the little Colonel via carrier pigeon, & I nearly got hysterics & choked to death. Then the civilians left, & we got down to an hour of hard conference work, with the men & Hobby firing questions at Knox.[36] After that I rushed the Colonel down to the White House. Maj. Powell, Jere Knight (the very fine public relations gal in our office) brought me home, I washed my face & beat it back to the Colonel's, & we took out for the Hotel Washington. It had gradually developed that I was to introduce the people as they hit the line, & it also fell to my lot to tell the gals in the line where to stand—boy, how I like this shoving generals around. The Colonel had invited all the service women in town, & we had a most wonderful collection of uniforms. Everybody was inquiring about everybody else's uniform, & we had a most lovely time—I with Squadron Officer Hunt, head of the WAAFs here, among others. Old Knox & Hobby hit the gals right between the eyes—Knox looks holes into you when she meets you. She made a little impromptu speech—a nice greeting. At 9:45 Gen'l Knox & party left, & the Little Colonel dropped me off on her way home. Tuesday we all go to Des Moines for two days. Don't ask me what, after that. How's that for a week-end, doves?

7.　*Betty Bandel to Mrs. Bandel*

October 16, 1942

Your letter arrived last night, several hours after suit, which is in good condition and for which many thanks. You sound a bit bemused by my adventures—that's funny—so am I. I cannot now stop to tell you of our lovely trip to Des Moines, except to say that a highlight was sitting on the floor of the plane, between Gen. Knox and Col. Hobby, watching the tigress general polish our Little Colonel's shoes. Hobby and I both expressed such wonder over the state of the Englishwomen's shoes (they shine like old mahogany) that Knox got out her little box of polishes (as full of gadgets as a pistol nut's box of little hammers, cleaning rags, etc.), took off her coat, rolled up her sleeves, and gave us a lesson in how to polish shoes. Most amazing sight you ever saw—this faultlessly dressed, every-eyelash-groomed Englishwoman, with her eyes that look through you—solemnly polishing away at the Colonel's shoes as if she were playing a Bach concerto. Then the night before (Tuesday) I took Subaltern Grayrigge on a blackout convoy which the motor transport school at the fort was staging—a trip in a jeep, creeping along silently among 13 other vehicles, with nothing but the cat's eye red lights which are used for blackout convoy work to guide us, snaking through the corn field and country roads around the fort, with a moon and shadowy trees above us. It was a thrilling night—the English girl went nuts over it—she was brought up in the country, and said she hadn't had a good breath of air in weeks. Had so little time in Des Moines, couldn't even call Gwen—saw Reilly fleetingly.

Am now in office of general at munitions bldg., waiting for Little Colonel to get through conference. Potomac is swollen with floods—we are in *new* offices across river in Arlington (mammoth Pentagon bldg.)—took me over hour to get to work, with traffic on few bridges open. Am leaving Monday for 2 or 3 week trip—*may* not be able to write—can't stop to explain trip now.

In late October, Bandel travels to England with Hobby and Eleanor Roosevelt, who has been invited by Queen Elizabeth to see how the women of Britain are aiding the war effort. The trip lasts three weeks, in which time, at Roosevelt's suggestion, Bandel and Hobby also visit General Eisenhower and visit the British ATS and other military women counterparts to the WAAC.

8.　*Betty Bandel to her family*

Excerpts from letters written, November 11 to 19, 1942, upon returning from England.

I had known that the L.C. was going over for several weeks, but when she called me into the office with three or four of our ranking staff officers sitting around, and said, "You are going with me, if you want to go"—can you imagine how I felt? I think I must have been stunned, because she stopped me as I got to the door with "Just a minute. Don't you want to go?" I turned and said "Yes," and she looked at me a minute, grinned her funny little crinkly grin— she never does anything by halves, smiling or frowning, approving or disapproving—nodded and said, "That's all. Make the necessary arrangements."[37]

As you know, we went over with Rover,[38] who is very nice and exceptionally like most people, and so healthy she wore the press down to a nubbin. Miss Malvina Thompson, a nice old shoe who is Rover's secretary, was also along. Because she had known the L.C. before WAAC days, she called her "Mrs. Hobby" and me "Lt. Bandel," to the no small confusion of the British press.

The plane is, of course, secret, & so is even the country, but I will tell you it was Ireland, knowing you can be more discreet than I am. Because it is neutral territory, the boss & I—in high heels, black suits—travelled as Mrs. Hobby & Miss Bandel, government officials.[39] The Irish ask only that you save their faces, & they think it is a lovely, old fashioned game of smuggling, at which they can claim a somewhat distinguished history. Rover and Miss T. went as "Miss Brown" and "Miss Smith" & that threw the British porters off so badly I had to spend five minutes at the London station explaining to them that, yes, Rover did have some bags, & these were they.

Well, we landed in what the British would call a bit of weather, & were happily grounded for a day. American embassy people appeared out of the hedges to whisk Rover off to the castle of the local lord—who favors the American cause, which makes all the villagers very happy about aiding the planes and passengers as they come and go. The American Consul took the boss & me to the local inn, where some lovely quiet Irish people watch the mad antics of visiting Americans with understandable amazement.

The village, the inn, the road, the castle—it was all so typical I could hardly bear it. But that was the real surprise for me in all of Great Britain—how much it looked like what it was supposed to look like. I really felt as if I had opened my eyes in a dream world, because no world of reality could possibly approximate so closely what one had pictured. We had a wonderful drive through the countryside, thanks to the Consul, & the L.C. bought some lace at an old convent. The next a.m. I was whisked thru country lanes to a plane which took Rover & the rest of us over to England.

Incidentally, you may judge of my Texan's character when I say that after 3 whole weeks of travelling, & the necessary inconveniences of travelling in a war-torn country, & eating potatoes & cabbage 3 times a day, & being cold until Nov. 1 (when they were allowed to light fires)—she was still laughing over the wild things that would happen to us. The British have a passion for doing everything right on schedule, and the L.C. has the usual southern tendency to arrive one minute late, with fourteen porters streaming along behind her with the coats, bags, etc. Inasmuch as I am charged with such details, my hair is turning white by inches. Well, whenever anything didn't hit right on the nose, the British would say apologetically, "There's been a slight change," which delighted the L.C.'s soul so much that it became our slogan. Every time there were no more stewed prunes (only fruit you could get, about), it would be, "There's been a slight change." It was funny until we got held up five days in Glasgow, the world's dirtiest city, waiting for a ship or plane weather on the way back—then it wouldn't have been so funny had it not been for the L.C.'s peculiar inability to cry over spilt milk. She has the most amiable spirit under adversity I have ever seen. The moment a disappointment occurs, some peculiar something happens in her mind to bring all her gaiety to the surface. She shoves her hat back on her head, sticks out her lower lip, and says, "Come on, my pet, let's go to a movie"—unmilitary, perhaps, but absolutely life-saving at times.

We landed, from Ireland, in Bristol. Incidentally, all place names are secret at which aircraft land. The Irish landing, in fog and rain and on water, had been something—when Miss Thompson saw she had to transfer from our ship, merrily pitching in the waves, to a small and slippery boat to take us to shore, she said thank you very much but she was going back home. The Bristol landing was perfect, despite weather (and a little doctor who rushed aboard and asked us if we were all right—Rover laughed at him). We transferred to a private train, where Ambassador Winant—a lovely, serious Abe Lincoln American—met us, as did Maj. Bailey, American officer assigned as the colonel's aide during her period of duty in the European theater.[40] He is a swell fellow, most helpful and, after he got over his initial fright at lady colonels and lieutenants, full of a quiet vein of shy fun. Toward the end he adopted a slight fatherly air towards me, advising the colonel to see that I got enough carrots, etc. (They eat them as often as they can get them to sharpen their vision for the blackouts.)[41] Like all the rest, he was charmed by the colonel, and I think really enjoyed his tour of duty with the Waacs; despite the ribbing he took from his fellow officers. He carried my briefcase the length and breadth of England, and was much amused at my running around opening doors for him, etc.

Anyway, when the train reached London, the King and Queen were there, and a specially-rolled-out carpet, to greet Rover. The Little Colonel was also introduced, and the rest of us craned our necks out the door of the little train to see. She is far lovelier than you could possibly imagine from pictures, the Queen—I would call her radiant.[42]

Well, after about five minutes' chat, Rover looked back in the car and waved, and she and the King and Queen got in a car and drove off. I stepped out, and there was the L.C. being greeted by General Eisenhower—the nicest overgrown Iowa farm boy I ever met—and General Smith, his Chief of Staff. The Colonel presented me, and I was so overcome by the display of stars that I came to a smart attention, and just stopped myself from saluting in the nick of time when the clicking of my high suede heels together reminded me I was not in uniform. They are wonderful men, Eisenhower and Smith—the former big and booming and straight-from-the-shoulder, the latter quiet and scholarly and suave. Both are very American—a quality you come to cherish when you see a number of American officers making fools of themselves by acquiring pseudo-English manners, after a short tour of duty in the European Theater of Operations. Just before we left London Eisenhower asked Hobby to lunch. You may judge the stature of the man when I say that he remembered, with all the things he then had on his mind (it was just before it all began in Africa),[43] that she had a lowly lieutenant of Waac with her, and had his aide call up at the last minute and say he wanted me to come too. So we had a charming little luncheon—the Commanding General, European Theater of Operations, his Chief of Staff, the Director WAAC, and Bandel—in General "Beedle" Smith's rooms at the Dorchester—and I never had a better time in my life. General "Ike" couldn't get over the L.C.'s and my standing back to let him go through the doors first. He would throw back his head and howl, and say where he came from a lady was a lady. He was talking so hard when he put us into the lift that the operator did not hear him say "7th floor," and let him off at 3rd (his own, rather than Beedle Smith's). He pounded on the door, still talking, and I was afraid to butt in and say what was wrong. Nothing happened, and when he finally stopped long enough to say, "What the hell's the matter?" I said, "You're on the third floor, sir, not the seventh." He said, "How the hell did I get there?" I explained, and he turned to Hobby and said, "Now, y'see? You've always got to have some lieutenants along to be the brains of the outfit. Let's get out of here quick, before somebody opens that door."

He and the Little Colonel were at Ambassador Winant's for dinner one night, when Rover was being honored, and the L.C. was dying for a cigarette. You aren't supposed to smoke, if the King is to be toasted, until after the toast, so the boss gestured inquiringly across the table to Eisenhower, and he called up to Winant, "Mr. Ambassador, are we going to toast the King?" The answer was no, and General Ike reached in his pants pocket, hauled out a package of Camels, and sent it spinning across the table practically into the Colonel's lap. That same dinner, by the bye, almost cost the Colonel dear. She and I were both initiated into the Short Snorter Club by the crews of our planes—originally the only members were those who had made the Trans-Atlantic flight, and when you are initiated you must give every Short Snorter present a dollar (it cost me $5). They then sign your dollar bill, and ever after you must keep it with you, because if any Short Snorter ever asks, "Are you a Short Snorter?" and you don't have your bill, you must pay every Short Snorter present a dollar! Well, General Ike boomed out to the L.C., over the heads of the dignified diplomats, etc., "Are you a Short Snorter?" and she like an idiot answered "yes" before she remembered that her bill was in her other purse. He saw her face, and gleefully said it was going to cost her $80 if she didn't produce her bill in 2 minutes. But he reckoned without the Colonel. The Ambassador was giving his dinner in Claridge's, where we were staying, and the L.C. shot out of that staid dining room at a dead run, scattering British dignitaries like quail, tore to the lift and up to our rooms on the 5th floor, got the bill and was back down inside the time limit. General Ike refuses to go to all the social functions he's supposed to—he sends his complaining staff officers instead. He goes to Buckingham Palace occasionally, because he likes the King—says he's a "nice fellow."

The L.C. had me leave our cards at the Embassy one day, and the very next day, when we came in our room, there were two neat, white cards—"The American Ambassador." I asked the Colonel if she thought there was the slightest chance they might have been delivered in person, and she said if she did, she would go out and howl. We were both much taken with that old Vermonter, with his sad, granite-like, shy eyes of a thinker.

I also drove the English nuts, because they couldn't imagine a full colonel going anyplace with only a lowly shavetail in tow. We tried to explain we were an army of (a) 1 colonel, (b) a mess of second lieutenants, and (c) lots of privates—so that everybody would have a fair and even start—and they thought that was a "frightfully interesting" plan. Our hostesses really were Sr. Controller Leslie E. Whately, Deputy Director of ATS and Air Commandant J. Trefusis Forbes, Director of the WAAF. Both are keen top-flight women, Whately a little more brittle than outdoorsy, horse-and-dogsy Forbes. We spent days with those women, traveling to their many training centers, hotels, and military installations. The number of jobs the British women are filling is really amazing.

So—we went to Claridge's, where they had reserved for us the suite the chief of staff had on his visit over there—two bedrooms, two baths, and a living room. As the boss said, "Wouldn't it be wonderful to be rich all the time?" Thank God our expenses were paid. (Don't give out this tid-bit to the community.) The final straw was two buttons, for the valet and maid, placed so you could ring them while you were stretched out in the bathtub. The boss said one more night, and curiosity would have overcome her, and she would have rung one of the darned things. It got to be funny, how much she looked after me, despite my "aide" status. She would ration me a Hershey bar a night (one-half a one—we shared) to eke out the British diet, and after we went to a bookstore (Southeby's that Dickens loved) and got G. K. Chesterton's "Short History of England," she would read to me aloud just before we went to bed. One night she got a nightmare, and woke up calling, with no end of formality, for "Lt. Bandel" (she always calls me "Betty" when she's awake). By the time I tore from my bedroom across the sitting room to hers, she was standing by the window, about to throw the curtain back to see out—and the lights were on! I said, "The blackout, Colonel!" and she said, "Yes, it is black out." By that time she came to, and we had another Hershey bar and went back to bed.

Incidentally, Rover got the brilliant idea that "Lt. Bandel or Mrs. Hobby" should spend "a whole day just following an ATS through her schedule, from Reveille to Lights Out." Wonder what she thinks we've been doing up at Des Moines? We said, yes, that would be jolly. I earmarked all the places I want to see, really, when I can go as a visitor.

And in London we had some wonderful bits. Duncan took me out several nights, when the Colonel was tied up.[44] Once we went to a Red Cross shelter where she had worked as an ambulance driver, and where an old lady sits and takes care of the place—in her third year underground! Another night we had fish and chips in the New Zealand club, where I had an opportunity to talk to two WAAF corporals, and find out how they really felt about their jobs. Incidentally, that was my main purpose in life—to fall out of the official party and chat with the girls and junior officers, to find out what the score was, as much as possible. One day Duncan drove the Colonel and me through the market district, and as we crept along between the push-carts, the car door was suddenly opened and a grinning Cockney thrust three apples inside, saying, "For America." Apples are so scarce, his gift was like a gift of gold. Incidentally, the food is plentiful but lacking in variety. The Colonel says if they would just give up boiling everything to death they would begin to make some headway. Lord Woolton had an article in the papers which drove us close to hysterics—he said there were fourteen ways of cooking potatoes, and the public should try them all. We thought we had.

On our flight home, we stopped at a far northern point, and had a wonderful day with American troops.

Well, that's all. I thought of you all, from Anthony to Grandma, every minute, and I wanted you all with me.

The following three letters from Tucsonans at Fort Des Moines relate some of the stresses of aiming for officer candidacy, and of being a noncommissioned officer.

9. Auxiliary Emily Brown to Mrs. Bandel

Brown is training as an auxiliary after not passing the officer training course earlier in the year.

[November 9, 1942
20th Company, 3rd Regiment
Army Post Branch,
Des Moines, Iowa]

My dear Mrs. Bandel—

So far I have only availed myself of the flashlight you so kindly gave me on the two occasions when I had to arise before reveille to serve on kitchen police. I have been snug in my little bed every evening before lights out—I am that kind of a girl now—I shudder to think of the consequences should I sit up until 10 p.m.

The training period has been fun—a little strenuous, but fun, nonetheless. We have one week more & then we are turned out—either to specialists' schools or to duty. I wandered into public relations office this afternoon on an errand & was greeted with joy—the lieutenant who talked to me said there was a crying need for newspaperwomen & that she would personally see to it that I was assigned to her office—I would consider it a definite break if she is successful. The chances of making officers' school are very slim in the light of the hundreds of well qualified women already here—the jobs open now for auxiliaries are not too exciting & the prospect of doing public relations work is the best so far—I am the envy of the girls in my squad room.

I am enjoying looking at life from this side of the parade ground—I am free of any responsibility, happy, well-fed & not sad with my lot. I am looking forward to seeing Betty & know how proud you are of her & how happy you are that she has been given such a good slice of WAAC life.

Affectionately, Emily.

10. Helen Harris to Betty Bandel

Harris was in Officer Candidate School at Fort Des Moines.

[November 22, 1942]

Dear Betty:

Just a note to tell you how happy I am for you in what you are doing. I think it is swell. They couldn't have picked anyone better for the job.[45] I also want to give you my new address—so you will know what I am doing. Co. 3, *1st* Regt.—Yes, and the same building. I wish I could have had your bed. It might have brought me luck. *And* luck!! I will need a lot of it. They are certainly picking us to pieces at every turn—and hinting all the time that only a few of us will pass. I hope it is just to put a scare in us, and that the results with us are the same as the other classes.

Any way, keep a good thought for me. I need it, as I believe you know how much it means to me.

Love, Helen

11. Bessie [Edna] Floyd to Betty Bandel

4th Company, 1st Regiment
Fort Des Moines, Iowa
November 29, 1942

Dear Betty:

Don't be misled by the address—I'm only the poor pursued and greatly harassed supply sergeant—and I love it. I can't ever remember enjoying working hard but I have really worked in the three weeks I have been here. I got here for the last two weeks of this company and it was my pleasure to get pinks for them to graduate in. The supply room seemed to be in a hopeless muddle for days and then suddenly all the girls were gone, all their old clothes were gone, the laundry was gone and I had mopped the floor. All this week we have been receiving new girls. We thought we'd get a rest but Monday 24 came in from Daytona and yesterday and today the others have been coming. There's never a dull moment.

I was very happy to escape from the warehouse. Now that I'm away from there I can admit that I wasn't very happy there. However, I learned a lot that has helped me here—in fact, I think it is an excellent place to train prospective supply sergeants. I was fortunate to have the warehouse for a back ground because after one week my supply officer was transferred and I was just about on my own.

You can't imagine how excited I was when Reilly brought us the news that you were in England. I think that's swell. I looked at all the pictures in the papers and in the newsreels, but no Betty. Betty the Brain and Betty the Big Shot. Do you remember once when you were first assigned to Public Relations and still wanted company work that I told you you'd be running the organization? You will.

I dreamed about you last night. Dreams are such peculiar things. I was sitting on the church steps listening to my primitive Baptist uncle preach (he's really my second cousin's husband on my father's side but I always called him uncle—and his preaching was one of the family secrets that I don't usually reveal) and you came along and sat down on the steps too. I don't know why neither of us didn't go inside. Anyhow, I recognized you and we just about broke up the service. Then I woke up and the noise wasn't people talking but my radiator gurgling.

My boss writes that he has had six stenographers since I left and he'll be glad when the war is over. I'll be qualified for any job he has by that time. Last week I went down to the Quartermaster and got three huge boxes of overcoats and two or three boxes of skirts and jackets. There was one man, the truck driver (a Waac) and one girl from the QM. And I. We four loaded the truck. There was no loading dock, the warehouse was in the basement, the boxes had to be lifted into the truck. We did it with very little effort. It is surprising what you can do when you put your mind to it.

I wish I had had to do kp duty. Everything else has happened to me. In October I had a two day pass and went to Chicago with another Waac who had friends there. That was really a week end. I hadn't slept in a bed for three months and we stayed at the Sherman, and at service rates. We visited the Chicago Servicemen's Club and the Mayor came up and introduced himself. (I understand that some things about him are questionable but when hot dogs and coffee are given to me I don't ask questions.)[46] We were the first Waacs to visit and they were quite pleased with us. I had never been to Chicago so I had to see Marshall Fields, eat at the Palmer House and see the Lake and everything else. We were supposed to be here by reveille on Monday. We had a sneaking idea that we wouldn't be in if the train left Chicago at 11:30 so before we had dinner Sunday night we went down to the station and asked. The gentleman at the information desk told us that the train for Des Moines left at 8:30. It was then six. So we went out in search of a steak and found one for $3.00 so I had fish. At eight we left for the station. At eight-ten we arrived at the station and were told that the train was just leaving. I got on but when I looked back poor Frances was fifty feet behind with the bag—and she is smaller than I. The conductor said, "She'll never make it. If you want to stay with her you'd better jump off." So I jumped off and there we were, AWOL in Chicago. We were so afraid that we'd miss the next train that we didn't leave the station. A friend of mine was our first sergeant so I knew she'd believe us. But this is the Army—she was transferred into a Headquarters Company over the week end. Fortunately the new first Sergeant was a friend of Frances'. We weren't even reprimanded— I suppose because so many Waacs missed the same train that it was obvious it was the truth.

I didn't know I was writing such a volume. It may be a little disconnected but you can blame that on the fact that I was interrupted by people wanting sheets or overcoats or fleece-lined gloves. Or people who just wondered who was typing.

Bye now—As ever, Bessie

12. *Betty Bandel to Mrs. Bandel*

November 24, 1942
Washington

Just a note, to say I am alive and kicking and happy and working my fool head off. Maw, I got all the interesting clippings—many thanks. Incidentally, will you tell Alexander I know I am a heel for not writing, but durn it all I expect to be spoiled by her, just the way I have been for ten years and more, and where the heck is a letter?

Naturally, living is costly here. My meals never seem to run under a dollar, and taxis are really an item, since I am always tearing breathlessly from one end of town to the other. I get $6 per diem when I am travelling, but by the time you pay $3 or $4 for a hotel room, plus meals and tips and taxis, you come out on the short end of the deal. This last week-end, in New York, the Little Colonel insisted that I use some of her paper's (The *Houston Post*) advertising scrip, just as she did, to pay the hotel bill—but that was a windfall which doesn't often happen, of course. If we had been on per diem in England, we would both have been broke for the winter—but fortunately such was not the arrangement. Needless to say, don't read to my constituency anything about the army's financial arrangements—which are always a mystery even to the Finance Corps. But I haven't the time to see any shows (my last was the Gilbert and Sullivan number in Scotland, preceded by Noel Coward's grand movie about the British navy—which we saw in London and loved) or music, and the shops are always closed by the time I leave the Pentagon. Incidentally, that building will be the death of me—it is way over in Virginia, in the first place, and it takes you ten minutes after you get in the thing to reach your office. It is built like a giant spider-web, & it takes you 3 weeks to find your way around. One of our girls found a lieutenant-colonel wandering around lost the other day, asked him if she could help, & received the answer, "Don't try to tell me how to get to my room—just take me by the hand & lead me."

The boss gave a talk in New York Sunday before the American Women's Association (Ann Morgan [*sic*] presided—a nice old gal—she kept mistaking me for the Little Colonel, every time she turned around & found me under-foot).[47] We got in fairly early, stayed at the Plaza hotel near the Park, & went for a brisk walk down Fifth Avenue—the Little Colonel insisted she wanted some practice in marching (she is trying to stretch her stride to the prescribed 30 inches, under my tutelage), but ended up by nosing around looking in the shop windows, after Maw's best manner. Then when we came back to the hotel at 1:30 am. (& had to get up at 4:30 to make the plane & train home) we ordered chicken sandwiches & milk, & ate our heads off. Incidentally, the good souls at the hotel were slightly confused over the reservation—they had made it for "Col. & Mrs. Hobby, & Lt. Bandel—one double room & one single."

I had a wonderful time out at Leavenworth—Col. & Mrs. Schmahl (executive officer) entertained me, while Gen. & Mrs. Truesdell entertained the Colonel.[48] All the cream of the regular army. Mrs. S. put me in her daughter's room (she being away to college) & proudly exhibited me as a living Waac—party that night, etc. The L.C.'s family at Houston was adorable, from fat little Governor to Anne-like Jessica. I am getting so blasé about travel I didn't even bother to go out & look at the town.

13. *Dave Brinegar to Betty Bandel*[49]

11/26/42
[Public Division,
Barrage Balloon School,
Camp Tyson, Tennessee]

Dear Betty,

Pardon me for writing like this—after all, *you* are the field soldier, and my role seems to be that of the "desk soldier"—but I can't help but say that your success has been very, very thrilling personally to me. (You should know that!) I am glad you have a Little Colonel you can admire and serve well, and I hope (if you want to be) that someday you can be a Colonel yourself.

I know you're too busy to write to me often, so I don't ask that. But drop a line when you can. And *if you ever have low moments,* remember that down in Tennessee is a lieutenant who is for you and feels you are a grand success and that you're doing a very important job that no mere man could do.

Love and kisses, your friend Dave

P.S. *I am very glad you joined.* You have the supreme satisfaction of knowing you are serving in a way where your own ample talents can be exercised best; that you have proved yourself publicly as well as privately; that you have evoked the sincerest admiration for yourself. Your replies to my letters have been valued greatly by me. There probably would have existed no excuse to ever write you on any subject had you not joined. I almost didn't then, for it seemed that what you did was so much more worth-while and better than a mere man's enlistment there was very little comparison, and my poor congratulations were superfluous, but I wrote. In the natural course of events this correspondence will no doubt die; but it has helped me do my job, and if it has brought you any pleasure I am doubly contented.

I suspect you feel as idealistically about this matter of being in the army as I do—that service thrills you. If you do, we stand together under our own flag, as a brother and sister and as fellow soldiers, in a way that civilians never in the service can hardly understand.

14. *Betty Bandel to Mrs. Bandel*

November 27, 1942

Thanks for the lovely letters—I found them waiting for me when I got home from the Little Colonel's, where I was invited to supper—a lovely, home-cooked meal prepared by chocolate-colored Nettie-Mae, which together with the letters, kept me from being homesick over this Thanksgiving week-end. I had no time to be homesick Thanksgiving Day—I worked until 7:30, & then went out to dinner with Gretchen Thorp.

The L.C.'s husband is in town, & I think it was in a rush of motherliness that she asked me home to supper with them tonight—she never acts as if I were a scant seven years her junior. Helen Gruber came over to have supper with us.

Did I tell you about the Rover Club? It formed spontaneously one day in England—composed of everybody who has ever spent one day trying to keep up with Mrs. R. We are to have annual meetings—one year in Tasmania, the next in Utah, the third in Afghanistan, etc.

And did I tell you about our pipe? The L.C. bought a churchwarden in Scotland, to give to her brother, & she & I got so bored sitting in that hotel in Glasgow we took to smoking it one night, to the amusement & amazement of dear Major Bailey.[50] The L.C. told her husband about it, & he thought it was very funny; but she told a bunch of "old army," & she said you could have cut the silence with a cheese-knife.

Of course I met lots of nice Englishmen, young and old—one lovely Scotsman named Angus Malcolm—but all for 10 minutes, in flight. I didn't stay longer than that in any one spot.

15. Betty Bandel to Mrs. Bandel

December 4, 1942

Maw, your cake was such a howling success that I almost had to protect my rights. The mob discovered it, asked if they could put a piece in their lunches to take to work (the food at the Pentagon is absolutely horrible), & how could I refuse? It melted fast.

The boss is going to N.Y. Tuesday, & we will both be off again Wednesday for Daytona Beach (the new training center) for a day. Then back to Wash. for a week before going to New Orleans for a big conference, to return just before Xmas & start off again on another trip that will keep us travelling Xmas day— itinerary not yet known. So no leave, my dears, much as I would like it. But I hope to spend most of January quietly in Washington—if nothing else breaks loose. Please don't mention to anybody the possibility of my travelling Xmas day—they might think it a little rough, not knowing the necessity for such trips, & anyway it isn't settled yet.

More & more, I am getting nice research projects to do—you know how they delight my soul. The boss turns me loose to find out this or that army method, or to suggest a plan for this or that project or procedure, or to draft this or that speech or outline for a speech. Whatever an aide is supposed to do—& I have never had time to find out what it is—I am sure I don't do it, but I certainly do everything else in the world. Dotty would have died of hysterics if she could have seen me give the L.C. a manicure the other day, when she suddenly had to go to lunch with Gen. & Mrs. Marshall—I almost had to use type cleaner, there being no nail polish remover in the office.[51] The hidden talents this war is developing!

The news of so many Tucson deaths is startling—poor Elspeth Duncan's American fiancé, Gen. Lyons, just died of pneumonia—she will be quite done in by the news, I am afraid.

16. Dave Brinegar to Betty Bandel

December 10, 1942

Dear Betty—

It occurred to me today that you, too, might be expecting promotion, so I got a pair of sterling bars and am enclosing them in hope they will bring you good luck.[52] I will consider they have if you're double-promoted and never need them.

I think the feeling that you are fellow soldiers is very general. I have heard it on the radio, in camp, everywhere. We don't have any Waacs here, but I know all of us wish we did. It isn't that civilians are *per se* bad; it is just that most of us feel an army post is no place for a civilian. I know I particularly resent civilian young men holding jobs on army posts. They are outside the chain of command, do not understand the army, often are very discourteous and sometimes even overbearing, and in general just look terrible (to me). So the entire WAAC movement, plus a movement to get *men* in *too,* meets with most army folks' approval.

Let me know how you fare. I'm with you always, heart and soul, and I'm proud to be.

17. *Betty Bandel to Mrs. Bandel*

Dec. 12, 1942
Washington

I returned from my last trip to find I had a room—the ever-efficient Gunston Hall Waacs had had one member leave during my absence, and, since she had held the one single room and I was the oldest inhabitant left in the place, they decided I deserved it and moved me over. This new one adjoins the kitchen and has no door, but is nevertheless endowed with a desk, bookshelves, and divers other riches.

I am enclosing a letter from Dave Brinegar, because I think it one of the loveliest things that ever happened to me. I must say it makes me feel like a calf that has been over-vigorously licked by an affectionate mother cow. I also got a lovely note from Mrs. Helm—I sent her some roses, and she responded with this: "Dear Betty Bandel: Your note is one of the very nicest I have ever had, so nice that I am going to keep it to remind myself what a note should be. Then there is the heart-warming thought that I have a new friend, so I am enjoying that idea and the lovely roses. Thank you. Is there any chance that you will be here on Christmas Day? Could you come to a mid-day dinner? I hope so." So I, drooling at the thought of missing one of her dinners, wrote back my profound regrets, etc., official business, etc.

I received dear Alexander's letter—tell her, yes, I was along when Eleanor held Franklin Pig in her arms.[53] That was the one day we had with the WRENs [*sic*]. It was, as the British say, "laid on" for Mrs. R., and was one of the things Mrs. R. expressed a wish to have us in on. We had to wait to make up our final schedule until she had picked out the days she wanted us along, and this was one of the two or three. It was the Canterbury, Dover, and way stations between expedition, with Lady Reading along guiding things and with Franklin Pig showing up at the Women's Institute exhibit of war-time preserving, etc., in one of the lovely Kentish villages en route. They bombed Canterbury the next day—I presume they had gotten wind of a possible visit there—but we were safely out of range, and only heard an alert—a very mild thing which made Elspeth Duncan say with scorn the next morning, "What a shame! I was hoping we'd have some fun—I would have come by to take you out in it." She had the most touching faith in my eagerness to be "out in it."

Alexander says she was "concerned" for fear I might be left in England to help establish Waacs—there is nothing I would like more than a tour of foreign duty, but for the first time the L.C. is letting drop little hints as to which way my fortunes may fall. Her policy is, as it is in the Air Force, to rotate officers frequently, so as to keep them from going stale and give them the broadest possible experience. She is also thinking already about junior and senior officers' schools, such as the British have to keep the women on their toes on new policies, plans, methods, etc. So I have no doubt I will be sent out into the field for a time, and perhaps sent to school, but I also gather—although she has certainly never actually said anything on the subject—that she wants my permanent assignment to be more or less around headquarters, although in just what capacity I have no idea. Already my job is anything but an aide's job, and they will probably have to find a new name for it—although "aide" would be a perfectly legitimate term when the L.C. hoists a star—which she should do as the Corps grows.[54] A unit of 15,000 men is commanded by a major general, and our present goal is 150,000 women. But the wily Little Colonel does not want to rock the boat by even the breath of a suggestion that anyone inside the corps is asking for a general's rank for her or for any woman—if they want to give it to her, after the Corps is well established and is actually functioning in the field, and has proved its worth, that will be a different thing, of course. Actually, for the Corps, it would be a very good thing—army people think a lot about what kind of gadget you wear on your shoulder. Don't breathe any of this to anybody, of course.[55]

Just now, we are undergoing terrific changes of policy and plan because of the sudden lifting of our 25,000 ceiling by the president's executive order allowing us to train the whole 150,000 women allowed by the original law. One of my principal jobs has lately come to be the digesting of all kinds of nebulous plans and projects into short, readable outlines for the L.C., and the addition to them of comments, based on whatever I can find out from our various divisions, as to whether the plan would work, how it might be made more practical, etc. She has a true newspaperwoman's 24-hour deadline sense, and the way War Department people will take a week or two to make up a plan, when some big thing is being held up waiting for it, drives her wild. They work thoroughly and well, and she would be the last one to advocate sloppiness or error, but, as she often says, "We can dot the i's after the war is over." I think my newspaper deadline sense is what makes me useful to her—when I get an assignment in the morning, I break my neck to get it back to her in the afternoon, cutting whatever corners must be cut to do it. Incidentally, the working day runs from 8:30 a.m. to about 7 p.m., most days, and is frequently followed by an evening of added work. But then I get three or four days of travel every week or two, with plenty of time to sleep and rest on the trains and planes.

We got grounded out in Des Moines, and I, out of pure ignorance that although you can have priorities on a plane for an emergency war mission you can't have them on a train, got us out of the place by calling up Chicago and announcing, in a decided tone, that there would be three of us there to pick up tickets the following afternoon "on priority." Evidently I sounded so sure of my ground the fellow thought there was some rule out he hadn't heard about, because I got the tickets even though the train had been closed to reservations for three days—travel east of Chicago toward Washington is almost impossible now, because of the congestion on the trains. Craig McGeachy had egged me on to make the call, when it became apparent we were grounded and our priorities would be no good, and I told her—when I found out what I'd done—that I'd probably be court-martialed. She said, on the contrary, I'd probably be given a medal—she said if I could get it in writing, I would have established a useful precedent. The Boss thought it was very funny. I also turned into a travel agent to get us the R.R. tickets back—wrote out the Transportation Requests, on some blanks our Administrative Division had had sense enough to give me.

Then, after a short 24 hours in Washington, we flew down to Daytona in military aircraft, and spent a day and a half as guests at the home of Col. and Mrs. Faith—excuse me, since yesterday GENERAL and Mrs. Faith. The Boss recommended him for promotion, on the basis of the establishment of our new Training Command, to coordinate and direct all WAAC training. They have taken over all the available hotels, and are training the Basics in them. Some of the girls miss the old Post, and the life which can only center around a parade ground and barracks, but others enjoy the dispersal of Daytona, and the challenge to women officers to make their arrangements for study, living conditions, etc., work, out in some outlying hotel, when the army men at headquarters are way down town instead of right at hand to ask questions of. They drill on that magnificent, sandy beach. When you drive up to the principal hotel, you see the waves pounding the beach, through the great Spanish archway that your car noses its way through—then you get out and go into the hotel, and there, neat as you please, are the old army cots lined up side by side in what used to be palatial quarters. I saw Gwen, who was enjoying her work immensely and looking very good, and lapped up all I could find time to tell her about England. She says she will be home on leave after the first of the year, and will come over to say "hello." We ate in a WAAC mess—a wonderful lunch—and agreed again that the women cooks are doing a marvellous job—everybody says the food cooked in quantity by them is much tastier than that the men prepare.

Maw and Dotty, I have enjoyed the clippings and news immensely. The [Tucson] *Star* has been giving the WAACs a nice play. Yes, I wear the uniform to parties and everywhere—haven't had the civilian suit on since I got back from England.

I like to think of you all at 1025 [N. 2nd Ave., the Bandel home]. Now, keep the peace, my cherubs. Maw, DON'T work hard. Do take the $40 a month from my check, and use some of it to get a part-time maid. Everything you set aside let's figure toward the mortgage, with the idea of paying it off while prices and wages are high. After [dinner with the Faiths] the L.C. and I retired to our ad-joining rooms, we got into one of our long-winded discussions of life and art and the modern economic system that lasted till the wee hours. The boss says I am a deterrent to the war effort.

A group of naval officers have moved in next door to us, but I haven't been around enough to meet them—the girls say they are all nice. This Air Force fella that Arthyeta and I picked up the day we sailed down to Mt. Vernon, occasion-ally calls up to chat with me about "down home" in Texas-Arizona, and his wife and kids, but I seldom have time to see him—the other night he took me out and bought me spareribs, and insisted I eat them in my fingers, Texas style.

CHAPTER 3

Acting Deputy Director

Betty Bandel's first Christmas in the WAAC is celebrated far from home, but she writes to thank her newspaper colleagues for their many treasured gifts: "How did you know that, to one who is living out of a suitcase and in a uniform, a FLAT sewing kit is more precious than the crown jewels? But of all the precious things you put in my box, none gave me quite the nostalgia for one glimpse of the *Star*'s lovely messy newsroom, that I got from the sheet of paper with 'Merry Christmas,' and your names, upon it. I sat and read them over, one by one, and as I read each name, I saw you signing, and grinning, and stopping in the middle of a hectic day, right close to deadline—gosh!"[1]

Bandel is one of eighty WAAC officers promoted to captain in late December, in response to a great need for higher-ranking officers to be in charge of Waacs in the various army commands. While serving as Director Hobby's aide, Bandel accompanies her on numerous trips to promote the WAAC, encourage women to enlist, and inspect the newly established WAAC training camps in Florida and Fort Oglethorpe, Georgia. Hobby also assigns Bandel to act as deputy director in Washington during Hobby's frequent absences in the field. As Bandel's letters reveal, Hobby is away from Washington so much that many of the planning and policy decisions for the WAAC are conceived by Bandel in her absence, to be implemented later, with Hobby's recommendation, by the army.

Bandel's experience as a writer leads to her liaison with the Writers' War Board, a group of well-known writers and journalists who have pledged to aid the WAAC in recruiting and publicity campaigns by writing about life in the WAAC. Together, their work will reach a wide segment of the public, through popular magazines, newspapers, and film.[2] In March and early April, Bandel meets with them in New York with Hobby, and later accompanies ten members of the board on a visit to Fort Oglethorpe to observe the Waacs in training. Bandel is clearly in her element amongst them. She uses her writer's sense to observe the motley group with a humorous and perceptive eye: obviously, she likes them all and finds them deliciously quirky and engaging.

But in spite of attempts by the army and the WAAC administration to publicize the contribution that Waacs are making to the war effort, the WAAC encounters some critical problems and undergoes changes in the first half of 1943. A congressional mandate to increase its forces to 150,000 by the middle of the year is an almost impossible task that is complicated by a "smear" campaign beginning early in 1943, which alleges that Waacs are behaving immorally and that the army is aiding and abetting their behavior. Although Bandel seems not to have experienced much enmity personally, she and her fellow Waacs comment upon this problem as it manifests itself in the field.

During this time, the tenor of Bandel's letters begins to change. She comments on the "perfect team" of women working at headquarters. More and more, she involves herself in WAAC policy planning and administration, as well as doing her part to convince the army officers with whom the WAAC will be working of how valuable the WAAC can be to the army. The WAAC, with the support of the army command structure, begins a drive for a congressional bill integrating them into the army. Bandel's part in this effort is substantial. In March of 1943, she also travels to the Command and General Staff School, an advanced leadership-training course for army officers, to meet with the first Waac attendees and to talk about the WAAC at the school. Bandel has indeed become a part of the central administration, in spite of her half-serious concern during training that she would be assigned to the WAAC band, or be heading up a public relations office in some out-of-the-way post. In a letter to her mother, she reflects on how her rapid rise in status has affected her, and on the meaning of success: "I don't believe my present dream-like existence will bother me, when I leave it—so far as I can see, my one virtue is that I am always happiest with whatever I am doing and being at the moment, and still am never desirous of doing nothing but vegetating. As you know, my idea of success has nothing to do with locality or time element or people involved—it has to do with the development of the mind and spirit, which are not bound by time or place or people. Therefore I can be most successful (to my way of thinking) anywhere, anyplace, anytime, provided I develop my mind and spirit to the limit of their capacity. To my way of thinking, my most successful day was the day on which I finished a very bad novel, and thereby proved to myself I had the will-power to stick at a demanding mental job for one whole year, despite every type of interruption which life can put in the way."[3]

But she makes clear that she is, and will always be, willing to serve the war effort in whatever capacity is required. There is a moving statement of her commitment in this chapter. Reflecting upon her high status, the "regular" army, and career ambition, she avows that "all I really care about, at this moment, is making the Corps to help the army to help the country win the war—and if the Little Colonel tells me they need me most playing "Reveille" on the bugle at Des Moines, I'll go, with never a second thought."[4]

1.   *Betty Bandel to Mrs. Bandel*

December 28, 1942

Well, Maw, after I called you that night, I began entering upon the holidays. Of course, the boss's presentation of our captains' bars in New Orleans was what really began it, but it gathered momentum as it went. She told us not to say anything until it was official, so I carried mine around in my pocket, reaching in to feel if they were still there every 10 minutes.[5] It was a great thrill to go up to captain—most of the gals who did are in some executive position, and I really didn't expect to make the grade. It's fun still to be the No. 3 Waac in the country, even though I know I will have to give up that place when they begin promoting the women who are now serving as WAAC Service Command directors to rank equivalent to their responsibility—but they won't do that for several months yet, until the women have proven themselves.[6]

When we got back to Washington, Col. Catron, a nice old regular army man who is our executive officer, made a pretty little, shy speech, and read off the list of those in headquarters who had been promoted.[7] I was going to refrain from wearing my bars until the boss got back to pin them on, but we had a visiting Elk in town—one Controller Falkner of the British A.T.S., so it fell to my lot, as aide, to call on her, present the Director's compliments and the keys to the city, etc., etc.[8] Naturally, I wanted to put on as much side as possible, so I wore my bars. So I resigned myself to being "captain," for good and all.

I had a lot of fun with the telephone operators today. I was calling Des Moines, and said, "Captain Bandel wishes to speak to Major Payne." The operator there said, "Put Captain Bandel on," and grew incensed when I insisted Captain Bandel was on. Finally I said, "It's a she captain, not a he captain," and the operator at my end, evidently listening in, chuckled, and said, "They don't know about these things yet, do they captain? This is WAAC headquarters calling, operator. You ought to join up, and learn." The other one said, "Why don't you join up?" And mine said, "Gosh, I would, but I've got a child." And I said, "Come on in, girls, the water's fine." And by this time, I have no doubt, poor Major Payne, who was trying to get on the line and answer the phone, decided the world had gone mad.

I have told you about our perfect team, haven't I? Helen, Gen. Gruber's wife and very much old army, who is handsome as a picture, stylish, warmly friendly, the perfect gentlewoman, and a very good egg generally; Lois Hill, pert little Texan stenographer, lovable, smart as a whip, the perfect ingenue; and myself. We get along remarkably well—there is no clash of temperament whatever, and I cannot remember ever having worked in an office in which everyone in it seemed so confident in the other workers, and so willing to cooperate and help. Helen had a quart of champagne for me to take home, as a means of celebrating my promotion "properly."

[Describes her Christmas] I came home, and ran over next door to the naval officers' house—10 nicely mad chaps, most of them recently from civil life. We had two magnificent turkeys, cooked by some of the gals. One of the army men toasted the navy, and the senior naval officer toasted the army and the WAAC, and I, as senior WAAC officer, had to toast them both, and then one sentimental youngster from the navy got up and said he wanted to toast what was in all our hearts—our homes, and the thought that we might spend next Christmas in them. After dinner we danced, and this youngster turned out to rhumba well, and I did the "jarabe tapatio," and we had fun.

2. Betty Bandel to Mrs. Bandel

Bandel comments on why the WAAC, unlike the army nurses, opted be a military organization, and on her own hopes for an executive position.

January 3, 1943

Did I ever answer the question in your own Christmas card about how to address the L.C.?[9] All the old army men, like General Marshall and General Somervell, who knew her before the WAAC and who, in fact, were responsible for putting her in it, call her "Mrs."[10] Most of the army men in our headquarters say "Director," and most of the Waacs "Colonel." You see, the rub is, in the old army the nurses made a point of remaining a professional, non-military corps, not saluting or going through any of the military rigamarole. Our problem is an entirely different one—we do not represent one trade or profession, we have enlisted personnel whom we must house and keep living and working together harmoniously and efficiently, and we are rapidly growing so big that the only way we can accomplish that end is to have a real military organization, with military control. This control, and the esprit de corps which makes possible such control (which really, strangely, is based on cheerful and intelligent willingness to work unquestioningly with a group, under a leader) can only come when you have the trappings of salutes, etc. Hence the adherence to military titles, with us. I called up Mrs. Helm the other day, and when the message finally got to her that "Captain Bandel" was calling, she picked up the phone and said, "Did I hear aright? What on earth did you do to deserve to be a captain?" I said, "I can't imagine, ma'am."[11]

Would you mind too much calling Margaret Knight, of the Women's Overseas Service League? Tell her one of our greatest ambitions—we women who are serving in this war—is to live up to the example she and other members of the League set up by their service in the last one.[12]

I was reading over some of my old mail the other day, and was overwhelmed by the amount and variety of niceness there is in the world—everyone seems to wish those of us who are in uniform well. Even though uniforms almost outnumber civilian clothes, people push me to the front of lines, on buses, etc. And in this town that is something—I have never in my life seen anything like the mobs. You wait interminably for the simplest thing—a bus that can take one more person, for instance (Bandel rides the taxis)—and often you go into three or four restaurants before you find one that hasn't sold out all its food.

Back to the "Col. Hobby" situation, we of course substitute "ma'am" for the army's "sir." It is a little game we play, since most of us have never said it before. Actually, when I am alone with the colonel, or when we are with unofficial friends, I never think of saying it, and we all act just like ordinary human beings. But when I take some general into her inner office, or something, I "ma'am" till I'm blue in the face, jump up whenever she rises, stand back to let her go through doors first, etc. The other day we were walking away from a plane, and I was laden with many coats, bags, etc. She started to take some away from me, and I said, "Now, now, mustn't do it." She said, "Dawgonnit, Betty, that may be the army's idea, but it isn't mine. Army or no army, you aren't going to make me look like a clown. Here, give me some of that junk." So she loaded herself down with a lot, and we went wandering out of the station, like two civilized grown women, instead of like the traditional commanding officer and aide. She will play army just so long, and then will balk—especially when she thinks they're being silly. Col. Catron (old army to the eyebrows, but entirely flexible) refuses to let us play junior officer—he insists on holding doors open and letting us go through first, and I have finally given up on him out of sheer ennui—he is even more stubborn than I am.

Col. Macy, the boss, and I went to Col. Macy's apartment and had a drink to celebrate New Year. We were just ready for our first swallow when 12 o'clock struck, and the whistles and horns—very subdued this year—began to sound. We toasted the WAAC, and the army, and each other, and sat and talked until 2:30 a.m.

Don't get it in your head, Maw, I am with the L.C. for the duration—things don't work that way in the army. Also, I would like to do something really executive, rather than advisory, before I am through. I still yearn for company work, whenever I see our wonderful little auxiliaries around—they have such shining faces, and they seem so worthy of any amount of hard work to see that they get a square deal.

At present we are frightfully busy, with our expansion program. Resetting your sights for 150,000 requires some doing. I myself spend a lot of time on little research projects—things which don't quite jell, in the ordinary routine, and which the boss throws at me with "Bandel, see if you can figure out how we ought to fix that." I then study it over and present my newspaper idea of how it ought to be done, & the solution is invariably totally un-army, so then our Elder Statesmen work it over to make it fit into the army, & the boss takes the compromise & adds her own brilliant ideas (she actually has an excellent creative mind), & by this time nobody who worked on the project to start with could possibly recognize it. But we have fun. My latest has been a re-hash of the army "efficiency report," which has been a headache to the army for years, & which the boss simply refused to accept in its standard form. This is a form on which an officer evaluates the efficiency of officers working under him. If she accepts my idea—which is revolutionary—I'll tell you all about it. I really based my scheme on a study made by Gen. Hughes (whom we met in London) when he was a major—he described it to us one day, & I worked out from his plan.[13]

3. Technical Sergeant Emily C. Brown to Betty Bandel

[January 3, 1943
radio school in Kansas City]

Dear Betty—

Your nice Lieut. Nichol looked me up as per instructions. Seeing him, however, involved the breaking of these cast-iron rules:

(1) An auxiliary or non-commissioned Waac shall not be seen in company with an officer of the Army of the United States while wearing her uniform.

(2) A Waac shall not drink in uniform.

(3) A Waac shall not be lured into a man's hotel room.

My room-mate heard me consummating plans to meet the guy & as soon as I hung up, she turned to me aghast & said, "How do you ever expect to get away with all that!" and I replied, blandly, "I don't intend to get away with anything—I'm going to call the lieutenant & tell her what I am going to do." Poor Aggie (room-mate) was by that time completely flabbergasted—she stood by helpless while I called the lieutenant & damned if the old gal didn't give us her blessings on all three counts—in a tacit sort of way—so off I went for a very pleasant hour—In this matter as in many others, I found myself using my father's technique to great advantage—he always said to be sure & tell the commanding officer whenever you intended to break the rules & nine times out of ten you would get permission—I was apparently the first selected personnel of the WAAC that Lieutenant Nichol had ever conversed with & I think he was a little shocked to find me so completely happy and so entirely lacking in ambition—along military lines. He kept assuring me that I, too, would some day be wearing bars, but I kept assuring him that I, too, loved being a sergeant better than anything that had ever happened to me & was unconvinced that O.C. [Officer Candidate] was the ultimate. Seriously, though, something should be done to make O.C. more inviting. There are 280 hand-picked Waacs in the detachment, nearly all college graduates who held down responsible jobs in civilian life & not one has applied for a commission in spite of personal invitations from the officers in charge so to do. I met your lieutenant at the very end of my happy 32nd birthday, which was remarkable for the fact that that morning I had won the distinction of being the first Waac to build a radio receiver & the damned thing really worked! The rest of the class are starting on theirs & by the end of the coming week we will have completely whipped this business of receivers & will be ready to start on transmitters. The class continues to maintain its high academic average to the utter amazement of the army officials.

It's been at least two hours since I started this letter—being a WAAC is such a sociable affair. Everybody on the floor has been in to ask about the state of my health & remained to pass the time of day—I had looked forward to a long, peaceful afternoon with the symphony and my studies, but that afternoon is almost gone now.

I do hope the colonel comes out to inspect us here—I really would enjoy talking to you about this WAAC of ours. I'll never be sorry things broke the way they did for me because I've had this opportunity to see the thing from an auxiliary point of view—something which will be of inestimable value to me if & when I do move up to the more rarified atmosphere.

Congratulations on your further promotion—I fully expect you to be named assistant director of the corps & when that day arrives I'll be up to give you a few of my fine ideas.

4.   *Betty Bandel to Mrs. Bandel*

Ellipses here are in the text.

January 11th, 1943

We are en route to Ft. Leavenworth for a talk the Director will make this afternoon, & tomorrow morning we will stop in Kansas City long enough to see the Radio School where Emily is studying before flying home. Needless to say, I hope to see her. We are in the Chief of Staff's plane—occasionally it is offered to the Director when the Chief isn't using it (don't mention this)—so my life is simplified by not having to worry about the tickets, luggage, etc. We just step on & off the plane, & the pilot—one of the best in the country—says, "When would you like to take off, Colonel?"

Saturday was a big day. Yours truly appeared over the radio. It was supposed to be a round table among 4 service women, & when I got there it turned out to be a fancy luncheon called the "United Nations Club" luncheon, & I was seated between a brigadier general & a British naval commander. At the zero hour 4 of us poor souls—Lt. Palmer of the Waves (very good gal from Indiana), Lt. Clarke of the Canadian Women's Army Corps, & First Officer Biddle of the WRNS got up & read our parts in the script—I had given Meredith Howard, the woman who runs the show, the story about the 3 apples in London. They seemed to think it went fairly well.[14]

Also, lovely old General Peterson, head of the Inspector General's branch, was over to see the boss Saturday, &, as he came out, I started to help him with his coat, & he said, "By the way, you're the one that worked with my men a couple days last week, aren't you? . . . Yes . . . thought so . . . they came back & said, 'That Waac is a damned smart girl.'"

5. *Betty Bandel to Mrs. Bandel*

January 16 I think 1943

We have a new gal in our office—one Lieutenant Stryker, a southern belle from Mississippi. The work of aide-ing was getting so mixed up with a hundred other jobs that the L.C. told me to find somebody to share the chores. The boss wants me to stay in the office more, to kind of keep track of what goes on in her absence, and let Stryker do the aide part of the job—it will cut down on my nice trips, but I don't mind at all, since it will also mean increased responsibility, and increased contact with the inner executive activities of headquarters. Poor Stryker has to get used to something that was very hard for me at first—the boss's lightning changes of plan at the last minute. At first I would be dismayed by the thought of all the horrible little details that had to be changed, but now I think of it as a game to figure out how in the world I can accomplish the seemingly impossible, without letting the L.C. be worried by knowing just how many details there were to change. The boss was going to Philadelphia this week-end to make a speech at the annual Poor Richard banquet, and first she said it was such a little trip that she wouldn't need anybody along. Well, I saw the details piling up, and knew she was going to change her mind at the last minute, so I inwardly grinned and outwardly said nothing. Then Saturday morning, the boss called in and told Stryker she wanted her to go along. Poor Stryker turned pale, but didn't offer an objection or even a question. She seemed to realize what was needed, and, with a little prodding— not much—from me, got her own orders set up in whirlwind time, and was set and ready to go at 12:15. Actually, she will be much more help to the boss than I would be on the usual aide details, having travelled all over the world and had the usual southerner's education in things social. She can look after clothes, etc., in a way I never could—in fact, the boss looks after mine more than I do after hers. My life is getting complicated about now—Special Services is doing a movie for us, and I am the liaison guy. I went and talked with Col. Frank Capra—a very nice, quiet, efficient fella, incidentally—and sat up until 2 a.m. that night preparing him preliminary information.[15] Col. C. is to depart for Hollywood soon, turn it over to his writers, and, when they are ready, I am to come on for about a week there.

6.   *Betty Bandel to Mrs. Bandel*

She expresses her dedication to helping win the war.

January 23, 1943

Jeepers, what a week! It has not been my considered opinion that I have spent the last 30 years in a state of immobility, but, believe me, I had to join the WAAC to find out just how mobile I could become. Mental mobility, I am talking about now—my travels have stopped for a time, I fear. You see, the Little Colonel said to me, "Bandel, I don't know whether I ever want you for the final, permanent Deputy Director—I've been thinking all along that I wanted an older woman than myself—but you're the only person in the world I know who would act as Deputy Director for me now, because I need somebody when I'm out of town, and to take a little of this load when I'm in town, and understand perfectly if a month or six months from now I put somebody else in, or asked you to take some difficult field assignment that requires your youth. You wouldn't have your nose out of joint, and you wouldn't sit in a corner and mope. So I want you to be Acting Deputy Director, for now." So I looked at her tired little head, propped up on a weary fist, and said, "OK, boss." I thought it was to be just a kind of tacit agreement that I was to carry the ball while she was away, but Col. Catron was in the office yesterday, and said, "I wonder if you could think yet of someone for deputy director—I feel you should have one, with the amount of time you are forced to spend out of town, and the amount of work you are expected to do." And she said, "I can tell you right now. It's Bandel, on an absolutely selfish basis—from my standpoint. She knows it may be the most temporary kind of arrangement." So he said, "Very well— Bandel to Acting Deputy Director," and made a note in his little black book. I entered in the daily journal, "Director decided to use Bandel as Acting Deputy Director on a temporary, tentative, tenuous basis," and again thought that ended it, but just as I left the office tonight I noticed Col. Easterbrook had left a note for the administrative division to ask for a War Department order on the appointment, since he felt it would be "of interest to the entire corps." So I'm afraid the news is going to be quite widespread in the family—and I would regret that, if I cared a durn what anybody thought when, two months from now, I am shifted to a lower spot. I really don't, though—the one thing you learn in a job like mine is how many old army men, brilliant and loyal and devoted to country and job, cannot help but think of themselves and their assignments first—natural enough, to be sure, in men making a lifelong career out of the army, but a poor way to fight a war. For me, all I really care about, at this moment, is making the Corps to help the army to help the country win the war— and if the Little Colonel tells me they need me most playing "Reveille" on the bugle at Des Moines, I'll go, with never a second thought.

Actually, my work will differ very little from what I've done for the past two weeks. I've been trying to keep the boss informed on the activities of headquarters, and see to it that she stays in channels as much as possible. She is so busy deciding vital policy matters that she sometimes loses track of the activities of big chunks of her headquarters—I trot round and find out what is going on and gently punt her into reading the daily reports, etc., and asking questions that will keep her really informed. Then too, she sometimes forgets just how the army channel system works, and reaches down to give an assignment to someone way down in a division, instead of to the chief. I then run around and tell the chief, and the executive officer, in order to be sure everybody knows what everybody else is doing—an essential in intelligent staff work. The trouble with the army is it needs a good newsroom, with an editor sitting in the slot in the middle where he can see and hear everything, and can't lose track of some poor guy who is working away on a project which was vital when it was assigned to him, has since lost its value, and has been forgotten by the planners. She has a trick of giving me un-workout-able problems, which divisions submit in a form she doesn't like, to work out on a jackleg, amateur basis. I simply return to her my layman's commonsense idea of how it could be done, she approves or disapproves, and it then goes back to the Executive to be handed down to the proper division for a proper military dress. For the last two days I have been struggling with a tough problem anent our relations with the Air Forces—Col. Catron, the wise old owl, licked that one for me, at about 7 p.m. tonight.[16]

Don't tell anybody, except Alexander and Binda and Wicky and the Fullers, of course, about the deputy business, until I tell you.

There is a chance for one WAAC to go to Command and General Staff school (the army's cream of schools, except the War College), and the boss first thought she wanted me to go to it, but I think now she will send somebody else, this first time, and keep me at home at least until this thing is really rolling, policies are fairly well established, and companies are in the field in numbers—perhaps, if all goes well, by July 1. Gosh, how much there is to do! Miss Leis, our nice, hard-boiled, practical statistician-planner, said to me the other day, "My Lord, if private industry talked about expanding from 25,000 to 150,000 before July 1, somebody would lock 'em up!" She is new at headquarters, and, Lord, how she can think! She can make figures talk even to me.[17]

Incidentally, the size and the speed of this thing scare you to death, every now and then. When you analyze one little problem—what the Quartermaster has to do, for instance, to plan to get a uniform ready for one WAAC we are going to induct next July 1—it staggers you. Our whole supply branch, and every facet of the clothing branch over in Quartermaster, are involved—plus half the manufacturers in the country. It's a wonderful jigsaw puzzle.

But the funniest thing of the week was a little ceremony we had along about Wednesday morning. Col. Catron and Col. Esterbrook filed into the boss's office, solemn as two owls, and said, "Stand up, please." The boss, who can look like a little girl caught stealing jam, looked at me as if to say, "What have I done now?" We both stood up, and Col. Easterbrook read a document from the Commanding General, Services of Supply, to the effect that "Mrs. Oveta Culp

Hobby, Director, and Miss Betty Bandel, First Officer" had been awarded "the ribbons pertinent to the medals pertinent to the European-African-Middle Eastern theatre of operations" for service in that theatre. And then, as solemnly, he and Col. Catron pinned our little campaign ribbons on us—Col. Catron had thought it up, after reading that anybody who successfully completed a mission in that theatre, no matter how short, was eligible to wear them. He was as pleased as a child—or a grandpapa giving his grandchildren candy. I am the envy of WAAC headquarters.

Maw, aren't you getting in people's hair with tales of Betty? Imagine taking my picture to dinner! The picture was taken the first time I ever went with her on a trip, and I was yelling at the cameraman, "Wait a minute! I'll get out of the way!"

7. Mrs. Bandel to Betty Bandel

[January 23, 1943]

Betsy darling—

I love the snaps—the best yet of you—Gwen is right—the light shines thru. Such a nice note Wednesday, and such a precious letter today. Now "God's In His Heaven."

Who is Jess Rice? I *am* surprised you sent your "safety pins" to Helen—thot you'd keep them for Betsy Jr.—for of course you must *stay* in the army??[18] So you are talked about by Mrs. Roosevelt—I can no longer remain modest in the face of all this reflected glory.

Lovingly, Maw.

8. Anne Dragonette to Betty Bandel

Anne, aged seven, is Bandel's niece.

[January 27, 1943]

Dear Betty,

Can't you come home to me today or tomorrow. Because I am home sick for you.

Anne

9. Mrs. Bandel to Betty Bandel

[January 30, 1943]

My Darling Bet—

Your 2 grand letters yesterday overwhelm me. What can I *say* to make you know I'm "floored," with the spurs you are wearing—except that you are your father's own daughter and so could do no less. Of course fate has much to do with opportunity but—you no doubt were ready—and since all this can still hear you say "I'll blow Reveille if it's where I can best serve"—I'm sure you could be trusted with the Court of St. James.[19] The trouble at this end is I want to get out an Extra. But I'll be good and trail!

10. Betty Bandel to Mrs. Bandel

Jan. 30, 1943

I had thought I would go out with the boss on a long trip with Mrs. Roosevelt to Des Moines and Kansas City, but things are getting to such a state here that I asked yesterday if she didn't want me to stay in headquarters, and she said she did but just hadn't had the heart to ask me to do it. So of course I will stay, barring being called to Hollywood for the Capra business. I feel that between now and July 1 is our critical time—if we can get by then, we will have made the Corps. All our big decisions, on which the future running of the Corps depends, are being made now. A bill is before Congress to place us in the army, rather than with it; our budget, our future size, our methods of use, our methods of training—all these are being decided now. It means constant planning, constant conferences with those higher up in the war department. The boss does nothing but such work when she is here, and when she is away I can help her by keeping my finger on such problems as they come up, and being ready to shoot the facts to her when she gets back. She is a diplomat and a planner of the first water. Col. Catron knows the ins and outs of the army game from 30 years of experience. They make a good team.

A directive came in yesterday that caused us all to die laughing. It said, "By order of the Commanding General, Services of Supply, the Adjutant General will conduct a survey to eliminate all activities not essential to (1) winning the war, and (2) operating the Women's Army Auxiliary Corps." The boss collapsed when I read it to her.

11. Betty Bandel to Mrs. Bandel

February 14, 1943

I am doing more than playing deputy at the moment. The boss will be gone, probably until Mar. 8, and we are right smack in the middle of all kinds of definitive problems. If the bill now before Congress to put us in the army gets really hot while she is away, she will have to come back in for hearings. Otherwise, I will keep her posted of developments in our planning, etc., by telephone and wire. Tomorrow Col. Catron and I go up to a big meeting with G-1 and G-3 of the general staff (personnel and operations), to decide finally the dates by which we will be expected to produce our first so-many-thousand Waacs, and the priority on which they will be produced (how many to Air Forces, how

many to Services of Supply, etc.). Of course we already have companies flowing into the field, but we are increasing our training capacity with new training
centers, and we must know just how many we are expected to produce by when,
so as to gauge what extra training capacity to ask for, what extra clothing, housing, etc. Gosh, the ramifications of this job! I wish I could quote figures to give
you an idea. After the war, I will. If I survive this war, I should come out well
qualified for the diplomatic service—or the prize ring.

No, I don't have anything to do with WAAC ads—they are dreamed up by
the army's Recruiting and Induction Service publicity bureau, old and expert
hands at the business. It would scare me to death to think how many real professionals in how many fields are working for us, and more or less what my job
is supposed to be in relation to them—if I didn't think it was so funny.

Vincenta Torres [of Tucson] went over in the cooking detail, but her bi-
lingual ability may have changed her assignment. I saw her at the place from
which she left, along with 150 other of the happiest, most excited women I
ever saw.[20]

If the war were to end this year, whether we are in or with the army, we
would be subject to duty for six more months. Then I would sit under a tree, eat
the meat out of coconuts, and throw the shells at monkeys—for days and weeks
and months. As for the L.C., she saw some little dirty ragamuffins playing on the
street the other day, one with his socks all down and his hair every which-way,
and in a moment she was in floods of tears. She wants one thing after this war—
to get back to Governor, and William and Jessica, and run her home again. Of
course, being the L.C., she couldn't be there a month before she would be into
something extra-curricular—but after all she is executive vice president of a big
newspaper, which is a fairly good-sized job to add on to running a home.[21]

As for service in Africa—I have had kind of a half-way chance to express
a preference for foreign service on two occasions, but the boss kind of indicated
I might be of more actual service in hq—and that, of course, settled it.

Did I ever tell you, Maw, the thing that Alexander wrote me when I got back
from England, that seemed to me—well—a little overwhelming? Particularly
from my Alexander of the scholarly exactness. She wrote, "Anyway, we are all
bursting with pride and excitement and happiness over your good fortune in
finding rapid *opportunity* to reveal the worth that had long been as familiar to
us as the blue sky and the Catalinas and the vehement stars."[22] Whenever I am
feeling particularly incapable of doing anything right, I take it out and read it
again—and decide any goon could do well, with that to live up to.

12. *Betty Bandel to Anne Dragonette*

February 21, 1943

Dear Anne:

Thursday I had lunch at the White House! You know what the White House
is, don't you? It is the big old white house here in Washington where the Pres-

ACTING DEPUTY DIRECTOR 69

ident of the United States and his family live. Mrs. Roosevelt, who is the wife of the President and who is very busy with her children and her grandchildren and with all kinds of plans to help poor people and everybody else, almost, still sees to it that she has time to be nice to other people here in Washington, like me. She wanted to give a little party for the women who are in charge of the WAACS and the WAVEs and the other women who are helping the army and navy to win the war, so she asked my Little Colonel, but my Little Colonel was out of town, so she asked me instead. So Mrs. Helm called me up Thursday morning and said Mrs. Roosevelt had only thought this luncheon up a little while ago, so there hadn't been time to get out formal invitations, but would I have time to come to lunch anyway? I said, "Mrs. Helm, I'm busy, but I'm not that busy—I guess I can find time to come to the White House for lunch." So she said, "Fine!" And Mrs. Helm said, "Good! Now Malvina [Thompson] and I can fight over who gets to sit next to you."

Well, I didn't have a bran fresh new shirt when Mrs. Helm called me up, so I went out in the hall, and saw a Waac walking along who had one on, and said, "Just a minute. I need you." Then I told her I needed her shirt, so I could go to the White House all fresh and clean. Lois Hill, the girl in my office, combed my hair all over for me, and brushed off my uniform, and filed my fingernails, and cleaned my face with some little pads and powder and things.

Then at noon Florence Newsome and I went down and rode in a taxi over to the White House.[23] We walked up to the front door, and got there just when Commander McAfee, who is the lady in charge of the WAVEs, got there, and so we saluted and said, "How do you do, ma'am?" And she smiled and shook hands, and we went on into the big entrance room. Then an usher took us to a little table that had a drawing of a table in the dining room on it. I noticed Mrs. Roosevelt had the wife of a big naval man sitting to her right, with Commander McAfee sitting next to the naval wife; then she had Mrs. Marshall, who is the wife of the man who runs the army, to her left, and I was to sit next to Mrs. Marshall, since I represented our Little Colonel.[24] I didn't get to sit next to Mrs. Helm or Miss Thompson, because they had to sit a little farther down the table. Each one of us had a place card with our name on it. I told Miss Thompson I had to take mine home, so I could send it to my niece, so I slipped mine in my pocket.

We talked a lot, and Mrs. Roosevelt remembered how wet we got in England, and told some funny stories, and we all laughed. Mrs. Marshall got to talking to me a lot—she stayed in Tucson one winter, it developed—and I really had a lovely time.

Mrs. Roosevelt wanted to show us a wonderful bracelet that her guest, Mme. Chiang Kai Shek, the great Chinese woman, had given her.[25] It was small gold links, and with Chinese poems written in tiny characters on each bit of inlaid enamel. Miss Thompson brought a scroll of paper with flowers painted on it and with the little poems all translated into English and written out on it. Mrs. Roosevelt put on her spectacle and read us the poems, some of which were written by Chinese scholars as long ago as 500 B.C., and all of which talked about the beauty of the sea, and the wind, and flowers, and friendships. Everybody thought they were fine poems, and Mrs. Roosevelt read them very well.

Then Mrs. Roosevelt got up, and we all got up, and filed out into the entrance hall. Florence Newsome and I were the last, and Mrs. Roosevelt took both my hands and said she heard I had been working too hard, and I mustn't do that. And I said I understood Mrs. Roosevelt didn't exactly stand still herself, and she laughed and said, "Yes, but I've learned to play and rest in between the times I have to work hard." So we thanked her, and said "Good-bye," and went on out of the White House, and Mrs. Marshall drove us back to the Pentagon so we could go back to work.

Anne, your mother sent me your pictures. My, how nice you look as a Waac! And with a flag, and the Lincoln book, and—best of all—little Frieda Waac! You certainly are growing up. I see from your cap ornament that you are a WAAC officer—in fact a captain of Waacs, just like me.

Good night, Anne, and much love, Betty

13. *Betty Bandel to Mrs. Bandel*

February 25, 1943

No theatre party, because Controller Falkner was out of town again this week, and took young Subaltern Grayrigge with her. Grayrigge is an owl-eyed little English girl whom I like very much—just three months ago I was junior to her, and now when she calls me up she says, with true British regard for the forms, "Grayrigge here, ma'am." I scare the Navy to death by "ma'aming" their officers senior to me—they, you know, were commissioned directly from civil life (the key ones, that is) and didn't have our strict training in the mysteries of military courtesy and discipline. They have learned to salute by dint of hard practice, but they stick much closer to civilian practices than we do. Miss McAfee has a No. 2 gal from Indiana named Lt. Palmer who has a dry, droll sense of humor that is a lot of fun—at this reception of Sir John and Lady Dill's Saturday, Palmer and a marine officer and I were standing talking together, when a veddy veddy British officer came up and talked to us a minute, and strolled on. Palmer, with a very straight face and innocently questioning voice, turned to the marine and said, "Do you speak English?" "No, I never learned," he answered. "Do you?" And she, in her wonderful middle-western twang, said, "No, I never learned either."

14. *Betty Bandel to Mrs. Bandel*

March 4, 1943

I am under a dryer in the beauty shop of the Mayflower hotel—first time I have been able to get away from the office in time to have my hair washed in three weeks—& at that I will go back down tonight as soon as I get out from under this thing & try to finish a plan which I want to submit to the Director when she gets back here tomorrow night. We are hovering on the brink of being "in" the army rather than "with" it, & I am dreaming up a proposed change in regulations to make us fit—a kind of overall plan—which I hope the Director will submit, revised as she sees best, upstairs.[26] The detailed changes necessary in regulations are being dreamed up by our legal branch (a couple of good women lawyers), but I am working on the overall statement of policy, which I hope will simplify our procedure according to standard army practices & still safeguard a couple of exceptions to procedure which we consider essential to the efficiency of the Corps—like the fact that members shall have a right of appeal on matters of well-being (conditions of living & employment) up through the WAAC channel of women officers, when they cannot reach a satisfactory understanding with the immediate army commander. The British have this—& consequently never have to use it. We have a system which *requires* that certain matters go through WAAC channels—too cumbersome a system. All we need is the *right* of appeal. So I am dreaming up the policy. (Don't discuss these policies—they are so constantly subject to change.) We all think & work a lot over them, but it falls to my lot very often now to draw together the final statement, or to put in the briefest form possible the crux of the idea. Right now I have 3 major ones that I live with, eat with, & dream with—and as soon as they get resolved, others will pop up. I never thought I'd be a planner, with my feet firmly planted on the ceiling—but it's fun, like everything else.

My Lord, I almost forgot my Monday adventure! I broadcast in Spanish! I suspect I set Pan-American relations & the good neighbor policy back 10 years, but there was no one else in hq. who even admitted to reading Spanish. They made a recording to send to South America to be played over all their little radio stations. It was hilarious—you should have heard me stumbling around about the "estilo del uniforme [style of the uniform]" & the head of Minerva, "simbalo del sabituria y victoria [symbol of knowledge and victory]"—& ending up with an impassioned plea for continued union with our sisters to the South. Gosh, what this war is going to get me into! I just shut my eyes, take a deep breath, & jump in.

Another of my projects has been editing some lectures on sex hygiene! For Lord's sake. Incidentally, be *sure* not to pass this one on.

15. Betty Bandel to Mrs. Bandel

March 9, 1943

The L.C. is back, and things are popping. She appeared before the House Military Affairs committee today, and they asked her every question under the sun for most of the day. Then, instead of voting the bill out, they decided to continue hearings next Tuesday! Thus we are hung up another week, at least, before we can do much in a definite way about the regulations, etc., which must follow the bill itself. I am getting to be so much of a planner I feel as if I had my feet firmly planted on the ceiling all the time.

I now have an office of my own, in which I rattle around. I still like the old "city room" newspaper system, with everybody sitting around yelling whatever they want to yell across at everybody else. But in the army they are so anxious to put everybody in a little pigeon hole, and see that papers get held up for days while they flow from one pigeon hole to the next, that they have to put walls around you. The L.C. says they can't hurry on account of the emergency.

The staff meeting was nice. I wasn't scared after I got started—just talked to the kids a little about our present problems, and the reasons why some of them can't be solved overnight, and the importance of each department's keeping in close touch with every other one. Then I introduced Col. Catron, and asked him to explain the progress of some of our biggest plans, and they liked hearing all about that—keeps them informed, when otherwise they can easily lose track of things. Best of all, at the end they asked questions, and really got into some discussion.

16. *Betty Bandel to Mrs. Bandel*

She comments on her work on WAAC policy and public speaking.

March 14, 1943

What a week! I have worked morning and night over some major policy papers, involving our organization in the War Department, method of expansion, etc., etc., until I am green in the face. I have had the satisfaction of burrowing through War Department manuals, SOS [Services of Supply] books, regulations, and policies until I almost feel as it I were back in the dear old University of Arizona library, hot on the trail of a burning issue like whether London houses of the mid–Fourteenth Century had glass or just shutters. Even if I don't sell anybody else on my ideas, I have had the satisfaction of convincing myself what is the logical position and function of our headquarters, how it should operate, expand, and gradually change. I feel as if I had just arrived at the essential logic—the crux—of a plot.

I won't be making the Hollywood trip—the L.C. kind of intimated she wanted me to stick around just now, so of course I was flattered to stay. I must admit I am somewhat perturbed, to put it mildly, at the thought of speaking before 3000 picked army officers at the Command and General Staff school in Leavenworth the end of this month—but since I have put on this uniform, I have a kind of divine faith that I can do anything I am asked to do in it. I almost forget myself, and just go ahead and wade into whatever the assignment may be.

17. Betty Bandel to Mrs. Bandel

Bandel's adventure with the Writers' War Board begins.

March 20, 1943

The New York adventure was another one for the book. Wednesday the L.C. was to go to New York, accompanied by Col. Betters of Control, SOS, to discuss means of publicizing the WAAC with the War Writers' Board, a group of well known writers who meet once a week to figure out ways of offering their services to the government, in whatever line is most needed at any given time. She asked me to go along, so we flew up at about noon Wednesday. We were met by a gentleman—quite young—with a gray beard that grows only under his chin and sticks straight out like those affected by the English country squires of Dickens' day. He turned out to be Rex Stout. He took us into a little room, and there around a table were seated Clifton Fadiman, F. P. Adams, Paul Gallico, Russell Crouse, Margaret Leach [*sic*], and two or three others.[27]

They were all very swell—Adams is so much like his pictures, and his way of speaking, that he seems like a caricature of himself. It was just like stepping back into a newsroom—everybody lounged around and kidded everybody else and forgot all about army formality and said, "My God, that's lousy," over half the ideas, and groaned, and howled with laughter. Paul Gallico said what we needed was a whole flock of stories in which the Auxiliary, WAAC, always ended up with a lieutenant colonel for a husband. Then he said we should have a psychologist on our examining boards, to take care of women's problems. Adams said, "That's not a psychologist. That's a gynecologist." He looks like a gnome, sitting there with his beautifully ugly face all wrinkled up, and then suddenly he looks up at you from under his eyebrows and comes out with something like that. Fadiman is very competent, very kind, very helpful—much more a business man than the others. The L.C. gave them a simple, straightforward account of what we have done and what our plans are from a standpoint of recruiting, and they came back with many extremely helpful ideas. As usual, she won them all. After the meeting [Col. Betters of Control Division, Army Service Forces] took us to the Savoy-Plaza, where the L.C. had a suite reserved. Governor was coming on to spend the evening and the following morning with her—they had some business in New York—and she invited me to stay on for dinner and a play, before taking the midnight train home.[28] I demurred feebly, and stayed, of course. While Col. Betters took her around to call on Mayor LaGuardia and his wife, I went down and had my hair done. I fell asleep in the chair, and woke up with a part on the side, a roll of hair on top of my head, curls in the back and a bill for $3. But it was worth it to see the L.C.'s face, when I showed up at 6 p.m. Even Governor, who is far beyond noticing such details, said, "Say—haven't you done something different to your hair?" Someday I must find a way to tell the Little Colonel and her nice little fat round husband what they have meant to me, in this land of hard work and turmoil and that curious race of natives called Easterners.

These were my dissipations of the week. Otherwise, I had an interesting and swift-moving time. I accompanied the Boss and Col. Catron up to Gen. White's office (he is G-1 for the War Department) for a conference—and grew to like the little, quiet general even more than I had previously.[29] He is one of my favorite people in the War Department—makes you realize why the old army, with all its faults, was able to prepare, in peace-time, for the tremendous task which would face it in an emergency such as this. I like the scholar-soldiers.

I now have a helper—a cute little girl name Lt. Parker, who is a former reporter. She works like a beaver—good on quick research. A lot of the old bunch is in this week-end—we are sending them to Air Forces as the first WAAC staff officers to AAF [Army Air Forces]—Betty Clague from my old company, Arthyeta Van Dalsem, & others. I welcomed them this morning, & the L.C. made a little speech to them at noon.

18. *Corporal Emily Brown to Betty Bandel*

Waacs often received assignments that did not reflect their abilities and skills, as Emily Brown complains in her letter.

> Casual Detachment
> 3rd WAAC Training Center
> Fort Oglethorpe, Georgia
> [March 23, 1943]

Dear Betty—

I arrived here to be greeted by a very dismal little group—only 19 of the 72 in the original class had received orders. I hustled around & got the detachment commander's permission to organize a class in radio theory & that served as a good morale builder. The whole thing was the operators' idea—they ran into a lot of snags in trying to operate the equipment on the network during their last week at school & I tried to give them some idea of how to stabilize the frequency of a transmitter & stuff like that. The kids seemed to enjoy getting a little theory & most of the mechanics came along just for a brush-up. We were getting along fine & then I got hauled out & assigned to processing, where I spent one afternoon issuing utility coats before I got sick. They are holding the job for me, though—I understand the assignment is permanent for the duration of my stay here. There are about 25 others who have been similarly assigned but the majority of the group still lie around the barracks waiting—rumors of shipment are rife, of course, but to date only the 19 have actually gone out—to D.C., Scott Field & Chanute Field.

I am temporarily bottle-necked on O.C. [Officer Candidate status]. Now that I have finally condescended to offer myself for selection, nobody seems interested. The detachment officers fluffed off my questions with the remark that my K.C. [Kansas City] application probably wouldn't stand down here & I'd have to re-apply & what good would an application be without Lieutenant Tucker's rating & recommendation? After all, she's the only officer I've ever actually worked for. My platoon commander from ad school is here as a battalion commander & I might be able to launch myself under her sponsorship— but I hate to ask her to go through all that rigamarole. I guess I'll just have to wait until I get out in the field & see how they like my mouse-trap there.

We live a very primitive life here, but I am enjoying it—never a dull moment in my little military career—love, Emily

19. Betty Bandel to Mrs. Bandel

Bandel is at the army's Command and General Staff School.

March 29, 1943
Ft. Leavenworth

So much happens, so fast! I know this will all seem like a dream, five years from now. I have just finished lunch with Gen. & Mrs. Truesdell, Brigadier Dunn of the British Army, & Gen. Bruce & Gen. Tyndall of the American Army.[30] The Brigadier & I got in a fascinating scrap over leadership, how you define it, how you recognize it, how you achieve it. Old Gen. Truesdell had some swell ideas, & so did Gen. Bruce. Gen. Tyndall sounded a bit lost in the fog, but maybe he is not the talking kind. Mrs. Truesdell kept trying to put her oar in, & the General would say indulgently, "Now, Lassie, this is business. You keep out of this . . ." until I know she was ready to heave a plate at him. They are the loveliest survivals of the era of *Lavender & Old Lace*.[31]

In half an hour I'll go over to the big hall, where the SOS class here is studying a map problem (including our 16 valiant Waacs), will watch the class for an hour, & then will make my little speech on the progress of the WAAC.

I hopped the train Sat. night. In Kansas City Dot Muni & Emily Davis were waiting to greet me—as excited as all get-out. Capt. Rice (the general's aide) had asked them to get me, since he was picking up all the stray generals as they came in. There was a slight war dance & then we all went & ate & talked a mile a minute, & drove out to Leavenworth. Muni & Davis are among the 16 WAAC officers who will graduate Apr. 8, 1st women ever to take the Command & General Staff School SOS course.

6:10! Back from speech! All ok! There were about 400 officers, 16 Waac officers (Gwen Watson staring up at me from the audience with her mouth open), & 100 or less key civilians here to take the Army Orientation Course. I read all the speech except the introduction—talked a little too fast from very slight nervousness—but I think got my points over. They listened—applauded— asked questions. Afterwards the Waacs clustered around & asked a thousand questions. 'Twas much fun.

10:15 pm—Gwen has just left—we had a grand visit. Poor child, her fiancé has been across since mid-January, & she hasn't heard from him. She is doing beautifully in the school here—they all are.

20. Betty Bandel to Mrs. Bandel

April 4, 1943
Washington

You all sounded so let down about my putting off of my trip, when I telephoned last night, I was sorry I had called. But I wanted to hear your voices, and it was very good actually to talk to you.

I looked in a copy of Life that showed our five WAAC officers in a lifeboat after they had been torpedoed en route to their present station, and there in the front of the boat, big as life and twice as natural, was Elspeth [Duncan], her black hair streaming down her back. I wrote her immediately, realizing she had probably volunteered for service in Africa when her fiancé died, and my letter crossed one from her. She had done just that, and is now driving for the American forces. She and two other English girls were in the same boat our five Waacs were in. She is bearing up well, and sounds quite busy and full of some of her old sparkle.[32]

I got back here the day of a big conference—all our Training Center commandants were in. Then when I heard I was to go to Texas next week, to inspect three of our schools there, I thought, hot dog, here's where I get to Tucson. But this War Writers' Board trip has scotched that. At first I hadn't expected to go, but the Boss is having to leave the group a day early to get to Oglethorpe to receive an important visitor who will come to our Third Training Center there, so I have to go along to help ride herd on the writers. There will be a plane-load of them—Fannie Hurst, and some of the bunch whom we met the other day in New York. We will take them around to several posts where Waacs are serving, and to our own training centers. It should be a good three days.[33]

21. Lieutenant Edna L. Floyd to Betty Bandel

Floyd, assigned as a recruiting officer in Stockton, California, writes about recruiting problems.

April 6, 1943

Dear Betty:

War or no war I'm going to take a few minutes off and thank you for the bars. They are really beautiful and I brag about them all the time. Much prettier (that's not exactly an adjective for bars is it?) than G.I.[34]

Believe me, I was delighted to get back out West. I'm still a million miles from anyplace I'd like to be but I was ready to be satisfied behind the lone tree in Montana that our recruiting instructor told us about. I never dreamed it would be California. We were in Salt Lake City about three days. There were three of us and we were scared to death of the Adjutant. Of course, we never saw him. I'll never be scared of an Adjutant again.

Stockton has its advantages and disadvantages. It is a very poor town for recruiting. There are three Army groups here besides a cannery and ship building. We've talked until we are blue in the face—42 appearances in 16 days—quite a record—but still they don't swarm into our office as we'd like them to. If the army really needs the women, it seems to me that the only solution is to draft them. The young ones and the old ones want to join—also the too fat, too lean, and too blind. We had some people down from headquarters last week to initiate a new program—we now have 9 booths in department and dime stores and it keeps us hopping to see that someone is in each booth.

I really enjoy making speeches now. The first one scared me more than the thought of the adjutant. We arrived in Stockton at 11:30 and went to Rotary at 12:00. Then I had to make my first speech and into a mike too. But I lived through it. I spoke on the same program as André Maurois and met him.[35] His accent fascinated me.

I have a weekly radio program and that is the most fun of all. I write it and I think it's usually pretty bad but I'm learning a lot. The first time it only lasted 6 minutes and I nearly had nervous prostration but the last one lasted 13 minutes and I don't rattle my papers any more. I mentioned you once—it was approved by OWI [Office of War Information].

My audiences also include the American Legion and the Native Sons. I don't know which was funnier.[36]

When the people were here from San Francisco we had a parade. We got the air base band and six jeeps from the motor base. (I have influential friends at both places.) I finally got my ride in a jeep. The jeeps are my pride and joy.

I'd be so happy if I could meet my quota. Our quota is 47 per month and in three weeks I got two. I expect to be sent to Moffat Field any day now. I think that's where the air base sends all its renegades. Pretty soon we are going to requisition some straight jackets from headquarters.

Write again when you can and if you have any suggestions that might help me, send it on. I've thought about twisting their arms to get them to sign up, but somehow I don't think it would work.

Love, Bessie

22. Betty Bandel to Mrs. Bandel

Ellipses here are in the text.

April 11, 1943

Well, let's see, what has happened this week . . . Mostly a lot of close office work. Tuesday, however, I went down to Richmond and was a visiting Elk—

the two young recruiting officers there greeted me, "ma'amed" me, took me to dinner, and guided me to the studio of WRVA, where I gave a five-minute talk on the WAAC as a part of the studio's hour-long program in celebration of Army Day. I pulled out all the stops and told 'em what Army Day meant this year to 50,000 women. Everybody said it went all right. After the broadcast I made a mad dash for the train and caught it just in time to stand up for one hour and a half in the swaying, smoke and dust filled vestibule of a day coach, before I could worm my way inside to get a seat (no Pullmans available, as usual). Dotty said had I seen any of the bad travel conditions. Sounds of idiot laughter. I haven't seen 'em—I've been 'em. But you get used to it, and it's all part of the game. I got in at 3 a.m., my face so grimy I looked as if I'd stuck it down a coal chute. Picked up a cup of coffee and a doughnut at the little all night joint there at the station, along with all the other sailors and soldiers, and staggered home and to bed. Up at 7, for a bath before going to the office.

Tuesday I go out to give diplomas to our four gals who graduate from the Army Music School. I am holding my breath.

You and the Little Colonel, Maw, share a hero-worship of Mme. Chiang [Kai-shek]. Most of the women in the Corps feel something of the same sort of devotion to the Little Colonel. She's full of an old-fashioned simplicity and wide-eyed belief in the powers of good and the ultimate triumph of justice. Gosh, how I want you to meet her!

23. *Betty Bandel to Mrs. Bandel*

Bandel's adventure with the Writers' War Board continues.

April 18, 1943

Well, I arose at 12 today, fully rested from 3 of the nicest & most exciting days I have had in my lifetime. Our plane settled down on Bolling Field this morning at 1:30 a.m., after a 3200-mile trip which was both a holiday & a work assignment of the highest order. Last Wednesday afternoon Col. Betters, a very able fella in the Control Division of Army Service Forces (Gen. Somervell's particular pride among the staff divisions in A.S.F. as he reorganized A.S.F. a year ago), & I flew up to New York, in a big plane (the Great White Father's, actually, but don't tell anybody [GWF = Gen. Somervell]). I took a room at the Savoy-Plaza, & the Little Colonel flew in from Pittsburgh on a commercial plane about 1 a.m. I left a note, with her bags, in her room, telling her to call me when she got in, so that I would know she was all right, so she rang me up at 1:45, said, "All well," and we both went back to sleep. We were up at 6, and took a taxi over to La Guardia field, where, after a suitable wait for the late-rising New Yorkers, we were joined by our 11 guests [*see illustration 5*]. You know yourself what New Yorkers working in the whirl of the theatre-music-writing world—successful, much in demand, constantly on the fag-end of 3 hours' sleep in 24—are like when it comes to early rising; and I think the greatest compliment I can pay our 11 is to say they survived 3 days of early rising, late retiring, walking for blocks over big posts, constant take-offs and landings in planes when two of them always get sick on planes and one gets scared—almost without a murmur. I might add I think it is a compliment to us (the Waacs who entertained us wherever we went, Col. Betters and the crew of Gen. Somervell's plane, the Boss, and, I might add, myself) that never once did one or two of the bunch get away from the group, in that curious way that someone always has in any group of more than half a dozen. By the time we got back to New York we were lolling around on the plane in our shirt-sleeves, calling each other by our first names, typing away at a furious pace, kidding the socks off of each other about everything on earth from the way they all write to funny little breaks that happened along the trip. It was a story-book three days.

Our guests included Robert T. Colwell, a member of the Writers' War Board, co-author of "Life with Father" and other plays, a swell little fellow with a dimple in one cheek, big glasses, and that wonderful off-hand manner that I recognize almost immediately these days because it takes me back so instantly to the city-room. I don't know why it is, but the minute I meet a writer or musician or teacher, I have known him or her all my life—it is not so with business people, or even with the old army set, although I am getting so I experience that feeling of "belonging" with the latter group.[37] Colwell and Jack Goodman, a nice chap, Jewish I should imagine, who is advertising manager of Simon & Schuster, author of many successful short stories (Cosmopolitan, etc.), did the organizing and arranging on the radio script which the authors presented as the wind-up of the tour at Fort Dix last night.[38] Goodman is slender, short, rather handsome, and was completely white-faced during this trip because he gets deathly air-sick. You know, when a little guy like that will make such a trip as we made, knowing ahead of time what the plane trip would be like for him, just because the War Department asked the writers of the Writers' War Board to acquaint themselves with the WAAC and its reason for being, as part of their contribution to the war effort (what they write, either in fiction or fact, has a remarkable effect upon the opinion of America)—it really makes you take off your hat to him.

Katharine Brush was our star prima donna. She took me back vividly to Tucson—to the days and years when I saw so many of her kind floating to the desert country in the hope of recovering from that terrible urgency and insecurity of city life. She wears much make-up, and has the gallantry of those who have to take a thyroid pill at noon, a vitamin pill at night, something to relax them if they are riding planes, can't sleep if they are in strange places—and still do enough work each day for two other people, and drive themselves to make every contribution which they can make to life and civilization. Miss Brush has a picture in her mind of a plane nosing over on landing, and catching fire and she cannot get away from a conviction that that is the agreeable means she will take of ending her mortal career. She sees the picture every time she lands, and she usually reaches across the aisle to take hold of the hand of the person opposite, while she covers her eyes with the other hand. She looked at me with her white face and big eyes, grinned, and said, "Captain Bandel thinks I am a sissy—knows I am, in fact"—when of course I was thinking that she, more than any person on the ship, was brave, because after all it takes no courage for a person like me or good old Laura Hobson, who, as we both said, don't have sense enough to think about danger on an airplane, to fly. I liked Miss Brush, immensely.

Then there was Sally Kirkland, associate editor of *Vogue,* young, natural, a good egg generally, a typical army brat. She reminded me of a nice Pi Phi, if you know what I mean, Dotty—good solid kind of "heh, heh," plenty of brains but mostly interested in living a comfortable and pleasant and integrated life. I have seen hundreds of her kind at the University of Arizona. She wore nice clothes, was particularly interested in WAAC clothes problems, etc.

Toni Frissel, [*sic*] photographer, was a real find.[39] She is tall, gawky, wide-eyed, quiet, shy—the one of the whole group who struck me as being one of the earth earthy. She has a nice, deep, quiet voice, and she is just as easily excited over an idea as if she had never sold a picture in her life—she is actually one of the crack photographers of the country. She and the Boss took a great shine to each other, and I think she liked me, too—when we parted in New York last night, she said "Goodbye" once, started away, then stopped suddenly, turned around, came back for another handshake, and grinned as if she didn't know why she had come back or what she wanted to say.

Alice Hughes is a columnist and radio commentator—I gathered somehow that she was unmarried and had no children—the others mostly have families, or did have once. She wore a purple knitted cap on the back of her head, and purple lip-stick, and her skin is of that transparent variety you sometimes see on frail people, and when we got into choppy weather she would lie back against the seat, her eyes closed, and look as if every dip was probably going to finish her off. She and Brush were our patients, but somehow I think Brush took the trip better than Hughes—Hughes is a great realist, or rather pragmaticist, and I had the feeling she didn't feel quite the compensation in seeing the Waacs that Brush did. Brush was really tremendously moved, while Hughes was interested, artistically perhaps even excited, but also aware of the sleep she was losing. She was a good sport, though—she never mentioned it once—I just gathered that impression from watching her.

Oscar Schisgall was a nice Jewish fella who writes short stories for American, Liberty, Collier's, etc. Awfully regular kind of guy, whose wife and little son came down to see him off. Leo Margulies was a quiet little Jew who owns a tremendous string of pulp magazines, is touchingly grateful for attention paid him, hops around to get you things or carry your bag, and simply loved going along on the trip.

Sarah Elizabeth Rodger, who writes serials and shorts for Ladies' Home Companion and other women's magazines, interested in dancing and good times and making a hit with every man she meets, who surprisingly enough combines with that interest enough firmness of purpose to turn out a successful story at least once a month (a full length one, I mean, that nets her around $5000—and that ain't hay). She was probably the youngest of the group—in her late twenties, I should guess.

Margie-Lee Runbeck is a fat, jolly, good-natured woman, with one wandering eye, who looks like any family's favorite maiden aunt, utterly unexceptional in appearance, and who turned out to be probably the outstanding writer of the group. She writes for Good Housekeeping, Reader's Digest, etc., and has created what is evidently a very well-known character for American readers—"Little Miss Boo." She adopted a little daughter (somehow I gather she is unmarried), when the girl was two weeks old, and has brought her up to the age of eight, lavishing upon her all the affection and understanding in the world. Around her she has written the stories of "Miss Boo," and so famous have they become that today the teachers at the private school which little Margie-Lee attends call her "Miss Boo." The older Margie-Lee was bubbling over with enthusiasm for the Waacs, and turned out a page and a half of copy on them, yesterday morning at Oglethorpe, that was simply superb.[40]

As good and natural and earthy, in an entirely different way, as Miss Runbeck is Laura Hobson, contributor to the Saturday Evening Post, Collier's, etc., and former promotion manager—and I'll bet you she really promoted. She is a typical city business woman, of the forthright, nice variety. I imagine she is part Jewish. Anyway, she comes right out flat-footed and says exactly what she means, tries to talk in a slightly hard-boiled manner, and gets tears in her eyes when a WAAC parade passes by. She was as excited as a child by all that she saw. She seemed to like me—as a matter of fact, they were all very kind to me—and when we parted in New York, said, booming it out over all of La Guardia field, "Look, I don't know if it's against military courtesy to fall in love with a lady captain, but you're all right!" And shook hands with me until I thought maybe I would unhinge at the wrist.

Well, that was our motley crew. We flew to Fort Custer, where I saw my first WAAC company actually at work in the field. They have been at that somewhat barren and bleak post since January, are at present landscaping around their barracks, and have the enthusiastic assistance of every man on the post at planting trees, decorating their day room, knocking up shelves, and doing anything else they can think up that would add to their comfort. The girls are tremendously happy at having a real job to do. Our writers ate their first army meal there—nothing fancy, but good—and we pushed on to Des Moines. We arrived in time for retreat, and Col. McCoskrie had planned a colorful retreat parade. Boy, how the girls marched! I told old Colonel Mac I thought the first class should come back for a refresher. I had forgotten that the Little Colonel had never seen a retreat parade, with the officers marching "front and center" for formal "orders," and she was tremendously moved by the sight. Then afterwards Kadje Stull, just out there a week to take over Public Relations, attached one member of her staff to each writer as an "aide," and each one went off to a different company mess—a brilliant idea that Thorp had to get the writers to talk to the Waacs, instead of to each other, as they would have if they had eaten at the same mess. They seemed to love the idea. After mess, we all went on a tour of the post, ending up at the gymnasium for a good demonstration of mass calisthenics. Afterwards there was a press interview, arranged for the benefit of the local press, which fell rather flat—I believe the local fellas were a bit awed by the visiting writers. Then everybody separated for the night, the Boss and Stryker and I staying at the officers' club. Lillian Reilly and Kadje Stull came up to our rooms, and the boss lay in bed and listened while we hashed over WAAC problems and plans until after midnight.

Friday morning we arose at 5:45, and I went downtown and rounded up my writers, while the Boss stayed out at the post and talked to the officers and auxiliaries. We went to Fort Knox, Ky., where another post headquarters company is located. These girls are working for a post which houses the Armored Forces, and they proudly wear the overseas cap, just as the Armored Force men do, tilted on the left side of the head instead of the right, the way the rest of the army does. I was supposed to notice this detail, and, since I didn't, with the usual Bandel attention to matters of dress, they finally had to call it to my attention. I was then duly impressed. Of course the post commanders also turned out to pay their respects and offer the hospitality of the post at each place we visited. It was funny to see how each company had immediately become intensely loyal to whatever part of the army happened to be stationed at the post at which they were working—Armored Forces, or what have you.

We hopped off again for Oglethorpe, getting in just in time for a review which had been planned for the L.C. Brush and Hughes were in my car, and I was quoting Chaucer's description of spring to them—we had a lot of fun—by this time we were old friends. As soon as we reached the post—a beautiful old one, very like Des Moines—we rushed out on the field for the review. It was a simply magnificent review, with the best playing I have ever heard from a WAAC band. The writers were by this time hanging on the ropes, from admiration for Waacs. We put them all up at the WAAC officers' quarters—each officer had given up her room, and gone upstairs to share some other officer's, leaving soap and towels and cigarettes and things for her "guest." The women were all tremendously touched by their thoughtfulness. The men had left $8 back at Knox to buy flowers or candy for the girls who had served us our noon mess—they thought it so nice of them to dream up such a party for us. There was a girl back at Knox who had broken her ankle, and had it in a cast—and got Katherine Brush and the rest of the writers to autograph the cast.

That night at Oglethorpe we walked out under the Georgia moon, went over to officers' refresher classes, and ate a wonderful party meal during which the band, seated outside the entrance to our mess hall, played a grand concert of lively tunes. A chorus, directed by the officer in charge of the band, sang everything they could think of—and sang beautifully, outside the windows with the young voices coming to us in the quiet of the early evening. They have used the Pallas theme all the way through the post—the roads have been renamed "Pallas" and "Athene," and so on. Then yesterday—gosh, it seems a month ago—we had a very special event in the morning, a review about which I can't tell you for about a week or so.[41] Our writers were as excited and pleased as children. Then at noon we hopped off for Fort Dix, got in about 5 p.m., and wound up our three days with a hilarious evening meal with the company there, followed by a program the post (men and women) gave for us, and the broadcast of the writers, in which they sang the praises of the WAAC. During the evening meal the girls in the company put on the funniest fashion show I've ever seen—1 big gal with buck teeth and one of those funny-sad faces was the master of ceremonies. She told us later she had formerly been a Sister of Mercy, and after 9 years decided she was not suited to the religious life and applied for and got a special dispensation from the Pope to leave the order and resume her civilian life. She is still a perfectly good Catholic. Anyway, she put on a perfectly straight face, and, in typical fashion-revue patter, introduced girls modelling "what the well-dressed Waac wears upon arising in the morning." Some kid would come tripping down the aisle bundled up in a big utility coat, would unbutton it in that leisurely manner affected by fashion models, and would reveal one of those old fatigue dresses we wore in Des Moines for physical exercise. The company rocked with laughter—evidently they take exercises every morning. Then the M.C. introduced the "well-dressed office worker," and a Waac came out in skirt and sweater. The M.C. said, "After the post engineer gets around to throwing a few shovelfuls of coal on the fire, the Waac simplifies her attire thus," and the girl took off her sweater and went tripping down the aisle in her shirt-sleeves. The climax was "the ambition of every good Waac," and an auxiliary came out dressed in an officer's uniform with eagles on her shoulders![42] I thought the L.C. would die laughing. When she got up to our end of the room, she took her eagles off and handed them over to Col. Paullin, the commanding officer of the reception center, who had evidently lent them to her, and said, "Gosh! Busted already!"

During the broadcast the writers were all lined up merely to say their names into the mike at the very end of the program, except for Brush and two others, who did the real talking (Brush was scared to death). Everybody was very elaborately lined up, dramatically waiting the moment to say their names, and the program ran too long and they had to cut it just before they got to that part! My writers simply collapsed on the floor, on the stage, everyplace, and howled with laughter. I really thought we were going to have to pound Kirkland on the back. It was a wonderful evening. Then we flew back to New York, and I left them all and came back to Washington with Col. Betters.

24. *1st Officer Jean E. Melin, WAAC, to Betty Bandel, Acting Deputy Director*

Melin writes about ambiguities in command structure at this time in the Seventh Service Command WAAC contingent.

Omaha, Nebraska
April 19, 1943.

Dear Betty:

Thank you for your letter of April 13th. I have been on a much needed leave from April 12th to 18th, inclusive, and just today received your letter.

As this is an "off the cuff letter," there's no use to beat about the bush. You know that the situation here isn't what you thought it would be when you wrote me on April 13th. Since then, I understand, telephone conversations between this headquarters and Washington, D.C., plus correspondence, have been numerous, and to date the status of Gardiner, Bell, and Melin is still uncertain. At present, Captain Bell is the Director of the Seventh Service Command, for she has never been officially released from that duty; Melin was newly assigned Director as per the Director's teletype to the Commandant, Fort Leavenworth; the Commanding General this Service Command does not acknowledge this major change, and has designated Captain Gardiner as Acting Director in Captain Bell's absence.[43] You can see that the state of affairs and mental condition of all concerned isn't what you or the Director would hope for.

From my conversation with Colonel Gerhardt this morning, and observations, I am of the opinion that I am excess baggage in this headquarters. On paper I am one thing—and here I am another. Colonel Gerhardt suggests I interest myself in the recruiting angle. At present Captain Sweeney is in charge of all recruiters in this Service Command. Where do I fit in?

I am sure you know me well enough to know I am not worried about the loss or gain of an official title. There's work to be done and I joined the Corps to do my share. I dislike very much being drift wood. Captain Gardiner is doing a fine job, and from an angle of fairness to her and the Corps, I feel she should be kept in and officially assigned to the Directorship of this Command. Her six month's experience here, her association with various staff members, are something I cannot gain, especially with the feeling now present in the minds of superior officers in this headquarters. I don't see how I could possibly hope for the cooperation necessary to equal the work Captain Gardiner is doing.

Have you any spot for me in Washington or the Second Service Command? I don't care what the job is so long as I can feel I am accomplishing something worthwhile. My six day leave opened my eyes to civilian war production work and the shortage of competent war workers. At present I feel I was doing more for the war effort in my old position at Bauer & Black, makers of Surgical Dressings for the Army, and unless my point of view changes during that sixty day period before taking the oath putting us into the Army, I am very much afraid I shall feel I can do more in a civilian way.

Lt. Lutze would appreciate clarification of her assignment as Assistant Director, for as you know Captain Gardiner also has that assignment.

The earliest reply that you can get off to us would certainly be appreciated—and a reassignment for me in either the Second Service Command or Washington Headquarters would be all I could hope or pray for.

25. Emily Brown to Betty Bandel

Brown desires to enter Officer Candidate School. (According to Bandel, she had an outspoken, strong personality that delayed her acceptance into the OCS.)[44]

[Tucson, Arizona
April 21, 1943]

Dear Betty,

Your mother called this evening and said that you were anxious to hear all about me and my damnable voice, with particular reference to how long I will be held up.

I wrote you from Oglethorpe that I was the victim of laryngitis and nasopharyngitis but at that time I expected my recovery to be a matter of a few days.[45] For some reason (climatic, they finally decided) I didn't get well. The attending surgeon recommended at least a 21-day furlough for me so that I could come back to Arizona for treatment as well as sunshine. In addition to the laryngitis there is a strained condition of the vocal cords due to all that lecturing on radio at Oglethorpe with a sore throat and bad cold.

From the wire you sent to your mother, I gather that there is going to be some action on this specialist officer business or that the eligibility lists will be set up.[46] While I realize that I am a mighty minor character in this set-up, I certainly wish it were possible to go right from here to Des Moines instead of having to go back to Georgia and go through all that mess again. They will probably have mislaid all the records on me by then. The medicos at Oglethorpe wanted them to transfer me out of there but nobody seemed to know it could be done so they settled on the furlough. It seems sensible to stay here now and get well rather than go back and get a C.D.D. [Conditional Disability Discharge] for my trouble.

Needless to say, I am mighty curious to know what you have in mind and I hope that the information I have provided you is sufficient. I am knocking this letter off in my old morgue.[47] It makes me feel right at home only I think it would be more satisfactory if you could step in here and we could talk it over. You wouldn't know the *Star* office. The various new people hanging around seem to be not too competent. We'd look mighty good to the management about now, dove.

[Penciled note on envelope] What *did* I do? Emily made OCS—but how & when?

26. *Margaret Lee Runbeck to Betty Bandel*

Following the Writers' War Board tour.

New York
April 24, 1943

Dear Betty:

Make believe that all the proper official ceremony is on top of this letter. I think it, but there is so little time, and besides I have just finished writing something about the wonderful Waacs, and that has brought me to much affectionate remembering about you. Not you as an officer, but just a dear betty.

I was quite staggered to discover how many impressions had adhered to me. I made not one single note, except your address, but when the yellow sheet was flying from the typewriter's mast, impressions surged faster than I could use. Everyone who spoke to me, it seemed, had something unique and significant to say, and there'll be stories and stories I am sure.

This is not to prod you into remembering that Colonel Hobby said I might have the story which General Godfrey knows about the Waacs who behaved well on the torpedoed boat. But I am very eager to have it, because it does belong in this book, and is, of course, the only story we have of women in our forces.[48] We have British people of many kinds, and our own flyers, seamen, soldiers, marines and whatnot . . . and even children. So we must have some good little Waacs who are my favorite fruit.

When you send it, darling, don't forget that you promised to include the definition of gentility, which I remember so well that I nearly could reproduce it this moment. Only I want it exactly as you wrote it. For my own private treasury, of course.

It was such a lovely time for all of us. And your part in it was so gracious and skillful and dear that I think you'll find you have twelve good friends you didn't possess a week ago.

Most sincerely, Margaret Lee Runbeck

ILLUS. I. Betty Bandel, officer candidate, in her quarters at Fort Des Moines, Company 3, 1st WAAC Training Regiment, 20 July 1942. Photograph in the possession of Betty Bandel, and in the Betty Bandel Papers, Special Collections, Bailey-Howe Library, University of Vermont, Burlington, Vermont.

ILLUS. 2. Bandel's mother, Emma Frederick Bandel. Photograph in the possession of Betty Bandel, and in the Betty Bandel Papers, Special Collections, Bailey-Howe Library, University of Vermont, Burlington, Vermont.

ILLUS. 3. "WAAC women have just arrived at Fort Des Moines, Iowa, at the WAAC School. July 20, 1942." U.S. Army photograph.

ILLUS. 4. "Marching in review," 29 August 1942. National Archives.

ILLUS. 5. Writers' War Board on their tour of WAAC facilities. U.S. Army photograph.

ILLUS. 6. Bandel stand-
ing by jeep. U.S. Army.

ILLUS. 7. Eleanor Roo-
sevelt, Bandel, and
Hobby in England. Frank-
lin D. Roosevelt Presidential
Library.

MY TEN WAACS

Ten little WAACS all in a line,
One smoked my cigarettes and then
  there were nine.
Nine little WAACS, I gave one the
  gate,
She wouldn't kiss me, then there
  were eight.
Eight little WAACS, boy! This was
  heaven,
One was always hungry, then there
  were seven.
Seven little WAACS, knew all the
  tricks
One pulled a fast one, then there
  were six.
Six little WAACS, hoped they'd
  survive,
Forgot which one I'd dated, then
  there were five.
Five little WAACS, and this made
  them sore,
I called Mary "Hortense" and then
  there were four.
Four little WAACS, one was too
  free
With her address, then there were
  three.
Three little WAACS, one cooked
  some stew,
I took one taste of it, and then there
  [were] two.
Two little WAACS, and was I having fun?
One decided three's a crowd, and
  there was one.
One little WAAC, she sure knew her
  biz,
She married my colonel, That's all
  there is.

ILLUS. 8. "Smear campaign," poem from Army newsletter, *Fort Ord Panorama,* "My Ten Waacs." Photograph in the possession of Betty Bandel, and in the Special Collections, Bailey-Howe Library, University of Vermont, Burlington, Vermont.

ILLUS. 9. Mattie Treadwell, one of Bandel's Air-WAC officers. Authored an important history of the WAC in World War II in 1952. U.S. Army Signal Corps.

ILLUS. 10. Members of Bandel's Air-WAC staff in Washington, D.C., Lieutenant Madge Williams and Lieutenant Caroline Varn. May 1943. U.S. Army photograph.

ILLUS. 11. Bandel is promoted to Major. "The 'Little Colonel' muttered out of the corner of her mouth, 'It's you, butch,' and I howled, and the photographer snapped the picture." U.S. Army Signal Corps.

ILLUS. 12. Colonel Oveta Culp Hobby, Director of the WAAC/WAC. U.S. Army photograph.

ILLUS. 13. "Air WAC's High Command." U.S. Army photograph.

TUCSON LAUNDRY & DRY CLEANERS

Tucson Girl Makes History!
Betty Bandel Named First Lt. Col. in
W. A. C.

You, too

can have a part in

MAKING HISTORY!

LT. COL. BANDEL

Join the Women's Army Corps!

The eventful days of 1944, when democracy and freedom were challenged will go down in history for coming generations. You can have a part in this great program, and will be helping your country as well, if you join the Women's Army Corps. There are many opportunities for the ambitious and earnest woman in this work, promotions to be had, honors to be gained!

In addition, you are BADLY NEEDED! In order that every available man can be released for active duty, it is necessary that replacements be made through the W. A. C. If you've a brother or husband or sweetheart on the war front, you well realize how important it is that he be relieved and aided by a greater fighting army, made possible by a greater W.A.C.

For particulars call at the Army Recruiting
Headquarters, Federal Bldg., Tucson

This Ad Sponsored by *February 7*

TUCSON LAUNDRY & DRY CLEANERS

ILLUS. 14. A local ad encouraging other Tucson women to join the WAAC, February 1944, part of the All-States recruiting campaign. *Arizona Daily Star,* Tucson, 7 Feb. 1944. Used by permission from the *Arizona Daily Star.*

ILLUS. 15. Lieutenant Colonel Jessie P. Rice, Deputy Director of the WAC and creator of the All-States Campaign. U.S. Army Signal Corps.

CHAPTER 4

Chief Air-WAAC Officer

At Hobby's recommendation, Bandel is placed in charge of the Air-WAAC Division and promoted to major, the first WAAC officer so promoted. Her former fellow officer trainees express their delight at the news. "A few of the old 3rd Company drank a toast to you at the Officers Club," writes Lillian Reilly from Fort Des Moines, where she is head WAAC. Gwen Watson sends a tongue-in-cheek telegraph recalling Bandel's fears about being assigned to the WAAC band: "It is a far call from your anticipated bugler job." Captain Mary Spangenburg writes that "Company 3 is especially proud of you. After all, we can remember you leaping from bed to bed or typing away in more serious moments."[1] And Mai Bronson of the Green Guards, a pre–World War II women's organization that advocated for establishing an official role for women in the military, writes from Tucson: "Have been following your career & want to say: We are certainly proud of you & look for big things to come."[2]

Bandel's new command is challenging: the Air-WAAC Division comprises by far the largest contingent of Waacs in the army. This is due in part to the support of Army Air Forces Commanding General Henry H. (Hap) Arnold, who recognizes that the WAAC can be of enormous value to the AAF, both as part of the war effort overseas and in vital work in the United States. He reinforces his commitment to the success of the WAAC in the AAF by passing the word down through his command that the Army Air Forces will accept Waacs gladly and will find meaningful jobs for them.[3]

Bandel is gratified to find that, unlike her experience in dealing with the army while at WAAC headquarters, her ideas for utilization of the Air-WAAC are readily accepted and implemented by her AAF superiors. While WAAC headquarters has been routinely frustrated by their army liaisons and officers, and Director Hobby's proposals for WAAC organization and procedures too often ignored, by contrast one of Bandel's proposals to AAF headquarters, to provide air commands with Wacs equal to up to 10 percent of their personnel strength, is accepted so rapidly that recruitment cannot keep up with demand.[4]

In July, President Roosevelt signs into law the bill giving the WAAC full army status: it becomes the Women's Army Corps (WAC). Although the Corps' administrative and disciplinary structure do not change, Wacs are now eligible for army benefits and privileges: insurance, dependency allotments, and, perhaps most important in the long run, the GI Bill, giving veterans support for higher education after demobilization. Full army status also means that more women can be sent overseas, since they are now protected under international law if they become prisoners of war, and can receive hospitalization and death benefits if injured on duty. The Army Air Forces uphold their avowed support of the WAC by being the first to abolish WAAC officer grades and fully integrate Wacs. They will be the first to promote their WAC division director—Bandel—to Lieutenant Colonel, the highest level allowed by law.[5]

But the WAC is in trouble in 1943. The "smear campaign" takes a substantial toll on recruiting and on the morale of Wacs. It is fueled by columns in certain tabloid newspapers, such as John O'Donnell's article in the *New York Daily News,* that accuse the army of issuing contraceptives to women in the WAAC.[6] At first, the War Department attempts to downplay the slanders under the rationale that publicizing them would make matters worse and discourage women from enlisting in the WAC. This decidedly does not work. The WAC and the army look for sources of the rumors: are they "disinformation" put out by Axis agents within the United States, or are they expressions of resentment propagated by locals who feel Waacs' are crowding them out in stores and restaurants around WAAC installations? A letter from a fellow officer suggests part of the problem: in California, civilian women wearing uniforms resembling the Waacs' are observed drinking to excess and otherwise misbehaving. Mistaken for Waacs, they only add fuel to the smear campaign. A WAAC recruiter in San Francisco attempts in speeches to civic groups to stanch the rumors about Waac misbehavior by noting how few incidents there really are. This only increases gossip about such incidents.[7]

The reality is that much of the mudslinging comes from within the army itself, not only from enlisted men but from officers of all ranks. An FBI investigation of the sources of the slander campaign finds no Axis roots: the rumors are entirely "home-grown." Some of them have originated with the wives of enlisted men sent overseas, while Wacs are taking over the men's noncombat jobs on army bases in the United States.[8] Even vocal rebuttal by public figures like Secretary of War Henry Stimson and Eleanor Roosevelt does not stem the tide or completely restore the good image of the WAC.[9] The WAC never does entirely free itself of the negative publicity. Partly, it is the fault of the army itself, which does not fully commit to making the WAAC succeed by apprising the public of how important its role is to winning the war. When Waacs are given the opportunity to reenlist as a Wac—or to resign—the enmity of men in the army is one of the reasons Waacs give for leaving the Corps (*see illustration 8*).[10]

Certainly, however, not all army personnel dislike the WAC. Those in the highest ranks—army chief of staff General George C. Marshall, General Arnold, and such men—are certainly dedicated to supporting it. And most officers assigned to WAAC or WAC headquarters praise their accomplishments: Lieutenant Colonel Branch, head of the WAAC Planning Division, for example, expresses his "appreciation for the interesting and stimulating experience in being associated with the WAAC Headquarters, and my continued interest in the problems and progress of your Division" at the time of his transfer to another division.[11] Even those who are generally against women in the military make exceptions: one general in Washington, "who has a great prejudice against women and WAC members," is overheard saying that "his one exception is Colonel Bandel, 'who is efficient, brilliant, able, and without the usual woman's deficiencies in jobs.'"[12]

Many of the letters in this chapter and the next articulate the problems that Wacs are experiencing at this time. An officer writes about the prejudice against the WAAC that she has experienced at the Command and General Staff School (C&GS) at Fort Leavenworth, Kansas, a prestigious army school for leadership training. Enlisted Wacs trained in specialist work such as radio operation are often left twiddling their thumbs in the field if the local command balks at using them to replace men. WAAC headquarters goes through several organizational changes, partly because existing divisions are hampered by roadblocks set up by the army administration. As the WAAC ends its first year, there are many difficulties to iron out. In a letter not included here an officer notes, "As we celebrate our first WAAC anniversary, there'll be an added prayer for an organization we've all put so much of our hearts into. The future will need courage."[13]

1. Betty Bandel to Mrs. Bandel

Easter Afternoon [April 25], 1943
Pentagon Bldg.

I have a new job assignment! Don't tell anybody yet, because I always expect these things to fall through until I see them happen, but I am going over to the Air Forces, as their head WAAC. We would call it Deputy Director for Air, except that that title automatically places the person under the Director, who is over here under the Commanding General, Army Service Forces [EASF] (Gen. Somervell), and that would make the Commanding General, Army Air Forces, mad, since he is parallel in position to the CG, ASF, and thus should not have anybody on his staff answering to anybody on the CG, ASF, staff. Isn't the Army funny? Of course, what it means is that I am going over to Air Forces because we feel the need of a close liaison with this headquarters, and I will certainly be working for the Director in a very real sense—but we can't make it sound that way in my name. So they may call me "The Air WAAC," or something. We already have about 12 WAAC staff officers out in the various major air commands, and companies are beginning to go out to the Air Forces. Eventually, they will be using more Waacs than any other part of the Army—it is the No. 2 job in the Corps, a terrific challenge and responsibility, and one that will require all the diplomacy I never learned. In a sense, I hate to leave headquarters—it's such fun to work near the Little Colonel—but after all I am only moving upstairs—it might have been half across the world. And that is where she thinks she needs me most, for now.

Let's see—did I tell you about last week's trip? We had expected to pull the writers out of Oglethorpe before the President got there, and take them on to Jackson and Dix, but they were so tired we couldn't bear to move them, and anyway we figured they'd slay us if they found out later what they had missed. Of course they can't write anything about that angle, not having been accredited to cover the President's trip, but they did see it. And were they excited! Big-eyed Laura Hobson came up to me Saturday morning, just panting, and said, "Col. Betters knew about this two weeks ago!" I smiled, and she said, "Don't tell me you did!" I laughed. She said, "And Col. Hobby too?" I said, "Of course." She said, "My Lord. From now on I have complete confidence in our army. How on earth could you keep quiet about it? And you so innocently saying last night, 'We thought you might like to sleep late this morning, and skip Jackson.'" Then when the President's car came zooming onto the post (the Director and Col. Brown, the post commandant, had gone down to the station to meet him), and the 21-gun salute sounded, and the Waacs—the most excited kids you ever saw—let out a roar of welcome, and the band struck up the National Anthem—you should have seen the tears in those hard-boiled writers' eyes! It was a perfect Spring morning—dogwood and everything else in bloom—and 24 companies of Waacs gave a simply perfect review. The President said the band played the National Anthem better than any band he ever heard. He seemed tremendously impressed—grinned, and complimented the Director, and said it was "a great show." Falla got loose and raced over to join the Waacs—he was mobbed, and seemed to love it.[14] Almost a soon as it began, it was over. The big open car swept off the field and away, the companies were dismissed and everybody let out a whoop. One little girl said, "Well, I've seen Eleanor. I've seen Oveta. I've seen Frank. Now I want to see my Mamma."

Tuesday Laura Hobson came down here to write an article on us, and I put her up overnight—there wasn't a bed to be had in Washington, and one of the Waacs was away, so we stole her bed and put it up in my room.[15] We talked until 3 in the morning, and I learned all about her life, public and private, and she read me from the galley proofs of her new book—her first full-length novel—she is excited as a child, and well she should be. It is called "The Trespassers," and Simon and Schuster is publishing it next fall—has to do with the migration of the persecuted from the European countries in the last ten years. Very swell writing. Laura took a big chunk out of two of my days, but getting people like her interested in the WAAC is invaluable to us.

Henry and Tom Burges both looked swell, though much worked, at their graduation—that was a funny thing, wasn't it? One of the four girls I gave a diploma to that day turned up at Oglethorpe, when I was down there a week later, directing the band![16]

2.   Betty Bandel to Mrs. Bandel

[April 28, 1943]

Well, my fate is sealed. The Air Forces "accept with pleasure," & I am being ordered over to their headquarters next Monday as "The Air WAAC" (they have "The Air Surgeon," "The Air Engineer," "The Air Finance Officer," etc., etc.). The Waacs in headquarters have been kind enough to express great regrets; the Waacs in Air Forces, pleasure. Needless to say, that makes me feel good.

In honor of the occasion I am paying 20 bucks to a gentleman with a French name Saturday to have my hair "styled" & permanented. The Little Colonel thinks she has finally broken me down—but I drew the line at having my face half-soled & heeled. I said, "Now, remember, I belong to the Air Forces—you can't boss me around any more"—& she said, "You belong to me!"

This is a terribly challenging assignment—& yet not so hard to live with as my tight-rope-walking assignment in WAAC hq, where as a lowly captain of WAACs I was supposed to see that 30-year colonels followed the Director's policies, in her absence. They probably wouldn't have been able to put up with me much longer, if this other thing hadn't broken.

It will mean a delay of my visit home—but I know you can put up with that when you realize really how terrifically essential the WAAC is, & how important it is to get the air part of things established, now that companies are going out to Air Forces in numbers.

As soon as I see where I am, & am down in the saddle a little—perhaps two or three weeks—I will ask for a few days to run home.

3.   Mrs. Bandel to Betty Bandel

[April 29, 1943]

My darling Bet—

Where shall I begin. Ans. me this—do all Waacs go the pace you do? And survive? Well I'll hold my breath until the next letter which will tell me what the *new appendage* is?[17] I'm one of those old "stick in mud" type and don't want you away from the L.C.

I was about to say you need not have been so secretive about the F.D.R. visit for we had it in the afternoon paper and of course when we saw the L.C. decided you were not far behind. After all I think we've proved ourselves almost perfect clams—so, as a family I think we should not be made to wait so long between acts—it's really bad for my digestion.

Binda [Tuke] & your sister are worrying—"you are so occupied with all these women—there is no time for romance."

Even tho' they made you Director General I could not be prouder or happier for you.

4.   *Betty Bandel to Mrs. Bandel*

After her promotion to major.

May 2, 1943

I am sitting in my room, surrounded by yellow roses (from my house-mates): an empty champagne bottle, 1928 vintage (shared the eventful night—Friday—with the bunch here): my gorgeous orchid. It was wonderful to talk to you all yesterday. The L.C. asked me what you said, & I told her that you, Maw, didn't like it because I was "leaving my Little Colonel." She said, "Don't worry—you can't do that." And 'tis true—I never can leave the Little Colonel, spiritually, any more than I could leave Alexander, or Binda, or the Fullers.

Well, here is the latest chapter in the dream: Friday morning old Virg. Bock came in & stood in front of me, while I was talking over the telephone to the head of her Division (Personnel), & began playing with the sign on my desk that says "Capt. Bandel," pretending she was snipping off half the sign. I said, "What's the matter?" She said, "Congratulations, Major!" I yelled, "What!" And Jepson, who heard it all over the phone, said, "Is that Bock?" Tell her to come back here—I'll speak to her!"[18] Then it developed it was all to be a surprise, because the Boss wanted to tell me & to pin the leaves on. So I promised to look surprised again. Three other people found out about it, wandered in, & broke the news again—& 3 more times I looked surprised. Finally the L.C. got free, called me in, & pinned on the leaves—I couldn't look surprised again, but I suppose I looked enough what I felt to do. Then a photographer from the Bureau of Public Relations came in & took pictures of her pinning them on, & shaking hands with me. She said the gold leaf is so becoming she thinks she'll have to freeze all promotions at this level. There will probably be several more majors in a few days—Jess Rice, I hope, & some others. When I went out into the other offices, I was mobbed by Waacs who wanted to say, "Congratulations." It seemed to fill them with such pride in the Corps & in the L.C. that one of their own number—plain old Betty Bandel from Arizona, with no more pull than anything—should have become the first major. Their kindness was, to me, the greatest thing about the promotion. I came home, & found the kids had been waiting up for hours, with excellent champagne & lovely roses. So we had another party.

5.   *Mrs. Bandel to Betty Bandel*

[May 2, 1943]

My darling Bet—I am still spinning round—somehow just can't take this latest honor in stride. All Tucson *calls* to send congratulations also to your dippy parent. Child you've become an epidemic and I'm afraid I'll need "Sulpha" or something before I recover. The *Star* should swell its sales with your picture and write up today. All day yesterday I *tried* to write—and simply couldn't—only "Bill" or a Bernard Shaw could "coin" the feelings of your Maw.[19] And ever present, in all you do—"I hope her daddy knows." I can guess his pride and joy like mine, speechless.[20] Most of all I enjoy the L.C.'s "pinning the oak leaf." I never dreamed of this kind of career for you—felt it would be in the writing field—of that I've always been sure. Dot too will be heard from when her "baby days" are over. The thing I hear often is "Betty was the one girl." Were I a rich woman tho' I had to break my arm to do it, I['d] fly to Washington this minute. I see you all dolled up in the Gabardine, new hair do *and* the oakleaf going to church—feeling pretty humble about fates blessings to one Betty Bandel, who saw the light of a Sunday twilight at "Garfield"—not *very many* summers ago.[21] Before you came, I visited Congress with your father and Uncle Albert and "I dreamed dreams of 'a place in History'"—just as I did with my first—but certainly never imagined "A Major Betty."

Dot's reaction over the phone slayed me—ringing true to form, her first thot was "some men around" "goody." Emily said she didn't want to be a ossifer [i.e., officer] cause her friends were *not*. When I called Alexander yesterday I said "How are you?"—then dropped the bomb kinda casual like & back she came with—"How could you ask me how I felt, with such news."

Now my dearest child, you are my child aren't you major, each day I'll pray God to keep you well, for the task ahead. I know you'll win.
Lovingly your proud Maw.

6. *Dorothy Muni to Betty Bandel*[22]

Ft. Leavenworth
May 6, 1943

Congratulations, Major, both on promotion and on the new job. Everyone here was enthusiastic about both, especially the promotion. I hate to see you out of Hq, but assume that you really won't be far off.

I've been interested in where Kate [Fawcett?] is now located. My G-2's don't always come up with information which agrees. I know about Stryker—think that's fine—imagine Knollwood will have pleasant memories on her work re the Weather Observer's tests. Sorry about Miller though—that stuff hurts us so undeservedly.[23]

I'm not sure of the reputation the first 16 left behind them, but several instances have caused doubt about our own social security. One in particular, in very bad taste and not what one expects from the top man, made me very angry. I'd like to have had Col. Catron here. One of the girls was asked at the first hop by the top man himself why she wasn't in Kansas City getting drunk.[24] The question was asked in front of quite a large group of people. From the remarks of top officers and particularly their ladies at the Gen.'s tea our first Sunday, we feel quite unwelcome. Fortunately, no one stags it to the hops, no one gets drunk. Perhaps, the majority of us (not me—worse luck) are too good in class recitations; the men resent it—some have said as much. We don't expect to place as well as the first group, but we do not expect to fail. We haven't received back any pay problems as yet, but believe we're all right. The stuff is not too hard—I studied like this in school—but it's the stupid mistakes you make that makes you cuss blue blazes.

In an informal chat with Col. Pashley, I was tipped off to the fact that G-3 was watching the assignments of the last group.[25] If they do not go to the four places for which such instruction was intended—no more Waacs would be taken here. The Col. repeated this three times. He was a little disgusted (nicely so) that no Waacs flunked the T of Opns and Med. Eva in T of Opns problem.[26] Five of the group did not have to attend the extra session in map reading. I was not one of them, damn it. Computations!

Just came back from an inspection of the Waac barracks—are they ever fine—reconstruction of available facilities beats any new construction. These men are pleased with themselves when they do a good job like this one—and that should be. Col. Schmall tells me he has re-submitted his requisitions by spec. no.—doesn't expect to get all of them as some are highly technical. He prefers no Waac at all if they can't do the job called for—example: multilith operator. Old C.G. will have to get out the needle.[27]

Sorry Col. Branch left—I admired his thinking and most of his methods— got a little tired of hand holding, but learned a helluva lot about management.[28] Do you ever suppose I'll have an opportunity to sit down and mull over all the things I've learned in the last 10 months—my mind surprises me so by the very elasticity of its absorption powers. Recent Hq reorganization should put us back on an operating footing. The Planning group is just what it should be. How did we ever get into that other set-up anyway?

Betty Smith tells me the Training Command will be in there soon. We do not discuss it.[29]

I'm nuts about all this stuff—kids think I'm crazy to figure out more than is required, but I like doing it too well to stop. It has taken some time to see the value from Waac standpoint, but the value definitely is there. Of course, after the war, I'll be a bore to all my friends—women don't like this stuff and men prefer to be masters at war interpretation—guess I'll hie away to the Minn. cabin & tend to my fishing. For quite a while after the war, civilian life will be very, very dull. Suppose they'll keep on us females? Now if I can get a shot at machine gunning—life will be complete.

Dort

The staff & instructors spoke very highly of your last appearance here. I'm going to do a 10 minute thing—wish it were you. I'm going to kill Major Kreinheder if he doesn't quit calling the Little Boss "Oveta." Damn, that makes me mad.

7. *Corporal Emily Brown to Mrs. Bandel*

Emily, having received specialist training first—as a radio operator, in her case—applies to OCS, which is to supply the specialist units with officers qualified to oversee them.

Fort Oglethorpe, Georgia
May 12, 1943

Dear Mrs. Bandel—

I have been before the officer candidate interviewing board and have been accepted for admission to the [Officer Candidate] School in Des Moines—if all goes well, I will leave here early next week. As usual, it was a *Hairbreadth Harry* finish—I was placed on orders for Aberdeen Proving Ground, Maryland, and put on the alert less than 12 hours before I faced the board. There was some question among my officers whether or not I could leave "quarters" long enough to be interviewed—they finally decided to let me chance it, so I dashed over at the last minute with my shirt-tail flying, technically A.W.O.L., and breathlessly told the board members why I thought I would make a good officer—by the time I got back to the barracks, I discovered that I had been accepted as an O.C. (officer candidate) and "pulled off" the orders.

I have been having a lot of fun here—too much fun, according to my lieutenant, who called me on the carpet twice for giggling in ranks yesterday—fortunately, the commanding [officer] thinks it's a great joke. Affectionately, E. Brown

8. *Betty Bandel to Mrs. Bandel*

May 16, 1943

I have been running around like a chicken with its head off, but I feel that I have got something done—or at least started—in the right direction. When I hit the Air Forces, I found we were receiving companies left and right, with very little preparation, within the Air Forces, for gearing their method of requisitioning and receiving personnel to a new method which had been set up, for the army as a whole, whereby women are shipped as "casuals" rather than as units, to expedite delivery of the right person for the right job at the right place. I don't blame the Air Forces—we worked it out in ASF over a period of months (I was in on some of the planning down at WAAC headquarters), and it hit AAF all at once, although they had of course known of the general idea. So I have run around between the various parts of the air staff (Assistant Chiefs of Air Staff) practically at a trot for the whole two weeks, and I think we now have worked out the beginning of a pretty good system. I am up in a little cubby hole on the fifth floor of the Pentagon, way away from WAAC headquarters. I have

three Waacs in with me—Capt. Elrod, a former Aircraft Warning Service officer; Capt. Treadwell; Lt. Varn [*see illustrations 9 and 10*]. Elrod is a nice girl,
rather quiet, inclined to give the first impression of being slightly stuffy but
really just reserved; Treadwell, who graduated from Command and General
Staff school with the highest grade made by a Waac in that first class, and fourth
place for the entire class—men and women, is a fluttery gal with an Aunty
Mamie sense of humor that simply keeps you in stitches; Varn is young and
very attractive and thoroughly charming. Treadwell has been trying to get our
records started on where we have Waacs, and why; it has really been terrific—
she has had to go from WAAC hq. to Air Forces to the field and back again trying to find what has arrived, and where; the other day, while she was thumbing
through some of her stuff, I hung up the phone and said, "Oh, Treadwell, WAAC
hq. tells me there's a man who knows the entire history of every WAAC unit—
been keeping the records ever since they began—named Pifer." She kept right
on thumbing and said, "Where is he? Adjutant General's Office or St. Elizabeth's?"[30] Then we have WAAC officers scattered through the various divisions
of AAF headquarters—personnel, training, planning, etc.—who work closely
with us, back and forth, on figuring out all kinds of planning.

The job that I must begin immediately, and that I conceive of as my principal responsibility, is the job of orienting the women in the Air Forces—seeing
that they get settled on the job, that the posts learn what they can do, that their
housing and well-being and what not is all set up for them. But I can't even get
to that, until this preliminary planning is under way. Meanwhile, six hundred
people a day in the Air Forces who know little or nothing about Waacs but
would like some Waacs to work for them call up my office to find out what it is
all about. So, as you can see, I am not standing still.

And this morning I arose at noon and went down to the Catholic USO club
to cut a birthday cake for the WAAC's first birthday—we are a year old today.
The L.C. couldn't make it, so the one and only major doubled in brass for her,
shaking hands with a WAAC mother, handing the first piece of cake to a hungry auxiliary, cutting the first chunk (with considerable coaching from the
Waacs on the sidelines—one of the corporals said, "Beg pardon, ma'am, but I
take it you aren't a housewife"). All the little soldiers and sailors and Waacs and
WAVES who were in the club crowded around for a piece, and I told the nice
USO woman what a good job I thought they had done in making the place
cheerful for the service people, and they all bowed and scraped, and I bowed
and scraped, and it took about an hour, and then I went out and got breakfast.

I am sending you a picture of the L.C. pinning my leaves on—the one that
was in the Washington paper. The reason I am howling so is that I was standing, very stiff and wooden, and the photographer kept saying, "Major, will you
please . . . ," and of course I didn't realize he was talking to me, and kept on
standing, until the Boss muttered out of the corner of her mouth, "It's you,
butch," and I howled, and the photographer snapped the picture [*see illustration 11*].

My chief is kind of nebulous—actually it is Gen. Echols, head of MM&D [Materials, Management, and Distribution], but I haven't seen him; Gen. Whitten, under Echols, is my boss, but he doesn't know what the score is on Waacs and anyway he's too busy on a lot of other stuff, so when I go in to present an idea, he says, "That's fine. Yes, yes, I see. Yes, we must do something. Will you go ahead and do it?" So I do. One of these days they're going to wake up to just how much I am doing, and then I will probably get some supervision.[31]

Just heard the Army Hour—wonder if you heard it? The L.C. spoke, and it was mostly about Waacs, because of our anniversary today. Thought it was an excellent program—particularly young McCune, with her "The Skirted Soldier."[32] She was formerly with CBS, I believe.

9. Capt. Anna W. Wilson, WAC staff director for the European Theatre of Operations, to Betty Bandel[33]

A.P.O. 887, U. S. Army
[Great Britain]
28 May 1943

Dear Major Bandel:

Word has come to me, indirectly, of your change in assignment, and it sounds like a grand job. One thing is certain, you will perform it well. I have often thought of you over here, and have met a few people who recall your visit with pleasure.

I find the people here friendly and helpful, but of course, there are many problems. I think the biggest task I have is interpretation. It goes on continuously, over and over again to the same people and to the new ones.[34]

Best of luck Betty, in the new job, and I know you do not need it.

10. Betty Bandel to Mrs. Bandel

June 6, 1943

Dearest Maw:

Just a scribble, before I dash out to the National Gallery for a string quartet concert—I am hungry for music—haven't heard any in weeks. Jessica is singing here July 2.[35]

You would like the bunch I am working with these days. Little Pattie [Mattie] Treadwell has the darndest sense of humor. And young Caroline Varn, from Florida, is nice, very attractive, a perfect person to meet people and do the front-man stuff. Then there is Lt. Martha Selvik, not in my office but over in Military Personnel, AAF. She calls me "my major," in introducing me, and says, "Yes, ma'am," even though you know she never said "ma'am" before she joined the army. Little Lt. Bernard, also over in Military Personnel, AAF, is another cute youngster, willing to work her head off for the Waacs, big-eyed, saying "No'm, I can do it. It won't take very long." Kate Fawcett, who has been in the Air Forces from the beginning (last October, that is), will come up to my office shortly, from the division in which she has been working. Then late in June I will get one of the new graduates from Command and General Staff school. Quite a bunch, no?

11. *Betty Bandel to Mrs. Bandel*

June 13, 1943

I know I have neglected you shamefully, but I believe we will be over the hump, by the end of this week, and then I can do better. All my initial planning as to distribution of Waacs in the Air Forces crystallized last week, and is now being put into action by the various divisions concerned; this next week we will have a conference of WAAC staff directors serving with the Army Air Forces here, and will clarify our work and progress and problems; after that it will be a matter of making the program work, and settling into a good routine. My own one-day conference will take place tomorrow, and will be followed by a three-day conference which the Little Colonel has called for all WAAC staff directors in ground, service, and air forces. If I can just find enough clean shirts to last through the week, all will be well.

Thursday I received a phone call—"General Arnold wishes to see you at 11:45 tomorrow morning." So I reported to my boss (a new little lieutenant here combed my hair in the morning, so I would look presentable). He is a big, jovial man, rather red faced and white haired and middle-western. He doesn't strike me as the scholar type, as Gen. White (G-1) did, but he is very definitely a good soldier and a man of decision and character. He said, "Looks like you've been here quite a while, and I only just found out." I said, "Yes, sir, I've had a little time to get settled, but I know you've been out of town a good bit." He said, "What are you doing?" So I told him, in some detail, and he seemed much interested in the Waacs—like everyone in the Air Forces, he genuinely wants them, and wants to see that they are looked after. He asked how many I thought we needed in Air Forces, and what jobs they should do. What I said seemed to agree with what he had already made up his mind to, anyway (my view does not coincide with that of some of his more enthusiastic dreamers in Air Forces, but it does follow the pattern of his best staff people), so he said, "That's good. Go ahead and do it. Get tough with 'em if they ask you for stuff you can't give them." And I said, "Yes, sir," wondering, the while, just how I was going to get tough with some of the major generals who want "stuff we can't give them." But the four stars on his collar are a powerful bulwark behind which to stand, when you are announcing a decision. That's the funny thing about this job in

Air Forces—they seem to view me as the final authority on WAAC, and when I say something they all accept it in a way that scares me to death—I am used to having everybody brush off my view, and having to defend it for days before I can even get one little morsel of it incorporated in any plan. He said, "Anything else I should know?" I told him about our staff meeting this Monday, and he said, "I want to meet 'em. Bring 'em in at 11." So my little Waacs will get a chance to meet him. Mighty nice, when you consider that he is only running the whole air show for our entire country, in this present unpleasantness.

Friday the Little Colonel called me up and asked me to go to an Ordnance show with her. Poor Little Colonel—they have been slinging mud at the Waacs in the papers here, and she bears the brunt of it, of course. The rumors—about wholesale immorality and stuff—are utterly without foundation. If I weren't in uniform, and having to be respectable, I would punch the noses of a couple of reporters in this town—their disregard of standard newspaper ethics in regard to checking the accuracy of what they write is shocking.

12. Emily Brown to Betty Bandel

Brown has finally made it to Officer Candidate School. She argues on behalf of her fellow radio school graduates that they be assigned to jobs that utilize their training.

Flag Day [June 14] 1943
[Co. 8, 1st Regiment,
Fort Des Moines]

Dear Betty—

I have been wanting to write and congratulate you on your now not-too-recent promotion, but I have been waiting to see whether I found favor with the management at O.C.S. I can't seem to find out, so I thought I might just as well go ahead and write—As a result of a vigorous squad room campaign, I have succeeded in cornering the votes of my bunkmates so I guess I will depend on their support. (Remind me to tell you some time about how I ran for sergeant when we were at Oglethorpe's casual!) So far (at the end of three and one-half weeks) I have not been interviewed by an officer but I have hopes of being discovered on the roster some day, but perhaps it will be better for us if they never know—We are to be interviewed en masse, by classification and I am going to ask the permission of the company commander to talk to the classification lady in behalf of the four other radio school graduates in the company, as well as myself. They have asked me to represent them in the matter—we all have hopes, of course, of landing something in which our technical training will be of some value but after our various experience at Oglethorpe & Daytona we are prepared to be mess and/or supply officers of basic training centers. I feel more free to talk to you now than I will in a few weeks hence and for that reason I would like to mention just a few of the things that should be of utmost concern to you in your present very responsible position—I realize that radio-trained members represent but one of the many specialist fields serving the AAF but the suggestions I am about to make should obtain in any of the other fields. Overlooking the fact that a number of the radio-trained girls are being used as file clerks, librarians, shoe fitters and the like, there still remain certain things that are very definitely correctable.

1.   The girls who have gone out in the field and have actually been assigned to radio say that there is little correlation between their training and the work they are assigned to do.

2.   The AAF, in its training program, bears down on what it calls an ROM (radio operator-mechanic) yet the WAAC is training operators & mechanics independent of each other under Signal Corps specifications, not AAF.

3.   There is no radio-trained officer at any of the WAAC radio training schools either for mechanics or operators. I would suggest that those girls now being commissioned, who are graduates of the radio school, be sent to the schools as a remedial measure for situations 1 & 3 and that the training program be coordinated & be coordinated pronto to correct situation 2.

All of the girls in my section have been faithful in writing to me about the work they are doing & what they feel they lack in training—If you could know how hard they have worked and how hard they are working now and the interest they have in their jobs you would understand why I have no hesitation in presenting their problem to you on the very unmilitary basis of past association. I would like to see the radio girls (all specialists assigned to the AAF for that matter) built up into a crack bunch, representing real accomplishment by the Corps. I can never forget I am a newspaperwoman and in this connection I think great opportunity for some stories on what the Waacs are actually *doing* have been missed. In the first place some of the girls in my section are now at air fields and are actually going up on regular flights doing the radio maintenance work & if that isn't one of the best WAAC stories that has developed, I'm not the newspaperwoman I think I am—Also, why aren't our girls who go up regularly and draw flying pay given some kind of a distinctive insignia—what's wrong with some sort of WAAC wings—Another story: At some of the other fields our girls are teaching radio to the aviation cadets. At Kansas City the operators are getting their network experience under simulated field conditions—tents and all—I wish that I could talk to you some time and let you talk to some of the kids—They want so badly to know that they are *doing* something—That verb, "do," is a very important word in a Waac's vocabulary. Most of the morale problems come from the fact that the girls don't feel that they are "doing the job." Recruiting hangs on that verb, too. The answers to the question, "What can I do?" can only be badly answered by the girls already in service. I know you understand why I am writing you this way. I feel about the WAAC like I did (and you did) about the *Star.* Let's not have a style book unless it's a good style book and it is followed. By the same token, let's not have technical specialists unless they are properly trained and are given the jobs they are trained to—AND when we do have them on the job, let's let the world know about it.

If all goes well and I learn to keep my shoulders back, I'll be out of here by the end of this month, and all ready for mess officers' school or whatever other institution the WAAC has that I haven't attended. I can't imagine being a WAAC & not being a student.

Good luck to you & while you keep 'em flying, I'll keep screaming until my radio gals are both happy and justified.

White's letter came after I'd written this.[36] I know you'll be interested in what he has to say, even if you may not approve of the method of presentation in some cases.

13. *Captain Mattie Treadwell to Betty Bandel*[37]

Sent from Air-WAC headquarters to Bandel in Tucson.

June 27, 1943

Dearest Betty,

Just a note to report that our first week seems to be without calamities other than those you heard over the phone. Only, we always knew you turned out a lot of work, but never realized before just exactly how much. The girls have all done grand jobs, however. I feel Varn's shoulders every day to see if there are not wings, and I think there soon will be. Katie has been able to stay until 2:00 or 3:00 every day. Miss Lenz has struggled through a mountain of letters, and I believe that tomorrow they will lend us a girl from the pool to help her catch up.

Our secret operatives discovered when your birthday is, and I only hope that they have not sent you an alligator.[38] We really did mean to find you a greeting etc. but never got to town to get it. I see why you smiled so sweetly to yourself when we told you how we would revise the filing system, reorganize the AAF, etc. The other day when you talked to me from Arizona, the second time I had you on one phone, Betty Clague on the other, two visitors in the office, and Col. Catron and Stryker waiting downstairs![39]

The Waacs in Bandel's office write her affectionate letters while she is on leave in Tucson and at AAFFTC Headquarters in Fort Worth, Texas. In this one, Madge Williams alludes to the newly published WAAC pamphlet Sex Hygiene Course, Officers and Officer Candidates, *meant to be a more modest version of a course given to army men at the time. However, the publication is depicted in the press as a "supersecret agreement" of the War Department encouraging immoral behavior. It is particularly maligned by the syndicated column* Capitol Stuff, *which incorrectly states that Waacs are to be furnished contraceptives.*[40]

14. Madge Williams to Betty Bandel

June 30, 1943

Dearest Betty,

Presently I'll drop into "Major Bandel," but for the moment this is to our Mama.

Pattie is doing a good job, altho I'm afraid that before the deal on the sex course is finished, our poor Pattie will either be bald from scratching at her hair or else courtmartialed for a well-deserved case of mayhem. And I don't have WAAC Hq. in mind this time.

It isn't that we don't miss you or anything but Pattie has been working us just about like we were before you left. Yesterday between flights around the Pentagon, I tried to dash off a note to you, and did get as far as addressing an envelope. This is my afternoon off, so I am sitting here and just grinning when anyone opens her mouth and starts to tell me to stop wasting time. Very likely I'll be running errands before I finish this note.

Betty, the best thing that you could have said was just what you did about my going to Mitchel.[41] It made me walk on eggs and I was conscious the whole time that I was there that I was there as Pattie's and therefore your representative. I do think that I handled it o.k., as I was invited to spend a couple of days at Mitchel when I get some leave again. To Major Bandel I would like to report, ma'm, that the deal came off very well and that the only person even slightly upset was a lt. at the 2nd Service Command who is supposed to have charge of all orders, and who was very upset that said lt. had not seen the orders that caused the difficulties. Seems that said lt. would not have allowed the orders to get by if said lt. had seen said orders! As Capt. Durr had called them anon the matter and then gotten out a letter with exactly how the orders should have read to 2nd Service, no trouble from that end. And of course, Capt. Gilbert is extremely pleasant to do business with, and First Air Force is definitely letting her run the WAACs, and giving her all of the help and cooperation she needs. They all think so well of her that it made me feel good—kind of nice to know that other people back up your judgment of a person and a person's ability.

Back to Mammer Betty again.

You have an apt. Caroline found it last Sunday, and there will be all sorts of questions about it when we talk to you about furniture and such, so be prepared with all the answers.

So far only one person made Major: Emily Davis—what happened to the others? Not knowing Major Davis, I can't even make a catty remark or two, and I did hope that a couple of the gals that I know have done a fine job would be in your list of "several."

Capt. Downey is up here—got in yesterday, and we like her but are afraid that all of us with our occasional hells and damns and carambas may shock her—but I am sure that we'll have her cussing right along with the rest of us, just as our innocent little Pattie now does! She is an easy person to get along with and a very hard worker.

Instead of sending you the alligator, I finally broke down and cancelled it and will give you a certificate entitling you to one genuine Florida alligator, redeemable any time in the next year, for your birthday. O.K.? Then any time you want to feex up some one, can do!

This is from my cheeild [*sic*] from here on—Have a good time and don't hurry back but for gosh sakes come home soon—we all do miss you.

Madge

15. Caroline Varn to Betty Bandel

[June 30, 1943]

Dear Major Mamma Ma'am:

I feel that we have been very bad children because we haven't written you sooner—but then, say I, we have chatted with you quite a bit, and you have heard all our troubles, etc.

We have gotten along remarkably well since you left, but believe me, I sho' will be glad when you get back. We are at the zany stage now and in all probability, will be quite far gone when you return.

After La Lottman left, I started my good ol' pecking again, and Elenor and I are about to get caught up on the correspondence. Very little messy stuff has come in—thank heavens. This is about the worst typewriter I ever used.

Poor ol' Patty is about to go crazy with the sex hygiene, Madge went crazy with New York, and I am going crazy with any number of things. I've been working on that weather job for the last couple of days, and I honestly don't believe that there is a chance, and this morning Brother—I mean—Colonel Yates called and said that he absolutely had to have them, and I laughed up my sleeve, and told him to hold tight, and I am now thinking up a good story to tell him.

Your apartment is bought and paid for—but it's still rather void of furniture. I hope to be able to talk with you tomorrow and find out what you need. I have been rather hesitant about buying any for you, because I believe I heard you say something about getting some from the Director.

'Spect I had better get back to work. I can assure you that the correspondence that I have answered did not look like this! Come back soon.

Miss you muchly. Love Caroline

16. Betty Bandel to Mrs. Bandel

Upon Betty's return to Washington from Tucson.

July 4, 1943

Alack, the beautiful midwinter days of no travel by mothers & babes is no more. We are returning to the civilian ways but rapidly. One young gentleman just jumped upon my hat, & is now remonstrating loudly with a young lady of, say, 3, who is squawling in return. Oh, well—the rigors of war.

I did have the best time at home! You probably thought not much of me was home, what with my preoccupation with my job, but you must remember my mind has a trick of doing one thing with the front half of itself & another with the back half. So I have many memories stored away of how you all looked & acted to take out & amuse myself with when I get lonely for the beautiful desert & its inhabitants.

Anne, you had better not play the trumpet until I come home & show you how—you might get the mouth position all wrong & make it hard for yourself. Anyway, be sure to take care of it, so the little Christian heathen can play it when he grows up—you can play the piano while he plays the trumpet.[42]

Many thanks for spending the week *my* way.

17. Betty Bandel to Mrs. Bandel

July 23, 1943

I had a great and stirring experience last night. I went out to Catholic University, and saw Patty Treadwell's play given its premiere—WORLD premiere, as Patty put it. I have told you what a lovely spirit Patty is—sensitive and keen and full of fun and shy. All these riches showed up in her play, which was a hell of a good play. And the best part of it is Patty is enough of a critic to recognize its many faults—no strong motivation to launch it on its way, a too sudden and violent change from little forward movement to a melodramatic succession of events. But to my mind there are two kinds of plays—those that hold and develop an audience's interest, no matter what their faults, and those that don't, no matter what their virtues. The first type are plays, the second experiments. Patty had written a play, and I was as proud as a mother hen. Many Waacs came, and applauded and yelled "author!"

Before the great event, Madge and Patty and I went to the Mayflower, and had one of their usual splendid dinners to QUIET music, and—for the three of us—I presented Patty with one of those slender gold nameplates on a chain, which we wear around our wrists in the military service often. It has an Air Forces insignia on one side, and we are going to have the other side engraved. Patty, if she hadn't been unconscious already from excitement, would have gotten that way when we gave her the bracelet, I think.

And at curtain time we went back in, Patty too excited to join us. She had to be backstage. The play is about a woman who feels she has never received any real love—her mother is dead, her father a busy senator—and fails to realize she has not, simply because she has failed to grow up and accept adult responsibilities and serve in the way that brings happiness and normalcy, and, with them, the love of those who surround the well-integrated human being. Whenever she meets a new rebuff, she turns to a dream world in which an ideal lover talks to her constantly of happiness, meaning by "happiness" selfish satisfaction of every personal desire.

And after the play Patty had to take a bow, although they almost dragged her on stage with her feet braced. And after we got all through talking to the cast, we went down and found [a] hamburger place, and we sat and ate them and rehashed the show.

And today the Boss asked me to drive out to see a company with her—she is back after another trip—and found out about the play, and made immediate plans to ask Patty and Miss Malvina Thompson and me to dinner Monday night, and then go to the play. We got Patty on the phone, and the Boss extended her invitation, and I think if one more thing happens to Patty we'll have to pick her off the top of the Washington monument.

18. Betty Bandel to Mrs. Bandel

July 30, I think, 1943

Wednesday Madge & Patty dragged me away from work early, & took me up to a nice restaurant called *The Parrot*. We had sherry, & were ordering dinner—elegant fried chicken for me—with a bottle of sauterne for us all, when Madge solemnly laid in front of me a mountain of assorted packages, white with fancy blue ribbons. So, in defiance of all military customs, and while the assembled multitude stared, I unwrapped 2 pairs of nice stockings from Patty, 4 gorgeous white monogrammed handkerchiefs from Madge, a woven New Mexico tie from Caroline, & some Tweed Lentheric perfume from them all! And, to cap the climax, a bundle of large white handkerchiefs from Col. Breckenridge, a grand chap in the Air Forces who was a hard-bitten marine officer in the last war & got in at the first scent of gunpowder in this. He is in O. C. & R.[43] (Madge's division), & he likes "those Air WAAC kids" to the point of occasionally coming up & visiting. He saw Madge buying my handkerchiefs, said "What the hell kind of a handkerchief is that for a soldier?" & paid a personal visit to the Quartermaster store to purchase a wad of G.I. handkerchiefs. Can use them as individual, personally-owned doilies in my apartment, in lieu of a pipe for each woman.

Monday night Patty—as excited as possible—& I went out to the L.C.'s for dinner & on to Patty's play. The L.C., who gets terribly excited over the drama anyway, really fell for Patty's play—grabbed me & almost let out a yell when the hand of the Devil appeared around the door. While we were at the play, Patty received a telegram from 20th Century Fox, asking for a copy of the script![44] If she had been anybody else, we would have been picking her out of the spotlight. As it was, her comment on the evening—with that wide-eyed elfin look of hers—was, "You know, I often wondered why you thought the Director so wonderful. I guess it's because she's wonderful."

19. Betty Bandel to Mrs. Bandel

August the somethingth [9], 1943

Please forgive my long delay in writing, but I am really in the middle of the major crisis in my particular chore for this war. We are head over heels in the transfer of Waacs to full army status, & are at the same time completing our general planning as regards Waacs in the Air Forces. I have set Sept. 15 as my goal—if I survive until then, I think things will quiet down & a routine will begin to be established which will make it possible for me to write more often, to play with my little house more, & generally to emerge from my Pentagon shell at more regular intervals. In anticipation of that great day, & of the fact that we will by then hold regular commissions in the army of the United States, Jess Rice & I are planning a week-end in New York about then. Meanwhile, I am not working terribly long hours—not half so long as I often did for the *Star*—but my every working thought seems to be absorbed by the WAAC, or by Waacs. The second is quite different from the first: there are, in other words, a whole lot of people around here who take up time—time I am glad to devote to them—because they are my colleagues.

I wrote Alexander, & asked her to pass on to you the story of our Monday night celebration of Caroline Varn's promotion, so I won't repeat it here. Little Varn was so cute. She is quiet as a mouse, ordinarily, but she came bubbling into the office Monday morning, all full of her trip to Des Moines—she was just back. I was on the phone, but she came scurrying into my office, saluted, & said, "Second Officer Varn reporting for duty, ma'am!" Her shadow, Madge Williams, was right behind her. I motioned her to a seat, & she began telling all about the trip almost before I got off the phone. I said, "Varn, you're out of uniform." She looked down, much startled, said, "Insignia on the right side, all buttons on—what's wrong!" I said, "Can't you see?" She kept looking, puzzled, & answered some questions the others were asking about her trip. I said, "Ok, well, I guess I'll have to fix it," & reached over & took her 1st lieutenant's bar off her collar, substituting a captain's bar. She was talking all the time, & couldn't very well see what I was doing anyway, so I was quietly sitting back by the time she glanced at the desk, saw her lieutenant's bar lying there before her, jumped as if it had bitten her, snatched at her collar & dragged it out until she could see her captain's bar. Then she let out a squeal, & sat back utterly unable to say a word. Her surprise was really funny. She is young, but immensely able, & a member of the first class—nothing but her natural modesty could have kept her from anticipating that I would recommend her for a captaincy, as soon as I had a vacancy. It was a lot of fun—one has so many problems, it is delightful to be able to recognize a complete absence of problems.

The next two letters are from Emily Brown, 845th WAAC Post Headquarters, Alliance Air Base, Nebraska—after washing out of OCS. Clearly, she is not broken by this experience but more determined than ever to salvage what she can from it. As usual, she takes the opportunity to offer her views, in this case on the officer selection process and how to improve it.

20. Emily Brown to Betty Bandel

July 21, 1943

Dear Betty,

Well, it's taken me nine months to do it, but I've finally achieved the distinction of being the only Brown in the organization. But perhaps that's because I am the only anything in an organization. Yes, the total strength of the 845th WAAC Post Hq. Co., AAF, to date is one (1). It's a great experience. I arrived here Monday morning and was greeted by two excited officers who have done everything in their power since to make me happy and comfortable. We are expecting some more members within the next few days but, in the meantime, I can delight in my solitude. Never before have I been accorded such courtesy. All I have to do is step out of the orderly room and I am confronted with a convoy of jeeps and I may take my pick of vehicles for my momentous ride to the PX or to the 1076th Guard Squadroom Mess where I am given the personal attention of the mess sergeant. He, and he only, does the ladling.

I haven't been to classification yet but my officers have and they assure me that I am to be assigned to radio—probably, the control tower. I am to wait until some more gals arrive before being assigned. Now, I am more useful around the orderly room or in my fatigue clothes. There's a power of windows to be washed. I am anxious to get to work but I'd just as soon wait now and get my reenrollment or enlistment, or however it's designated, over with.

I'm sorry that you had to be home when the sad news of my failure to meet existing standards—as it were—was received. I know it was hard on you and I also know you've had your full share of Emily Brown. Thank you for your kind expression of sympathy and for all your activity in my behalf while you were home.[45] There is very little that I can say about it that I haven't already said except to express the same thought to you that I did to Captain Reilly when

I talked to her about it and that is if what I have to offer is worth anything to the corps then I feel that I was worth an hour or two or somebody's time to make an effort, if nothing else, to correct the most obnoxious things about me. I am going back, if I can. I have already talked to my c.o. here about it.

It was quite an experience to live with a company of "washouts." Most of them took their failure pretty hard and were inclined to be pretty resentful of the system. There's no doubt but that it is a brutal one, but those who weather it certainly prove their stuff. In all, I think that there are precious few mistakes made and I should know, I lived with them. If anything, it isn't the ones they get—it's the ones they don't get that are the real liability to the service. There is only one answer and that is more careful selection along the line further down. In short, O.C.S. should advise selection boards what they are looking for. I should have been thrown out on my posture and general appearance long before I ever hit Des Moines and not been admitted to O.C.S. until I had done something about it, or them! I think that getting washed out of O.C.S. was about the only way that I could have gotten to the field as an EM [enlisted man], everybody was so determined that I go to Des Moines as fast as it could be arranged. For that reason, I am very grateful. It will make me a hell of a lot better at the job I still want to do. I am, if you will remember, the determined type!

Thank you again, and pull the ripcord sometime when you are flying over Alliance.

21. Technician 5th Class Emily Brown to Major Betty Bandel

[August 13, 1943
Kansas City]

Dear Betty,

I have been meaning to write to you as soon as it happened—you having heard so much to the contrary. The news, of course, is that I have an assignment in radio. A rather choice one, I believe—sufficiently choice to make those around me a bit envious of me and my walkie-talkie. I am assigned to Base Communications and our principal duty is to service and align the radios on all transient ships and to stand by for the base command in the event of an emergency. In this last-named capacity, it is our function to set up the temporary power-lines for the control tower sets when the power fails (frequently, in Alliance) and to man the mobile transmitting and receiving station which is housed in a truck and trailer unit. When I left, I was busily engaged in learning how to handle the truck and trailer, slightly different from Tessie in maneuverability. And now it is time to explain the "When I left . . ." part. It is without the slightest degree of modesty that I report that I am here on a merit furlough accorded me for having the honor of being chosen the first Waac "Man-of-the-

Week" at Alliance, an interesting accolade, substantially backed by seven days of freedom, not entered on your service record. The honor was given me in recognition of my term of service as acting first sergeant for the 845th and my supporting attitude during those first few trying days of activation and conversion. But in spite of my best efforts (and, I will concede, those of my officers) we lost 29 of the first 77 sent out to our base.[46] In most cases, I think the Corps is the winner, but there were those who, for reasons of dependency and physical impairments, are a definite loss. We had three who were washed out for spots on their lungs, but the Corps loss will be Tucson's gain. I was right there with my words of consolation, good advice, and Chamber of Commerce folders! After all, I have to look to my future and the Chamber most certainly has the softest chairs to loaf in and those pink walls have always had a soothing effect on my beer and/or walbridge-jangled nerves. Before my leave started, I was in Des Moines on special orders to line up PRO on the WAAC angle of the base dedication, which comes off August 22nd in the proposed presence of the Undersecretary Patterson and others of note, both military and civilian.[47] I was also able to report the situation as concerns publicity in the field and took it upon myself to make a few pertinent suggestions in this direction. Although I was, as expected, referred to the Office of Technical Information in Washington, I believe that I planted a few seeds which may well be expected to flourish and flower. If nothing else, I left them drooling. I talked to two officers who leaned wistfully forward and kept murmuring, "Yes, yes, Brown, go on." So I went on to extol the delights of field service, not confining myself to its angles of presentation. The upshot is that I am going to bang off some stories and send them in to OTI with Des Moines' blessing.[48] They seemed particularly interested in the value of an overall story from the time of the arrival of the Waacs from the various schools and training centers, through the "settling in" period, to their ultimate assignment in the jobs in which they can at least see the big job being done. There is certainly a very impressive angle in this assignment business and one which would give every hardened griper in the Corps cause to pause. We were all interviewed by a classification officer and temporary assignments made and then the commanding officer of the base waited upon our company officers in a seven hour conference during which time these assignments were verified or changed according to the *wants* of the individual Waac, insofar as it was compatible to her training. My case, for example, was a typical one. As is to be expected, my six years as a working newspaperwoman loomed much larger in the eyes of the original classifying officer than did my 13 weeks at the Army radio school in Kansas City. So the assignment was made: PRO. My commanding officer, however, spoke to the Colonel about the matter and he indicated the base communications assignment. We have reached a neat compromise in that I am handling all the WAAC publicity on an after hours basis and maintaining my official assignment in radio. As you know, I am enjoying the newspaper work as much as I am the radio, so I couldn't ask for a pleasanter deal. My first PRO job was to get out a WAAC cover and lead story for "Boots and Wings," the paratroopers paper, and follow through with a WAAC inside page. (It's tabloid format.) Just before I left, the PRO called me up and asked me to join the staff for the handling of the dedication publicity. August 22nd will be a difficult day for me: I will be torn between helping to herd the visiting press around and performing in the base communications field demonstration which will involve the setting up and handling of a field transmitter. I do so want the taxpayers to see a Waac twiddling the dials, but then there will be nobody to haul the press around and show them what the other 76 Waacs are doing in the field. (My life always seems to present so many little problems like that.) I am representing the WAAC on the dedication plans committee and I presented the ideas that the gals take part in the demonstrations in the jobs that they actually do rather than in some all-WAAC demonstration. The integration is the point we want to make, I think. Most of the 845th members are highly satisfied with their jobs—and why shouldn't they be? Those of us who are down on the line, though, have the best reason for believing that we are the chosen of chosen. But now that I am out in the field and have seen and worked at the jobs which the Waacs can do in radio, I am all hot on another project. I am lobbying now for a crack at control tower school and there are hopes that I may get it. The operations officer wants to send on his gals over and the communications officer is sympathetic with my interest in it. There is a very definite shortage of radio-trained men in the communications system and the WAAC might work in very handily. I have sort of a double-barreled job in that, in addition to the actual service and maintenance work I do in radio, I act as the office girl for the 23rd Airways Communications Squadron which has the tower unit at the field. In that way I am learning a lot about the whole set up and getting a pretty good picture of our function. At Des Moines this week end I bid a sorrowful farewell to the girls who had gone up to o.c.s. with me from radio school who were departing to their "operational assignments." They are almost pathetic in their hope to draw down something in communications but classification has almost convinced them that theirs is a lost cause. The most persistent are still lobbying for radar but I am now of the very definite belief that the control tower units are the answer as, under the Army set up, they involve about 25 EM and a radio-trained officer. All of my conjectures in this connection make my job a lot more interesting than if I'd just stick to my soldering and reminds me of our quixotic efforts in behalf of *Star* style. But that made working on the *Star* more interesting, too. I talked to Reilly about o.c.s. when I was in Des Moines and told her ready-or-not here I come again. She sighed audibly but I think that she is resigned to the inevitable.

e brown

still of the Lightfoots!

I just read this over the day after its writing & it impresses me as being redolent of an obnoxious variety of smugness. There are sufficient facts of my life to warrant sending it on, however, and I trust that you will accept it in the spirit that it is offered. It just happened to be washed up by a wave of genuine enthusiasm for the Corps, for radio, and I must admit, myself!—Felicidades—Emily.

22. *Betty Bandel to Mrs. Bandel*

Ellipses here are in the text.

August 22, 1943

How the weeks fly past! And how dreamlike this whole experience will seem, 20 years hence! So much happens . . . I have been in the Pentagon so constantly of late that my Gremlins resorted to the enclosed "R&R" to get me out last night. We went to Caroline's brother's apartment, & she cooked a delicious chicken dinner—candles—good records—big, comfy chairs—lazy talk or none at all. All very relaxing.

Wrote a speech for the L.C. to give to my air people Tuesday—if she's too busy I'll have to. It's a wonderful system. She is working too hard, of course.

[Routing and Record sheet mentioned in letter above]

Subject: Getting you the hell out of this firetrap
To: Major (Pooped) Betty Bandel   Date: 21 August 1943
From: The Air WAAC Gremlins   Comment No. 1
                                jayceevee 4823

1. It is requested that you leave the Thing Building tonight at a reasonable hour (preferably five-ish), and follow one of the following itineraries:

 a. Have a steak dinner at Hammel's and go to an early movie (or the other way around)

 b. Eat a meal (probably scrambled eggs, etc.) cooked by Varn and Williams, Inc., at the "Empty Arms" (residence of Mr. Stew Varn, who at the present time is basking in the sun at a Delaware beach)—and then listen to records.

2. Request recommendation and/or concurrence.

Janet C. Varn
Baby Gremlin
AFDAW

Coordination:
Fifinella Treadwell: Navy willing
Gremlin Williams: GW—!!!!
[Signed: Concur. BB.]

CHAPTER 5

Lieutenant Colonel, Regular Army

In mid-1943, the Women's Army Corps is in crisis. After a period of months in which enlistments sag, in part due to the "smear" campaign, a new recruitment strategy is desperately needed. Morale among WAC recruiters is at such an all-time low that Director Hobby writes a letter asking them to find the courage within themselves for one more go at the recruitment effort: "I know the difficulties, the loneliness, the heartbreaking apathy you have faced. I know how hard it is . . . to dip deep into inner resources and start again. . . . If you can give of your own strength, your own conviction, your own faith and heartfelt patriotism, we will not fail now."[1] And they do not fail. The new "All-States" Recruiting Campaign conceived and implemented by Major Jessie Rice, former WAC director of the Third Service Command and now deputy director, invites each state to raise its own company of Wacs, effectively giving states a stake in the success of recruitment and the deployment of their own citizens. The campaign is hugely successful, bringing in more than four thousand new recruits in its first month. Director Hobby later affirms that Rice is, literally, responsible for saving the Corps in a critical time (*see illustration 15*).[2]

In September, all Waacs who wish to continue service reenlist in the army, having attained full army status. When that happens, the duties of the office WAC director become advisory only: Colonel Hobby no longer has direct command over WAC personnel, and many of her staff are parceled out to the Army Service Forces offices that have assumed oversight of WAC operating functions. She now has difficulty keeping in touch with her Wacs in the field except by direct contact, one of the reasons why her senior officers are always traveling. WAC company commanders are still responsible for matters of discipline, but sometimes their male counterparts try to assume that role, causing division and disorder in WAC companies. Although Bandel welcomes the switch to being regular army, the changeover complicates matters: WAC officers now have to compete with men for slots on station rosters. The AAF, ahead as usual of the other army forces in supporting the Wacs under their command, sidesteps this problem by authorizing the promotion of WAC officers without regard for allotments.[3]

Meanwhile, Bandel settles into her role as Air-WAC Officer. One of her main duties is to find places for Wacs in AAF units. She spends much of her time on the road, visiting WAC units around the country. She notes later that their isolation, and disappointment at being assigned to tasks no different from their jobs as civilians, erodes the morale of both officers and enlisted women. Her role, as she sees it, is to ensure that living facilities in the field are good and that Wacs are aware that their welfare is important to the Corps.[4] As part of General Arnold's plan to create an atmosphere within the AAF that will ensure the success of the Air-WAC by educating his officers about the WAC, Bandel speaks in front of the officers in charge of personnel in the air commands. The effect her talk has on them hints at Bandel's real influence in the success of this policy: she even gets a standing ovation when she is done.

Although many Wacs are assigned to jobs traditionally thought of as "women's work," such as typist, telephone operator, and food service workers, some do receive specialist training in a number of fields: radio operators, vehicle repair and transport specialists, aerial photographers, and chemical warfare technicians, to name but a few. Not all are able to use their training, however. Letters in this chapter illustrate that frequently they are not assigned to posts where their training is used. Even skills that Wacs bring with them from civilian life are often not recognized and made use of by the army: language skills, for example. Some AAF commands request Wacs for such unsuitable duties as laundry and troop entertainment.

Women do not serve on the front lines: they are more likely to replace men in noncombat jobs in the United States and abroad. Bandel recalls how Wacs saved the day for a combat division that was held up from going overseas by a lack of army cooks. One of her Air-WAC office staff conceives the idea of sending Wacs to replace cooks at military hospitals, freeing up male cooks for the division.[5]

In between her many inspection tours, Bandel is one of the so-called "chairborne infantry" or "paragraph troopers," as those working at the Pentagon are known in Washington—but she leads by no means a quiet life. There's a story that she loves to tell to illustrate the frenetic pace of work: "We had to write a little diary at the end of the day, what our division had done that day and send it up to the head cheese, who was in charge of personnel for the air force. And when I was frantically busy, I would always say to [my secretary], 'Routine! Routine!' And she would write "routine" and send it up. She came in one day, when we had had a rape at one base, a riot at another, and the possibility of murder at a third. All of which had me on the wire, trying to find out what was true and what wasn't. She comes in, she says, 'Diary, Colonel Bandel?' I said, 'Routine! Routine!' She said, 'Murder, rape, riot, and routine.' And she walked out."[6]

Early in 1944, Bandel makes a worldwide inspection tour of WAC installations with Colonel Hobby and General Barney Giles, chief of Air Staff. He
sends Bandel a letter of commendation: "Your observations & recommendations for more utilization of available WAC personnel in *overseas areas* will
undoubtedly be of great value in the determination of future policies. I was particularly impressed with your excellent military bearing at all times, as well as
with your executive abilities, all of which reflect great credit on you as an individual & on the Women's Army Corps."[7] While in Tunis, she learns that she is
to be the first WAC lieutenant colonel.

1.   *Jessie Rice to Betty Bandel*

*Jess Rice writes from Third Service Command headquarters, Baltimore,
of her efforts to keep in touch with the Waacs in her command, efforts that
are frustrated by administrative obligations. She also alludes to the nascent All-States Campaign.*

[ca. August 1943]

Dear Betty—

I haven't written a letter in weeks and I owe many letters to people who in
their charity write to me despite my negligence. Yet I sit down and write a letter to you for no good reason except that I some how feel like doing so. Of
course the work is piled sky high on my desk but my mind is like rubber with
all the stretch gone out of it. Most of the work concerns things I have to decide
what to do with. Since I seemed unable to think through them I was walking
the floor when I decided to write to you.

I had planned to take this evening off and spend it talking to my favorite
Army officer in this Command. He is leaving for the Army Ground Forces—
much to his delight—but Gwen Watson called me and wanted to come over.
Gwen is a nice youngster and I enjoy these young officers who are capable and
have their hearts in their work. They remind me of my youth—not that I was
so capable but boy I could get steamed up over things that interested me. (I still
seem to be able to about the Waacs and a few other things despite the load of
forty years.)

I think the reason I am writing you is that I have been wishing you'd knock
off the night shift for one night and come over for a few hours, at least. I offer
you a glass of wine, a loaf of bread, and a lobster on the side—at Miller's—
plus conversation with or without shop talk. You can decide. I've been trying to
remember what I used to think about before I joined the Waacs. If I could remember I'd think about it again—for a rest. I'm quite sure though that there is
much to talk about—things which have in them peace and beauty.

But to get back to the Waacs—are there any regulations or rather is there a ceremonial prescribed for Waac funerals? We have had two in the Service Command within the last week. Not knowing what else to do I worked things out as I thought they should be. I did have a bugler. I did not have a firing squad. I did not think there should be a soldier firing squad. Major Dunn disagreed with me. If I was wrong let me know and I'll have one next time—if there is a next time. I hope there won't be. I used details of ten or twelve auxiliaries and one officer.

I called Westray personally last night because I have a cousin 46 years old who called me yesterday and asked if there was a need for her in the Waacs.[8] This cousin of mine is pretty capable. She was originally a dietician but for a good many years has been the business manger and superintendent of a hospital at home. I told her to join up and asked her to see Westray. Therefore, I called Westray and in the conversation last night Westray said she was staying out more and more—that Colonel Clapham wanted her to.[9]

This afternoon a few minutes before the office closed I had a wire from Des Moines saying we'd have ten recruiting auxiliaries in tomorrow. I arranged for their rooms, got tickets for them to eat on tomorrow, got somebody to meet them, got them passes to a show, (with Major Dunn's help) and then called Kep because the telegram also had the arrival of the people in the 81st in it.[10] In the conversation she talked about staying out with the companies. I'm wondering if I'm falling down on the job. I do see my companies but I do it mainly on Sundays. I have been out eleven out of the last thirteen. However, when I go I feel I give the companies little in the way of detailed help they need. I do answer questions. I do give out all the enthusiasm and encouragement I can but that generally has to be crammed into a couple of hours because the Post Commander wants to see me, the Personnel Officer, the Medical Officer, and Heaven knows how many other people want to see me and I generally end with about two hours with the company officers and then I have to come back. As a result, I am planning to keep Hoffman out practically all of the time.[11] She can check records, straighten out details, check assignments, find out personnel problems. These officers need help on details. Handling the companies in the field presents some new problems when they have had only experience in the Training Centers. Hoffman can find out what is wrong and if it is something she can't straighten out or something that should be taken up with the Commanding-Officer of the Post and she feels she can't do it—I can do it when I go on short trips. Maybe I don't see things right but in my situation that seems to be a better plan than my staying out so much. I won't know what is happening to the Waacs in this Hqs if I am gone a week at a time because since Lt. Kerr left there is no one here who can handle the administrative end of things. Right or wrong we have run Waac affairs in this SC from this Branch because we've done the work. I haven't run Recruiting but with the new plan out I think that will soon be in good shape. I have my fingers crossed. Since February I have been doing the hardest and most subtle selling job I've ever tried for virtually the same thing the new plan calls for. I have talked over the things I think have been wrong with the Senior officer in each District (in confidence). I'm pretty sure most of them are going to measure up to the new responsibilities because I have been telling them what it would involve if Recruiting were turned over to them. The new plan gives Recruiting to Major Dunn and the Waac officers but I have some part in selecting the stations for the senior Waac officers and I have confidence that I shall be informed about the things that don't work. I hope I'm not fooled.

I'm trying to make my chief find space for this branch next to the Military Personnel Branch. With the new allotment plan I think we need to be there. It may not be possible. If it isn't, I think I am going to put my staff around Hqs so that I shall have a[n] officer in each Bra[n]ch or section of the Personnel Division with which we have to work closely.

Sometimes I almost laugh aloud when I suddenly realize that I work and plan at this job as though I were going to be here forever and I am perfectly conscious of the fact that I'm not promised twenty-four hours. That has never bothered me though. I joined the WAAC. The powers that be can do with me what they will and I don't think I shall mind. It's wonderful not to have to decide where you'll work. Even on my worst days I've never been sorry I joined up and on the worst days I've still been glad I had a chance at this assignment.

I went down for the graduation of the class at Holabird this morning. The Commandant of the school told me this was the best class he has had and he has been generous in his praise for the others. Monday I go to Edgewood to see about arrangements for the group that is to go in there May 1st. I know nothing about it. I understand it is an experimental group but I think we can work out the housekeeping arrangements all right.[12]

I enjoyed my trip to Pittsburgh. As usual, all the people who saw The Director were spell bound. I always am myself; so I'm not surprised. Despite the fact that I have seen her comparatively few times she is a great personal inspiration to me. I have known some pretty top flight women in my time, and I think I am of the opinion that she heads them all. Having been in the educational world so long I have long known of and respected Miss McAfee but she doesn't in my opinion have what The Director has.[13] In fact, I feel a little sorry for the Waves and the Marines because they don't have a Colonel Hobby to head their services. When this bloody war is over and I am no longer a Waac officer, I think I shall dip my pen in star dust and write a tribute to her in prose that sings. Come to think of it, you are no slouch yourself. And I would like to see you. If the dinner at Miller's doesn't seem worth the trip over, let me know what would make it worth while and I'll see if that particular thing is available.

Jess

Tell Gretchen I said you can't run a job like this and be forever making speeches. She'd better send them some other name. Did you tell Senior Commander Hammick that I said I thought she helped the cause. I do.[14]

2. Betty Bandel to Mrs. Bandel

August 16, [1943]

We are right in the middle of the final administrative details re getting the Waacs on full army status, & I am swamped with all kinds of minor adjustments to make by wire, long distance, telephone, etc. Then too, I am promoting a new recruiting plan for Waacs in the AAF, & am at the same time helping Jess Rice on a great recruitment scheme she dreamed up. She called me up a week ago—as she often does from Baltimore, whenever she wants to convince herself of an idea by saying it out loud—& told me her recruiting plan. I thought it was so good I got her to tell it to the Director, & as a result she is now in here on temporary duty driving WAAC hq. into a state of unaccustomed decisiveness by working them nights, Sunday, & every other time. When either one of us gets a moment, we have dinner together.

I had hoped to fly to Florida this week to look into WAAC matters there, but I am serving on a board of officers here & cannot leave. The president of the board is old Gen. Pearson, who drives me nuts by asking what works lines of poetry which I cannot place come from.[15]

The writing urge is getting strong again—if things quiet down to a routine this winter, & I stay in my present job & therefore close to Washington, I will begin work again. I just thought of a wonderful idea for a one-act—a bride on the ration system.

3. Betty Bandel to her family

She reports on the reunion of the first graduating class of officers, of which Betty is one.

August 29, 1943

This morning—one year after you pinned my gold safety pins on, Maw—I made a little speech at a reunion breakfast which all from that first class who are in the Washington area had—about 44 of us.[16] Gen. and Mrs. Faith and D-WAAC [Director, WAAC (Hobby)] were the only non-first-classers present. Major Emily Davis (Ground WAAC, like me [being] Air WAAC) was master of ceremonies. All very informal and nice. No side. Dorothy Bussard—a golden-voiced girl—led us in a couple of WAAC songs; there were the little talks; we left. Just the way I like things to be.

Did I tell you we have 18 more majors? All swell people—two Air Force (Mary Freeman, Flying Training Command; Betty Clague, Air Force).[17] They told me that I had to speak on "Memories," the Director on "Dreams." I screamed, "Don't you mean 'Delusions' and 'Nightmares'?" But that was at 6 p.m., after a board meeting since 10 a.m. (it went on to midnight, incidentally, and old Gen. Pearson very kindly invited us to come up to the Army and Navy club after that and "drink dinner."—We had two drinks, and then he went home, and the three of us gals went to an all-night hamburger place for food.) So at 2:30 this a.m. I got home, wondered what I was going to talk about this morning, but trusted to inspiration. I really only recalled to them one or two of the thoughts we all held that wonderful, golden morning—remember the great garrison flag over the parade ground, and the salutes those girls gave us as we filed back past the barracks?—and those we have grown to have since that time. They all were so much of my mind, that they were most sympathetic and flatteringly attentive. Then Gen. Faith said a word or so on what it meant to the army to have us. Jess Rice—bless her sentimental heart—talked of plans for the future, and said what the corps had meant to her, quoting a fine line: "Here I am, plain John Doe, not destined to be a hero, but accorded the next best thing: I have walked with tall men, comrade-wise."[18] And little D-WAAC, all sentimental too, said what we had meant to her—and what the whole business stands for to her—just the privilege of serving, really. 'Twas nice. I ended by saying I was profoundly grateful, as a citizen to Congress, as a soldier to the army, and as a person to "my Little Colonel" for giving me the things from which to make a magnificent memory. Us southern orators—how we drool.

4.   *Betty Bandel to Mrs. Bandel*

Bandel talks to the assistant chiefs of Air Staff about the value of the WAC to their commands, an initiative advocated by Director Hobby to improve attitudes toward the WAC.[19] Bandel also praises, compares, and contrasts Director Hobby and Jess Rice.

September 5, 1943

The great news of the week—sensational, in fact—is this: I have some furniture. I took Caroline (my arbiter elegantiarum)[20] into town with me Thursday night—after deciding that the whole durned war effort could stand still, as far as I was concerned, until I got some furniture—and started out at the top: Woodward and Lothrop's.[21] I got no farther, because I walked into one of those little make-believe rooms, and was so entranced by it I bought the whole room. Caro and I calmly tapped a salesman on the shoulder, led him over, and told him we wanted this—"this" being what he saw before him. After a slight and well covered pause for breath, he whipped out his book and signed me up on the dotted line. Then we were so pleased with ourselves we sat down in the chairs, rocked, and admired us.

The week has been terribly busy. Thursday I spoke to the A-1s from the various Air Commands, in here for a conference (they are the men in charge of personnel out in the commands). I spoke in the interests of eliciting their wholehearted cooperation in making the WAC program a success in Air Forces—said how much we newcomers to the Army needed their guidance and help. I had been much moved by the apparency of the need for their assistance just before speaking, and evidently that conviction crept into my talk, because they accorded me flattering attention. Men are such lovely babies. You cannot tell them women need help, without getting them ready to get up and fight for the cause—they actually were blinking hard at the thought of anybody neglecting to care for Wacs placed under their control, and there was some hasty blowing of noses when I got through. They did something contrary to military practice—rose and applauded—as I finished. It surprised me so much I had to duck out, although I had planned to stay and listen to more of the conference.

Later a bunch of them met up in my office for a conference on WAC recruiting efforts. I have a little conference table in my inner office (I insisted on a wall between myself and the rest of the office, a conference table, and a rug, simply because people here lay store by such things). I don't know whether I have ever told you that I have on loan in my office three little model airplanes—perfect replicas of the big ships—out of a collection of such models which is at the disposal of my M.M. and D. people.[22] Well, the durned little things are cute, but they are more trouble than they're worth—every fool man who comes in here wants them, and devils the life out of me for them. Well, Col. Morrison, the dignified, able, scholarly, fatherly A-1 from the Training Command sat and played with that durned baby plane all through the afternoon, and finally went walking off down the hall with it cuddled under one arm, holding me off with the other as I trotted along beside him begging and pleading that the thing wasn't mine and that I couldn't give it to him. I finally recovered it, but had to hide it in a drawer to keep one of the other 50-year-old babies from stealing it.

Yes, I got sworn in Sept. 1, by Gen. Faith—we all went down to a little auditorium in the building, D-WAC made a little speech, and Gen. Faith swore us in. Very short, rather impressive. Reminiscent of that day in Des Moines. It is hard to remember to write, "Major, WAC," instead of "Field Director, WAAC."[23]

One thing I can say for the Director in all sincerity: there is not only no one who can touch her in the Corps, but also no one who is even in her league. She is head and shoulders above us all. It is to her, and her alone, that credit goes for all a woman could do for this Corps—much of the job has of course been done by the army proper. But it is her personal magnetism, her deserved prestige in civilian life, her diplomatic acumen, her profundity of devotion and dedication to the cause in which she believes, that have made possible the recognition which the powers-that-be have given us, and therefore the progress we have made. That personal magnetism is a powerful thing; others might have done as efficient a job (many leaders of other women's groups have, as a matter of fact), but few could have commanded the glad, voluntary surrender of leadership into her hands by women of much background and of little, which she has won, and the equally spontaneous respect for her opinions which men who are parallel or higher authorities have given her. The rest of us make a good supporting cast, but she is the star, with no more conscious attempt to make herself a star than a beautiful young colt would make to show off his satiny skin and rippling muscles, as he frisked across a field for the sheer joy of kicking his heels. But everyone who saw him would see that satiny skin. And everyone who sees her knows she is the star. Jess Rice, who in my opinion is the No. 2 woman in the Corps, in many ways excels her—in sound scholarliness, in finding the simple, logical mechanic rather than the brilliant, difficult one—but she still cannot touch her in the all-around effectiveness of her leadership among all types and kinds of people. Although I must say that Jess has a homely, earthy, spontaneous touch which appeals particularly to WAC companies, and which I don't believe the Director has, or could have without the advantage of the 6 weeks' training in standard army procedure which the rest of us all had. We have a kind of unspoken understanding, those of us who unconsciously know the funny little ins and outs of saluting and the rest of the outward manifestations of the military framework. The L.C. has learned many of the outward manifestations, but did not first learn the simple skeleton—she is like a person who speaks English perfectly, but never learned the few simple fundamental rules, and is therefore always afraid it is some great mystery and that she is probably making a mistake. Only those who learned the skeleton first, and picked up the form gradually and after, can be at ease among the customs of military life.

5.   *Betty Bandel to Mrs. Bandel*

The All-States Recruiting Campaign comes to fruition.

September 15, 1943
[Fort Worth]

Jess Rice says this war will be forever associated, in her mind, with fish. I say it will be associated with airports. Today I have been in Roanoke, Knoxville, Nashville, Memphis, Little Rock, Dallas, & here—& they all look alike. That is to say—their airports look alike. It is so tantalizing to me to know I am within reaching distance of sights & sounds & smells that would be new to me, & cannot pause to go & find them. Ah, well, after the war I will go back & really look.

I am in Ft. Worth on a recruiting conference—the Air Forces are giving a helping hand in Wac recruiting. Jess Rice, who was recently transferred from 3rd Service Command to WAC headquarters, & is in charge of their recruiting efforts, is with me. Mary Freeman, my WAC Staff Director down here, came in

& discussed plans for the conference. She's a shrewd old Georgia politician—made her farm pay all through the depression.

We have had a day of conference, & things have gone well. Everybody talked—me included, of course—& I think we are getting up a fair-to-middling scheme. Lord, what memories we will all have after this war! I'll bet we all make a noise like the American Legion.

6. Alexander (Marie Padgett) Hamilton to Betty Bandel

September 16, 1943
[Tucson]

Beautiful:

My furniture just slip-covered, and I wish the only major of my acquaintance were right now ensconced in one of the glorified chairs. All day I've advised freshmen and helped them straighten out schedules. The love of learning—or of something—still seems to rule the feminine part of the world (I've had three male advisees).

Mrs. Henry, my visavee[24] at table, remarked that the WACs are safe because they have two smart women to run them, and so would not make the usual stuffy army errors. *Do* I ever stop to think what this year has meant to you? You mean Do I ever *stop* thinking what it has meant to you? "From Rookie to creator of captains in less than a year!" There has never been such a record as yours. *And wost tu why,* as the Wife of Bath would say?[25] There aren't many such people.

Do take care of yourself, Dearest love, Alexander

7. Betty Bandel to Mrs. Bandel

Sept. about 27 or so [1943]

Dear Maw:

The L.C., poor lassie, has had a sick husband and child to look after lately. The Governor had to have an operation about a week ago, and she was simply worried to death. She spent sleepless nights running out to the hospital to see him, trying to dig up a nurse (they are scarce as hen's teeth today), and getting somebody to look after young Jessica, who went off her feed the way children will when things are upset around them. Add to all this a small apartment, with young William and Jessica in it, and you have some idea of what that one woman shoulders, aside from what I consider the most trying job in the War Department. I have seen her drag herself together for a hard conference, in which everything hung on the phrasing of an idea's presentation, when she would have to pull herself up out of her chair by holding on to the edge of her desk—and yet when she went into it, five minutes later, with fresh make-up on, no one in the room would have dreamed she was anything but sailing along at the top of her form, full of energy, strength, composure. Don't ever tell any of this to anyone—she never even tells people in the office of her family obligations, and has almost a fetish for refusing to place herself in a position which would seem to demand sympathy. Which fills me with such sympathy that it is sometimes hard to bear. The other day she told me suddenly of her husband's illness; I started to ask if there was anything I could do, and found myself brought up short by a sudden and wholly unexpected full-grown set of tears in my eyes and throat; she followed suit, at the unexpected sight; and we both began to laugh, ending in near-hysterics.

A friend of Bandel's from Tucson writes to her about his command's plans to utilize a WAC unit in the AAF public relations offices on XX Bomber Command air bases. The tale of how Wacs were trained and how utilized in the field is the subject of the next several letters from both men and women in the armed forces.

8.   *Captain Frederic N. Finney, Air Corps public relations officer, to Betty Bandel*[26]

Office of the Commanding General
Army Air Base, El Paso, Texas
7 October 1943

Dear Betty:

Thanks for your prompt response, and I'm glad to see that we still think the same way.

My idea is to procure WAC enlisted personnel to an extent which will provide each Base PRO office with a Wac. Next, if and when available, I'd like to develop it a step farther, and provide each Base with a Wac officer for PRO. I realize that any Wac competent to serve in a PRO office of this command is hanging rotten ripe for OCS. I've selected 13 men to work for me. Eleven are now officers.

Regarding WAC enlisted personnel, I've no doubt whatsoever that we can solve our problem if we can get such gals. As to use of Wac Officers as Base PROs, this will still have to be sold to 2 AF, but I think it not only feasible, but the best way out of an increasingly insoluble situation.[27] As I see it, this idea of any plenitude of manpower is just a thing of the past. If 2 AF wants to maintain its present PRO set-up and policy, it must go to Wacs for any hope of the project. The class fives, limited service categories available are no good for PRO.

Sincerely, Fred

9. Sergeant Emily Brown to Betty Bandel

Probably in support of the All-States Campaign in Arizona, Brown is planning to write some articles about Wacs for a member of the Tucson Chamber of Commerce to use as publicity. She is also considering reapplication to Officer Candidate School.

Saturday, 9 October, 1943
Day of Grace of Our Lord
[Alliance, Nebraska]

Dear Betty,

I returned from my furlough at 0400 this morning, 20 hours ahead of time and my C.O. nearly fainted, I being the type who usually wants to leave early and come back late even if I only have a pass to town. There seems to be nothing to do in Base Communications but listen to the Michigan–Notre Dame football game, and like the various executives of The Arizona Daily Star (Allah, Allah) the men here seem to think that the only way to listen to a football game is with the volume control set at maximum gain, so if this missile be slightly disjointed, you will understand.

I had a very enjoyable talk with your mother while I was at home, although I always feel guilty after talking to your mother, because no matter how I put it, she always seems to feel that I have been shamefully mistreated and it is never my intent to leave her with that impression. She has come to be, however, one of the most interested spectators of the battle of Brown vs WAAC and/or WAC. We have agreed that I should once again toss my little bonnet into the O.C. ring.

In the meantime, I hope to utilize some idle hours (all planes are grounded here) by framing some pieces which Bernie believes might be book-worthy. It seems that the vice president of E. P. Dutton and Sons was one of Bernie's guests during the summer and he is interested in something "warm and human" about the Wacs and Bernie suggested that I, having been through most every phase of the WAC EM life might have something to offer.[28] I am trying to get to my C.O. now and tell her about it and see how much clearance I will have to have. I had thought of such sketches as "Duty to Hospital," "Maid Sergive" [a word play on maid service?] (The Aladdin Hotel episode), "Casual," "Calling Alliance Tower," "Ah, the Field," "Officer Elect," "Officer Reject," "And Her Shoes Were Number Nine . . . ," etc. My intent is more earnest than it has ever been before and I hope I have what the guy wants.

Speaking of writing, my one purpose in getting this off to you is to share a recent comment of the acrid Mr. White, which I think will be of some slight professional interest to you and of more than slight entertainment:

"Maybe I was inspired to write this by the new WAC poster I just noticed down the street, on which the advertising agency borrowed the gal they were using in their cosmetic ads or for the Kotex account and substituted her for the one who looked like a sex lecturer at a Girl Scout camp. She is a considerable improvement over her predecessor, a woman about as attractive as the one the Marines use, who wears an expression similar to that of a gal that drank six beers on the way to the beach and finally has made her way far enough out in the water to hide what she's doing. Of course, while we're discussing the expressions on the features of the come-on girls for the armed services, there's that Wave they borrowed from the Scott Tissue account, still looking as if she used sandpaper or a corncob."[29]

We were inordinately busy before I left. I was called out twice in the middle of the night to make workable the radios on bombers which strayed down here from Casper, Wyo., much to the delight of my company-mates, who were inclined to overestimate my ability as a radio mechanic. The real truth is that there was nothing that needed to be done but retuning. While I am happily engaged in "real radio" work, there are five operators who are graduates of Midland who are unhappy little clerk-typists in operations.[30] Rumor has it, however, that their transfer to a station where there is net operation is imminent. My only horror now is that I will be lumped with the "radio girls" and transferred too. It will not take long, however, for whatever management there be to discover that I am not a radio operator. Teaching beginners here and sitting in on the advanced code classes has improved my speed somewhat and I hope to achieve a low-speed (16 wpm) rating before the winter is out.

10. WAC Private Nina Timchenko to Betty Bandel

Timchenko, an acquaintance of Bandel's, formerly of Tucson, writes to complain about not being assigned to work that uses her skills.

Oct. 14, 1943.
[Lowry Field, Denver
997th WAC Training Detachment]

Dear Major Bandel,

About 2 weeks ago 175 privates of 11th Co, 3rd Rgt. 1st Training Center, Ft. Des Moines finished their basic and 9 of them came here—I was among them.

We are in the Photo Laboratory Technical School. It is *most* interesting, but what I ever knew about Photography was *so* little, that I cannot understand why I was chosen?! I thought—I could use my knowledge of French or Russian in some way or other. Hope I could do so in the future. To-day we started to learn how to develop aerial films—it will take some time and skill to be a good technician—hope I will not fail A.A.F. and so you could be proud of your fellow Arizonian!!

11. *Betty Bandel to Mrs. Bandel*

17 October 1943

Got a grand letter from Emily—she is still holding the fort—I believe she will probably get another crack at O.C. in the not too distant future—and I'm sure she'll do a splendid job, when she does. Some of our officers are not too hot, it's true—one can't hope to turn out five thousand all in the mold of the first select four hundred—but they are learning, and working hard to better themselves and do a good job for the army.[31] The trouble is, one simply hasn't time to attack all problems at once—if one did, nothing would ever get done. So while we work on better utilization of Wacs in the field, better classification, prompter shipments, etc., we cannot give our attention at the same time to every phase of the training problem. But we are whittling away, knocking off one problem after another, and hope gradually to iron everything out.

12. *Betty Bandel to Mrs. Bandel*

Halloween [October 31, 1943]

Did I tell you I had a newcomer in my office? One Elizabeth Wooden, a nice, 27-year-old girl from San Francisco—very quiet and conservative, and inclined to look wide-eyed upon the crazy antics of some of the rest of us. I think she likes us, though, and likes the work. She said she felt as if she had fallen into a nest of rebels—and well she might, with Patty, my shy, playwright faun from Texas; and Caroline, my winsome young Floridian; and Evelyn Neel, my roly-poly youngster with the brown doe eyes, from Georgia. The remarkable thing about my office is my civilian help—in this day and age to find two youngsters of 20, both willing and able to work like beavers, is almost unheard of. Miss Lenz, my Pennsylvanian, and Miss Lottman, my Brooklyn Jewess, sit there with big round eyes; grin at what must seem to them a pleasant form of madness in the rest of us—we work at such a pitch that I try to conduct my business something like a newspaper city room, with enough breaks from concentration and enough laughter to keep us from losing our balance—and work, work, work as I swear no other two stenographers in the Pentagon work. In any other office I have seen, the girls get off in little clusters and gossip together, or float out for a coke rather often, but my two just burrow in first thing in the morning, and type or file or take dictation until the last bell rings at night. I even have to make them go out for lunch, instead of having a sandwich sent in, and sometimes have to make them stop at night. And, believe me, in this day and age of tremendous civilian turnover in Washington, with everybody making unheard of salaries, that is something. The funny thing about my whole office is the way every durned one of them looks after me. If I weren't already hopelessly spoiled, I would be now. And you know, I am afraid I am beginning to cluck like a mother hen over my brood of thousands. I suppose one cannot help beginning to take a proprietary interest in whatever one is supposed to look after, and every Wac in the Air Forces seems to me my particular concern. When I think how scrupulously I have avoided messing in other people's lives, I laugh, sometimes, at the way I now glibly hand out free advice. But they come and stand so trustingly in front of me, and expect me to be able to move the sun and the stars, that I can't do less than give it the old Yale try, and shut my eyes and hope to Heaven everything will turn out all right.

Lord, how hard I struggled not to become Dean of Women, once! I hope after the war I can return to a job that you do, all by yourself, in which you influence words or other abstract objects, rather than people. There is too much responsibility connected with the direct administration of people to suit my sense of "Laissez faire." And it would be awful to become a busybody.

Jess's mother arrived back in town today. I asked her what she was going to do tonight. She said, "Just sit and look at her." When are you coming east, Maw?

13. *"Baby Gremlin" Caroline Varn to Betty Bandel*

Written while on a field trip inspecting recruitment efforts for the Air-WAC—and, clearly, gathering intelligence on WAC problems in the field.

[October 31, 1943]
Hotel Texas, Fort Worth

Dearest Major Bandel:

Since we're leaving at the bust of dawn, I'll just write you a quickie—but I do want you to know that we are alive and kicking, and our ears are flapping!

We had a good trip down—with the exception of some ice in the Carolinas. We stopped in Birmingham for lunch with General MacDaniel [*sic*]—and he muttered something about training Wacs for Photo Interpreters. He was talking with General Harper—so I guzzled my soup loudly and pretended not to hear—but I'm quite sure that I cringed visibly.[32]

We arrived here about six Wednesday evening, and had dinner with Freeman, and she poured her troubles upon our shoulders:[33]

    (a)   Stryker[34]
    (b)   the unkind people of the old TTC [Transportation Command]
    (c)   Stryker
    (d)   the need for personnel
    (e)   Woods[35]
    (f)   not getting stuff from hq.
    (g)   Stryker—Woods
    (h)   Col. Daly (Daley)
    (i)   and so forth!

Thursday we spent the morning with Freeman, a couple of hours with Captain Black, and went out to Tarrant late in the afternoon. A girl (Capt.) by the name of Clarke is the new C.O.—and when she reported (according to Freeman) the post exec. said she wasn't to be C.O.—he wanted to keep a little shave-tail [that is, a lieutenant] who would do what he wanted. But she is the C.O. now—and getting along fairly well—under the circumstances. Freeman is a bit wary of her because of her background. According to F., the whole field is a mess. Everyone cooperates yet there seems to be an undercurrent.

Yesterday, we visited Majors and Perrin—both okay—but they want consolidated mess so that they can assign the girls to responsible jobs and not have to pull them for K.P. And they want more Wacs! Both are working very hard in the recruiting campaign, and are having good results. Today—we spent the morning with Freeman and Gen. Harper and he told us all about the Air-WAC being in training! Poor man—he's very interested and definitely thinks we're his babies!

I'm very much annoyed with Freeman because she keeps screaming about not being able to get anything from Washington. I realize her position—but I do think it's unnecessary to ridicule us in front of the base C.O.'s and adjutants. They do have a definite need for an additional fifty temporary officers for recruiting—and they can use around six hundred operational officers.

General Harper is very nice, and I like him tremendously, but his aide—one Capt. Giles, is about to drive us wild with his fatherly attitude—but I suppose he's just doing his job!

I'll write you again as soon as we are settled (?) again. I hope everything is running smoothly. Give me [sic] love to Patty, Neel, and Lib—and to our precious L & L, Inc.[36]

Miss you muchly.

Your loving Baby Gremlin

14. Betty Bandel to her family

7 November 1943

Dearest Maw, Dot, Drag, Anne, and Tony:

Mother, the clippings you sent me are one more interesting evidence of what I consider Jess Rice's particular triumph and contribution to the WAC—the actual, active community interest in the WAC movement which her "All States" recruiting plan has engendered. We have talked and screamed "WAC" for a year, but it took Jess, with her sense of community and state pride, and of how people will rally around when it is a matter of outdoing another community or state, to get the American people to take up the WAC as their own particular project. You will note, from those clippings and others from other towns, that a *cross-section* has taken up this recruiting campaign, at the behest of the various governors—and thus the WAC organization is winning the incomparable community support which only one other organization that I know of has ever been able to win—the Red Cross. My only end of this recruiting business is the new Air Forces branch recruitment—and I believe that also will do much to stimulate recruitment, since the Air Forces—the new thing—have that fascination for the American people which all new things seem to have for them. I think it's a laugh for me to be in AAF, when the new thing always rubs me the wrong way.

15. *Captain Polly F. Pierce to Betty Bandel*[37]

Pierce describes her new assignment at the recently opened Third WAC Training Center in Fort Oglethorpe, Georgia.

8 November 1943

My dear Major:

This is an awfully good gang—only one real pain-in-the-neck—not an Air Forces representative. We are all housed in a not-so-large squad room. The one first prepared for us had to be fumigated. Our quarters have only mice and a very mangy-looking cat. After a week of that I moved my bed to the top deck from whence I can view the animal kingdom with a more suitable air of detachment. The latrine facilities would never pass muster for a field installation; nevertheless I'm enjoying group living once more. I'm gregarious.

Captain Linch is doing an excellent job as our instructor. We appreciate her all the more after we've had some one else for an hour. Of course everyone makes cracks at the Air Forces, but I could recruit the whole training center without turning a hand, from the top officers down.

Lillian Reilly was the only major when we arrived. Since then they've become rather common. Methinks it had better be about time for me to win a certain five-dollar bet. How about it?[38]

Since you've been here to see for yourself, I shan't dwell on the Georgia pines, or the gorgeous coloring on the mountainsides, or the rhythmic swishing of pinks skirts as the officers "front and center."[39] But I am very grateful for these two weeks here. I'm more like myself than I've been for a long time, though I find myself, doggone it, ma'am, missing you.

With due respect and a certain amount of restrained affection and unrestrained admiration!

Polly

16. *Betty Bandel to Mrs. Bandel*

She describes one of her frenetic tours around the country visiting Air-WAC installations, and the trials of travel during the war.

10 December 1943
On train—between Dayton, O., & Indianapolis, Ind.

I have to make a speech in Detroit, for Michigan Aviation week (celebration of 40th anniversary of Wright Brothers' flight), & I decided to combine inspection of some of the mid-west fields with the speech, so—to save time!—I asked for & got a little plane. First time I have asked for a ship for myself, & I must admit it is fun to order the destinies of an airplane. Incidentally, don't pass on the fact that I am allowed a ship for a flight of my own—they are not ordinarily allotted to officers of my rank, but the scope of my responsibility was the determining factor. The Detroit shindig is a week-long celebration of the advance of aviation, with Edsel Ford & others taking part.[40] I talk on "ladies' day," at a meeting sponsored by the Women's City Club. They wanted me to talk on "Women in Aviation," but I hastened to point out they were way over my head—so I am talking on the WAC in the AAF, with a suitable bow to women in aviation industry & to the women pilots (WASPS).

I like my new shop very much, except my new general has a disconcerting way of popping into my office at all hours, out of interest in the WAC program. In the old days I used to have to hunt all over the building for anybody from "the front office," if I wanted them—now I have to keep my coat on all day for fear of visitors. Gen. Bevans is a good man—able & interested. He gives me a lot of support.[41] I am wondering what we will all do after this war. There are two schools of thought as to whether I will come back to Tucson—my own, & everybody else's. The L.C. just grins when I talk about it, & shakes her head.

17. Betty Bandel to Mrs. Bandel

Detroit, Michigan
15 December 1943

This Detroit soirée has been funny. We have had a grand inspection trip, staying at weird hotels in these crazy middle-western towns (Lord, aren't they ugly!), & trotting happily around airfields reporting to headquarters without any fuss or flurry & being received like any two officers from a higher headquarters. Then we hit Detroit. We have made Detroit our holiday time—last night we saw our first ice show (Sonia Henje starred), & tonight we dined in our living room, with suitable flourishes. The people of Detroit fall all over themselves to be nice to service people—one woman offered us a ticket to the show, & another asked if she could take us home afterwards.

This morning the tom-toms began to beat. Two women & a man, egged on by the very fine recruiting officer & PRO here, interviewed me & shot pictures of me. It was awfully funny—they were nice people, & we had a good old newspaper talk. Then I left there with my coattails flying & hit the radio station just 5 minutes before I was to be interviewed on the air, & had to read & edit the script. But we did it. Then we dove for the Women's City Club, where the local Mrs. Flaccuses received us with flattering interest & much confusion as to who & what we were.[42] The men had laid on a "ladies' day," without getting the ladies to get behind it, with the result that I spoke to about 20 people. But they all panted with eagerness, & I think will go out & carry the gospel to the wilderness. Then I was yanked to a defense plant, to view women at work, which I dutifully did, & at 6 p.m. we were allowed to escape to our hotel. Thus endeth the Detroit saga.

Last night at midnight I ate a bowl of chili in a Greyhound bus station, & thought of the lovely border country, & you all. When are you coming to see my house, Maw?

18. *Betty Bandel to Mrs. Bandel*

3 January 1943 [1944]

So much to tell, and so little time to tell it in! I am waiting for them to clear the circuits and get a call through to you. Central just told me there will be a five to six hour delay in getting through tonight, so you will probably hear from me around 1:30 a.m.—but I'm durned if I can let the Christmas season quite go without a call.

New Year's Eve was the most wonderful night. I arrived home, to find all three *Tucson* packages, and Maw's lovely Christmas letter. Jess was in the dumps, and I had had difficulty convincing her she must come to my house for a midnight glass of sherry, but she had promised finally, and Patty and I had gone on in to my place. So Patty stood by, as a most satisfactory admiring audience, while I opened each one, string by string and paper by paper. Shades of my beloved Mexico!—seeing, feeling, tasting your love and thoughtfulness and care that each single tiny thing within each package would be something to make me sit back and mentally lick cream off my fur, while the memory of the desert and all it means to me in family and friends and the dear, remembered things that are the fibre of my being rose up to surround me, to cradle me in strong, protecting arms.

New Year's Jess and I got away about 5 p.m., driving to Richmond to spend the night. We went up to the old Jefferson, where Jess wheedled us a room for the night—she can talk you right out of your ancestral home, if she puts her mind to it. Sunday we slept late, rose to a leisurely and gluttonous breakfast—pancakes, eggs, and Virginia ham—and drove on to Williamsburg.

The call just came through! How wonderful you all sounded! And how grown up Anne sounded!

Must tell you one story to end. The L.C., home at Christmas, was sitting in the living room reading when she heard her angel 7-year-old slam down the phone and say, "G—— D—— it, it's broken!" Jessica then walked into the living room, saw her mother, and gave a foot or two. Her mother said, "I gather the phone is broken." Jessica said, "You heard what I said." The L.C. said, "Jessica, I have said 'damn' many times in my life, but I don't believe I have ever taken the name of the Lord in vain. I think you had better go upstairs and ask God to forgive you." Jessica said, "God is busy. It's Jesus' birthday." When Jess

Rice asked the Director what she did then, the L.C. said, "Do? I sat there. What would you have done?"

19. Betty Bandel to her family

She writes of her worldwide inspection tour to WAC facilities with Colonel Hobby, and of her promotion to lieutenant colonel.

5 or 6 February, 1944
Alexandria, at last

Dearest of families:

Ye gods! 29,000 miles in 26 days, four continents, two oceans and three seas (Mediterranean, Tyrrenean (?), Adriatic), a glimpse of the Northern Lights and of the Southern Cross. I tell you, after this war, the story of how time and space have been telescoped will make a marvellous tale. I see that the Air Transport Command's routes across the Atlantic were published in a recent issue of *Life*, so, if you look up those maps, you can see where I have been: Iceland, England, Africa (Algiers, Tunis, Cairo), Italy (not by ATC [Army Troop Carrier] ship, but by another type of military aircraft), and home by way of Khartoum, Akkra, Dakar, Natal (in Brazil), then up the Caribbean, and Washington.

It was all so crowded, and so much happened, that I am afraid I will miss something really important if I try to tell it chronologically, so I will dive into highlights.

I went on this trip on about 24 hours' notice, and was not too anxious to go because I had too many irons in the fire here, but Gen. Giles asked Col. Hobby to go on an 8 or 10 day trip to England, and then asked me to go along, both to see how Wacs are getting along there and to stimulate a flow of news about Wacs serving overseas from the various theatres.[43] His and my particular interest is, of course, the Air WAC program, but the L.C. had all Wacs to worry about. It made an ideal arrangement. The only hitch was that Gen. Giles had to buy something for his wife every place he went, and he wouldn't buy it until he had showed it to "the ladies"—much good my judgment would do him. I'll bet his poor wife is still shoveling out from under the pile of junk he brought back—perfume, oriental goods, leather purses, etc., etc. But I consoled myself with the thought that I was leaving Patty [Treadwell] in charge of my outfit, and Jess in charge of the Boss's—and two better people never lived. Off the record, Jess is the best officer in the WAC, when you couple temperament and native ability with richness of civilian experience and a good crack at army experience. Many people have one or another of these requirements and some have several, but I don't know another who combines the lot in quite such sound proportion. I recommended Patty for promotion just before I left, and she became a major about a week ago—much to the delight of all who work with her, and her family. And yesterday Jess became a lieutenant colonel! So our cup runneth over. And the WAC grows up. There are now six lieutenant colonels, all promoted since I began the rush a couple weeks ago—and I expect that will be about all we'll have for a little while. They are the deputy director and executive officer of the Corps (Jess and Mary-Agnes Brown), me, a nice gal on the General Staff (General Marshall's staff), a gal who is assistant commandant of one of our training centers, and the two women who are WAC staff directors in England and Africa.[44]

As for my trip, when I once got started of course I had the world's best kind of time—in such company, on such a route, who could help it? The L.C. and I think the same things are funny, and it's wonderful to be sharing new experiences with someone who, when you steal a glance in his or her direction, is inwardly laughing at exactly the same things which are causing you to double up.

I found this second ten days in England rather wonderful, because the first had been so rapid and so dreamlike that I wasn't sure whether it was just as I thought it was, or whether I had it confused with a Dickens print. But no, it is still that way—still wonderful green lanes and trees, still an amazing amount of sleepy, rural country, despite all the little factories and airfields which have been planted all over the tight little island, still that look of nice, disorderly age and lack of rhyme or reason which somehow makes sense, for those people in that place. And the sight of the Wacs everywhere, doing a magnificent job and fitting so smoothly into our American army picture there, was enough to make me swell with pride, particularly since I had seen the set-up before any Wacs moved in.

But, since England was something I had seen and tasted before, the fascinating new thing on this trip was, of course, the latter half—Africa and Italy and the trip home. We flew down from the British Isles to Africa in one magnificent moonlit night, and woke in the morning to a blue sky, and fleecy white clouds, and hot, piercing sun, and earth that looks what my desert-rat soul thinks earth ought to look like—brown and clear and dry, instead of like chocolate pudding or something. I took one look, and said to those two Texans, Gen. Giles and the L.C., "Move over, Texas. Arizona, here I come!" And from then on nothing could hold me. I would get out of doors every moment I could, and just sniff the air, and look at the sky, and think, "This is the life! This is the earth!"

As we drove from the airport to the villa—we only stopped for breakfast, though when the Boss saw the sunken bathtubs she thought we ought to stop over long enough to try one—we passed Arab after Arab, walking along beside the road, rag upon dirty rag over his flowing, once-white robe, his dark face and beard showing beneath his hood, a long staff in hand, a little donkey trotting along before him with straw or pottery or some other ware tied to his back. Little boys in red fezzes rode on the backs of other donkeys, and women in flowing robes carried jars of water from wells to their homes, on shoulder or head. And there were black men, of course, there in western Africa. I had my nose pressed to the window, and nice old Col. Lowe, a man who used to be here in Air Forces headquarters, and who was one of my pets (he used to help me out with a lot of WAC problems), said, "Yes, they stepped right out of the Bible, didn't they?" And so they did—out of the Bible, and out of the great Moorish conquests that swept across Africa and up into Spain.

After breakfast, we hopped back in the plane and flew a couple thousand miles over to Algiers, arriving just in time for afternoon cocktails. Yes, Algiers is everything the movies say too. There is the Caspah, and a magnificent bay, and the city hanging on cliffs alongside the bay. Gen. Giles had had to push on, but he left Col. Rowe, who had met us when we landed in Africa, to look after us for the next few days, until we would catch up with him again. He is a slow, soft-spoken Georgian, very homesick for his nice wife and terrier pup (he carries their picture in his pocket), and, before we left, we had voted him into the WAC, and asked him to attend our veterans' meetings after the war. Then our Wacs met us there—Major Westray Battle Boyce, now head of Wacs in North Africa; Capt. Dorothea Coleman—she was in that first bunch that lived together in Gunston Hall and worked in WAC hq.—a wonderful, fun-loving tomboy of a girl, just as able as she can be; Capt. Ann McIlhenney, former able and hardboiled newspaperwoman who is now doing a public relations job over there. Dorothea is going to take charge of Air Wacs in that theatre of operation. She is brusque and hearty and middle-western, while Westray—whose 17-year-old daughter I have promised to write to—is soft and Georgian and the type ideal of the southern gentlewoman. Two of the Wacs from nearby came in and looked after us—one cooked our breakfasts, and the other drove us. The little one who cooked apologized for the first meal (which was wonderful), but said it was the first time she had cooked for two people since she joined the army—150 is now her style. She is going to be married soon, to a paratrooper over there, and we are going to write her married sister here and tell her how nicely she is getting along, and how happy she is.

The apartment had the usual French plumbing—I swear, the more you travel, the surer you become that Americans are right when they confuse civilization with superior plumbing. Why the French always separate the toilet from the bathroom I will never know, but at least their plumbing facilities operate mechanically a little more satisfactorily than the British. I ranged, on this trip, from Claridge's, where L.C. and I each had a bath; each bath had a special dressing room beside our separate bedrooms; there were (1) bath, (2) shoulder shower, (3) head showers (encased in glass), (4) footbath, (5) basin, (6) toilet, (7) two mirrors, one full and one half, (8), warm pipes on which stockings would dry ideally, in each bathroom; to a stopping point along the ATG [Air Transport Group] route in Brazil where, because of the mild tropic climate, the showers are lined up in an enclosed patio back of the nurses' quarters, where you calmly take a cake of soap and prance out under the sun and/or stars, turn on the faucet, and take a shower on a long piece of duck-board, with nothing around you but space for more people to take a shower next to you. I asked the L.C. what she thought they did when it rained, and she said, "Not turn on the faucet."

The L.C. had her birthday there in Algiers, and I had been carrying around letters which her devoted office had written to her, congratulating her, and which I had promised to deliver to her on that day. I gave them to her after she was in bed, the night before, because I could see she was very homesick for her two little bambinos, and I think her staff's thoughtfulness touched her very much—at least, she called me her "third child," which is as near as she ever gets to saying "thank you," or anything. But the funny part of it is, she is as much my child as I am hers—one of us is always taking care of the other.

Everyplace we went, the L.C. spoke to all the Wacs, and they seemed so glad to see her, and to hear about home. They have wonderful morale, and do a magnificent job—but one Wac, on "fire watch" in London of an evening, will write 12 letters home, some of them ranging to 10 pages each, their officers tell me.[45] In one gloomy old Italian theatre, after she had spoken to a group—she has a hushed way of talking to them which stirs deep emotions—one little girl came out, blinked in the light, saw her company commander, walked up to her, and put her head down on her shoulder as if she had been a first grader running to teacher during the recess period. The officer patted her on the shoulder, said, "Why, Jane, what's the matter?" The child said, "Nothing. She just makes me happy." *Don't* circulate this story, please—mishandled, it could look like the wrong kind of homesickness, whereas it was really just love of home.

We flew to three towns in Italy, including Naples. And in Italy we saw the war-bombed cities, hungry people, a field evacuation hospital a short distance behind the front into which they were bringing casualties after a big attack. That last is a scene which I will never forget, but which, I think, would make anyone fight to finish the war the sooner. And yet there is much normalcy. The Neapolitans, today as always, I understand, volubly try to sell you things from every street corner. The town is dirty as anything—they say it always was, like Marseilles and other seaports—but it has as beautiful a bay and harbor as I ever saw. And old Vesuvius smokes away, through the haze, back of the city.[46] Pompeii is just a short distance away, and they tell me the soldiers and Wacs, on leave or furlough, go over and visit the ruins.

I think perhaps the highlight of my trip was the stay in Tunis. By this time most of the business was done, and we were heading homeward, by a circuitous route. Carthage! Dido's ancient city![47] Again, a magnificent bay. This time, it was all ours. There is a villa on the cliffs overlooking the bay, which was built some thirty years ago by a Frenchman and his half-French, half-American wife, now known to all and sundry as "la baronesse." La baronesse is about 80 years old. Her husband was a painter "of delicate health," and they settled in Tunis for its mild, healthful climate. They must have had money to burn. Their beautiful home is a great pile of stuccoed, Moorish type building, set on the side of a hill looking down over terraces and orange trees to the bay below. As the bay sweeps around, an Arab village hangs along the hillside to the east, and the nearest building to the villa is the mosque, from which I heard the clear, wild call to prayer, several times a day. There were Arabs and donkeys down at the shore of the water below, and American planes overhead. This is cactus country! I almost got out and hugged it. La baronesse, whose husband I gather has been dead some years, immediately offered the villa to American forces, retiring herself to one wing of the villa, where she was kind enough to receive the L.C., Westray, McIlhenny, and me. There she sat, an exquisite little old lady who has travelled the world, graciously receiving what must have seemed a strange new animal to her. She immediately began to inquire about our families, and discovered to her delight that Westray was about a 64th cousin by some of her American kin—she said Westray must call her "Cousin Bettina," which stopped Westray cold.

I don't believe I have ever seen so much beauty packed into the range of a pair of eyes as I did when I first stepped out on the driveway in front of that villa. Below, the ground falls away in terraces to the sea, and there, lapping gently against the beach, is the most magnificent turquoise sea I have ever seen. The purity of its many colors is quite beyond description. And, in contrast to the turquoise, overhead is a sky of piercing blue almost equal to Arizona's. The silence of the place—except for the little village on the hillside, it stands alone, with the countryside behind it, makes it one's own, for however long one stands there. We stood, the L.C. and I, just lapping it up. And then, for some unknown reason we picked up an orange that had fallen off one of the trees, and played catch.

Our bedroom was something to behold. They had planned to put the L.C. in one by herself, but she took one look and got scared at the size and sent out a reconnaissance party to find me (I was over in the East Forty). The room had a bed sunken in the wall at either end, and McIlhenny, who was sharing a similar one with Westray, said it was so far from one bed to the other that she would have to get up in the morning, trot up to Westray's side, and report for duty. Furthermore, there were only three army blankets on each bed, and North Africa and Italy are under the delusion that Tucson was under 25 years ago—that they don't need heat. So the L.C. and I pulled the blankets off one and made up one bed of 6 blankets, in which we found ourselves nice and warm, once we could get in and get our feet off the stone floor.

'Twas here that I learned of my promotion! Westray came tearing into our room, fluttering up to the L.C. with a piece of paper in hand, and, when I started toward them, said, "No, you can't see!" So they were very mysterious until dinner time, when we went down and joined about 16 generals and colonels, American and British, who were staying there (including Gen. Giles), and, when we were all gathered, the L.C. read the cable from the War Department announcing my promotion. There was much hilarity and much pounding of backs, and the L.C. and Gen. Giles each pinned on one of the new leaves. Good old Major Burgoyne sacrificed to the cause a pair of lt. col.'s leaves he had gotten in London to take back to a friend of his in the States. And it ended up with everybody kissing me—even the three British generals, who first fortified themselves with another drink, however.

Of course dinner turned into a celebration party, and I was really made to feel wonderful about the whole thing. But best of all was the way the L.C. seemed genuinely pleased to have me have it. And equally best was the way everybody in my office here seemed pleased when I got back. I thought it tremendously thoughtful of Gen. Bevans to cable the news over.

In Tunis we visited the Caspah, or native bazaar—all the dirt of a thousand years is gathered there, with all the rich rugs and tapestries hanging from little shops that are so close, across streets made too small even for burros to go up them, that one can reach out and touch one on either side. In a perfume shop, where we stopped while Gen. Barney got his wife some perfume, the proud Arab showed us a picture of his family (no wife showing, of course), and stated that it was a fine family: "four children and a girl." "What?" yelled the L.C.— I thought Gen. Barney would collapse. He has been telling that tale all over two continents, ever since.

And so home, by way of Central Africa and the west coast of Africa. Lord, what a big continent that is! And how much desert you fly over. One little black girl ironed a shirt for me, at Dakar, and I said, "Thank you," and she grinned, and curtsied, and said, "Pas de quoi." She spoke no English. You are in malaria country down that way, and you rub mosquito lotion all over your face, and sleep under mosquito nets—quite an experience.

Natal, in South America, is a wonderful place—no mosquitoes, a holiday kind of place, again with a lovely bay and a city rising above it. And such fruit! The last morning we left Trinidad, had breakfast in Puerto Rico, and were in Washington by night!

One story, before I stop. The L.C. told this one on a man whom I consider one of the great men of the generation—Gen. Marshall. He is absent-minded as anything about names, and he has a secretary who has taken his dictation for 3 or 4 years, named Nason. He calls her Miss Mason. The other day he was dictating a letter, and as he dictated used somebody's name entirely incorrectly. She couldn't stand it a minute longer, and corrected him. Then she said, "And while we're on the subject, my name is Nason, not Mason. And, furthermore Col. McCarthy is named McCarthy, not Reilly." (Col. McCarthy is just General Marshall's right-hand man on the General Staff up there.) She came out and was telling us what she had done to Col. Sexton, secretary of the General Staff. Col. Sexton said, "Good lord, while you were doing it, why didn't you tell him my name is Sexton, not Taylor?" Don't relay this one.

CHAPTER 6

Fighting for Wacs, Caring for Colonels

Bandel returns from her worldwide tour of WAC facilities in February 1944. Her work as Air-WAC Officer continues apace, and is sometimes complex and demanding. As Bandel comments in a letter: "'Twas a dark and stormy night on the Erie Canal. One of the horses had the heaves, and the stove pipe fell down. The day has been, in other words, not without incident."[1] One of Bandel's important duties is to work with AAF officers, not only to bring the message of the potential value of Wacs to the men who will be directly involved in integrating Wacs effectively into their units and commands, but also to educate those officers who are taking part in the recruitment drive for Air-Wacs (*see illustration 14*). Clearly, she is good at this. Her popularity at home remains high as well, with her successes often celebrated in the local papers (*see Tucson recruitment ad*). And General Arnold continues to let the AAF command know that he wants them to support the Air-WAC. In February 1944, he writes to the commanding generals of all domestic commands, stating that lack of respect for Air-Wacs by airmen or officers will not be tolerated. Bandel will later characterize this as "one of the greatest single aids ever given to the WAC program in the AAF."[2]

Bandel also works with the National Civilian Advisory Committee, established at the recommendation of General Somervell when D-WAC is transferred to the G-1 Division. The advisory committee is comprised of the chairs of each service command committee and, in addition, twelve prominent civilian women selected by Hobby, who serve a variety of functions in support of the WAC. The committee is designed to be not only professionally but also racially and religiously diverse, and the civilian advisers are especially helpful in promoting WAC recruitment, each in her profession or constituency.[3] Each woman also consults with the WAC on issues relevant to her particular expertise. Marion Kenworthy, a prominent psychologist, for example, advises on the problem of morale in remote posts in the Pacific Theater of Operations.[4]

Bandel's letter of 5 March 1944 is an uncharacteristic articulation of the burdens and frustrations of her job as a WAC officer, with no real authority to command the Wacs under her or to implement policy. She can only recommend to her AAF commanding officers, who then take action on her suggestions if they concur. It does not help that her friend and fellow officer Jess Rice undergoes an operation for cancer at this time, just when WAC headquarters is moved from the Army Service Forces into the War Department's G-1 Division, General Staff level, part of a major reshuffling of the WAC administration. In the summer of 1944, Colonel Hobby takes a six-week medical leave to recover from exhaustion and illness, obliging Rice to return to work while still under treatment herself.[5] Thus, the people to whom Bandel usually turns for support and consultation are preoccupied with their own difficulties.

In spite of the pressures of work, Bandel spends some weekends in New York City and attends plays in Washington. Remarkably, her letters written shortly after D-Day, June 6, do not refer to this event, one of the most important battles of the war. Many of her letters in the summer of 1944 are chatty discussions of dinners out with fellow Wacs, plays seen, and her fascination with geopolitics (the study of the effects of geography on history and governments), born of attending the lectures of Father Edmund Walsh, a Jesuit priest and founder of the Georgetown University School of Foreign Service. She and Jess Rice are the first women to attend the school.

Bandel is clearly looking toward the end of the war by now. In several of her letters, she dreams about what she will do after demobilization.

1. *Betty Bandel to Mrs. Bandel*

Sunday, 21 February 1944

[In response to the suggestion from her mother.] Of course I think the L.C. should be a general—but Congress evidently got a horrible vision of hundreds of lady generals running around the country, and introduced into the bill a clause limiting the Director of the Corps to a colonelcy, and all others to "such subordinate ranks as the Secretary of War shall direct." This is again off the record. I believe they'll change it, when the corps is large enough. England has a major general, a brigadier, and 12 colonels that I know of in the A.T.S. (like our WAC) alone, plus a major and brigadier general and some colonels in the WAAF (serves with the RAF). The WAC in this country does the job which both the ATS and the WAAF do in England.

I have been having another flurry of Gen. Arnold interest in the Wacs, and when that happens it takes all my time to get him soothed. This time he wanted to know what he could do to help expedite a certain project which happens to be very near to my heart, so of course I took advantage of the opportunity to get some letters out of him (which we write, of course) to commanding generals of the various air forces and commands, putting the case before them.[6] A letter with the magic name of Arnold at the bottom is worth more, in the Air Forces, than all the orders that were ever given.

I trust you will agree with me that the enclosed clipping from the New

Yorker is the funniest thing ever written. The first time I read it, not noticing how the L.C.'s last name was left out in the first line, I didn't see what was funny about it, but the second time I got it, and collapsed. The L.C. did likewise, when we showed it to her. Patty said, after reading it, "And they didn't even know you!" Evidently she thought it particularly appropriate.[7]

2. Betty Bandel to Mrs. Bandel

She continues the story of her world tour.

27 February 1944

I had an amusing thing happen the night I took Grace to the Mayflower. The boy at the parking lot asked me how long I would be, and I said an hour and a half. When I came back, the car was buried behind a lot of others, and I said, "How come?" He said, "You said two hours." I looked at Cousin Grace, and she said, "No, you said an hour and a half." He said, "Lady, I was in the army once, and if I never learned nothing else, I learned not to argue with a woman or a colonel. You're the first person I ever seen that was both. So it was an hour and a half."

My homecoming celebration, over the lt. colonelcy, was pretty much just what I wrote—a simple dinner, with just the inner circle present. We were so busy that we had no time for much hilarity. The air staff was terribly nice to me—even the men who have been there a long time, and were in my grade or lower, congratulated me, which I thought pretty swell of them.

Iceland was quite a wonderful experience. In the first place, it was the first wild, open country I had seen in months, and it made me think of the desert, even though it is so different. It has a rocky coast and rolling pasture country inland, now, of course, all covered with snow. The wind howls and blows, and the snow scoots across the fields. The troops are housed in those snug little rounded Nissen huts that you have seen pictured, I am sure. We stayed in a big affair made of several of the huts put together, called the "Hotel de Gink" (name the Air Transport Command gives all its hotels for transient bigwigs, etc.). We went out, our one evening there, to the Red Cross building. Some of the men were fighting their way, on foot, through the snow from their barracks to the building, which is practically the only place of entertainment thereabouts. The Red Cross women are doing a wonderful job there—one girl, who was a language major in the states, stayed with an Icelandic family six months, learned to speak the language, and now teaches it to soldiers. We happened in on a class in progress. They are almost the only women (American) over there, and they are doing a beautiful job of helping the fellows out. The boys who come from Michigan and Maine, and spent all their lives hunting and fishing, think they are in Paradise—but the city boys, and the boys from the South, get awfully homesick for bright lights and warmth.

3.   *Betty Bandel to Mrs. Bandel*

5 March 1944

This has been a week when I have had little heart to write: Jess has been in Walter Reed's for an operation, and the Director is moving to the War Department General Staff from the spot she has been in under the Commanding General, Army Service Forces, and has asked for Patty to be on her staff.[8] So I have spent my time gyrating between the hospital and the Pentagon, reorganizing everything I could get my hands on. Jess is doing beautifully now, and Patty and I have gotten used to the idea of her not being in my office and have found some good substitute help for me, so I am once again feeling fine, and you needn't feel badly for me. Of course you have realized many times that a job like mine involves many disappointments, many impossible assignments, much dislocation which bears the more heavily upon one because it involves the lives of so many other people. I know you have known, even when I could not, of course, cite particulars, that I had plenty in my job to offset the trips abroad and the visits to the White House. Hard work, challenging assignments—all that I not only do not mind, I love; but problems which involve the lives of my Wacs, and which I cannot work out because the system is so much bigger than any one individual—those are the things that cause any staff officer to pace the floor. You see, when you are a command officer—when you have a regiment or company under your command—you can do anything in the world and, if you are wrong, you alone take the consequences. At least you have the satisfaction of knowing that you tried the best way you knew how. But a staff officer can only recommend to his commander—in my case, to the Commanding General, Army Air Forces. The thousands of Wacs in the Air Forces look to me as their head Wac, and yet I have not one shadow of command authority. So I must be smarter than a commander—I must recommend the thing which ought to be done in such a way that their actual commander does the thing which will benefit them most. That is the thing which keeps staff officers on their toes—planning how to present a program, how to discuss a problem, so that every other staff officer on the commander's staff will see it as you want it seen, and will throw the weight of his recommendation with yours, so that the commander will decide as you want him to decide. You will understand what I mean when I tell you that I was actually dismayed when I learned I was to go on this last foreign trip—so far I have come from my aide days!—because I had irons in the fire which I simply did not want to leave.[9] Of course, once I was on the trip, I relaxed and enjoyed it immensely, but if you can picture Betty looking forward to a trip to England and Africa with dismay, you can understand how thoroughly one gets absorbed in staff problems—and how much there is in this job to keep you from thinking of it as all sugar and spice and everything nice. It was because Patty has been my right hand in working out such problems—in saying the unerring right thing to the right person at the right time—that I felt keenly the necessity of having to let her go. But I knew the Little Colonel, going to a new spot in the War Department with a reduced staff (no larger than mine, as a matter of fact), would need expert help, and so I was glad to let Patty go to her. Patty rose to the occasion as nobly as only she can, and immediately set out to find me other expert help. Caroline will move up into her spot, and I am getting two new people. Actually, Patty will be working for me and the Air Forces as much up in the L.C.'s office as she has been in mine, so we will probably profit by the deal.

As to Jess—she is, as I imagine I have implied many times—one of the world's grand people—one of those rare, radiant, strong spirits whom it is always my good fortune to find, someplace in my life. She means as much to me as Alexander [Hamilton] and Peggy [Waddell] do, so you can know how worried I was when she learned she had a cyst in her right breast which had to be removed. They cut it out Tuesday at Walter Reed's, and decided it would be better to remove the entire breast, so she had a very major operation. But she did wonderfully, began to use her arm the second day, and is improving now at a rate which amazes the doctors and nurses. They do not know her brave spirit as I do. I have spent most of my evenings getting her mother on the phone, down in Griffin, Ga., and assuring her that all was well—poor Mrs. Rice has two boys overseas, and she says she guesses she was worrying about the wrong part of the family. But she, too, despite her 70-odd years, has what Jess calls "a good country raising," and so is holding up nobly. I wheeled [Jess] around in a wheelchair today, during visiting hours, while she smoked a cigarette.

L.C.'s executive officer has to leave tomorrow on a special assignment that we could find no one else to fill (so well)—so it is probably just as well Patty is going to the L.C.' s office tomorrow—it is practically denuded of key people, just at the time when it is transferring to the General Staff. That is a good place for it, and one where I have always wanted to see it land, since it deals with all parts of the army.

Well, that is how I have spent my week—organizing and re-organizing, until finally, yesterday afternoon, a little order began to come out of chaos. And as soon as I knew Jess was going to be all right, everything else became more or less all right. I should have hated, more than I can say, to have had anything happen to her, both because of the WAC and because of what I know the WAC means to her.

4. *Betty Bandel to Mrs. Bandel*

12 March 1944

This has been a far, far better week for me than was the last. Patty is getting settled into her new job, and is depending on me most flatteringly for advice, etc. Jess is getting along amazingly well. Patty and I go out and sit with her every evening visiting hours, and sometimes sneak away 15 minutes after "lights out" at 9, but she is doing so well that she doesn't seem to be at all tired at the end of the evening. She has it all figured out that, if they don't let her out permanently by [Sunday], she can get a pass and come out with us for our traditional 12 o'clock breakfast (yes, I have converted them all to that). We are using much of her gasoline ration to get the infernal distance out to Walter Reed and back, but I am saving enough tickets to go and get her when she can come home. It's amazing to see a WAC in anything but uniform—all the WACs who go to visit Jess comment on how different she looks. And who wouldn't, in a white and green dressing gown, against a white pillow, with her hair brushed softly away from her head, and make-up on? She is not the type to look her best in the dull tans and browns we wear, or in a stiff collar and tie—she is far too southern. Besides, I suppose no woman of 42 will look as well in uniform as a trim young girl of 21 would.

Maw, your inspiration re the flowers was a stroke of genius.[10] Jess said, "How much that bouquet looks like your mother!" And then I remembered she met you, fleetingly, in the old days at Des Moines. She said, "Oh, yes—I remember her very well—and I remember how you looked at her, when you introduced us to her." I didn't know Jess well in those days, except as one of the two scholastic people in my company. She used to sit on the back steps of the barracks, and tell me about her final mad year of graduate study at Columbia. She was so sick of study when she joined the WAC that she didn't do a lick of work in O.C. school—and still managed to pass with flying colors.

Well, Patty and I are now living in the lap of luxury. Georgia is taking care of us. Dusky Georgia, with her white flash of grin and slow, ambling gait, is a marvel of efficient service. I am getting so spoiled there will be no living with me. She washes our clothes. She makes our beds in the morning and washes our breakfast dishes. When we come home at six o'clock, she has dinner piping hot on the table. I handed her money and ration books and said, "I don't know how to work these. You feed us." So she grinned and said, "Yas'm." And since that time she has done exactly that. I don't know what she buys, or where, or how she works the ration books—I suspect she can't read—but we certainly get fed. I asked her where she learned to cook, and she grinned, and dug her toe in the floor, and said, "What little I learned, I learned at home." It is enough to make us feel that we have a real home. She adores Jess, and is just waiting for her to get out of the hospital so she can feed her.

My general (Bevans) became a major general this week! All the division chiefs filed in and congratulated him Thursday morning, and when he got to me he leaned down and kissed me, although he had shaken hands with everybody else (maybe because they were gray haired, and 50, and male), and everybody laughed and thought that was good fun, myself included. My beloved Col. Du-Bosque, ex–Wall Street man who is one of the brainiest men in the War Department, said, "Now you've been kissed by one, two, and three-star generals. Will you let me know when you are kissed by a four-star one?" And I promised to do so.

5. *Betty Bandel to Mrs. Bandel*

21 March 1944

Today we brought Jess home, and so are about to resume a more leisurely pace. I am at this moment sitting in Jess's living room, since I have promised to stay with her the first few days, until she gets her sea legs under her—she would come home, and the doctors (I think very wisely, in her case) let her go. With a person of Jess's strong and restless temperament, and an operation of this sort, it is terribly important to begin an active life again as soon as possible—and a useful one. So Jess will spend a couple hours in the office each morning, go to the hospital around noon for the dressing, and return home for the afternoon.

Georgia had three places laid out on the table when Jess and I got home tonight, and I said, "Why, Georgia, how did you know? I forgot to tell you Col. Rice was coming home." She flashed her ivory grin and said, "I had a dream she was comin' home today." After that she followed her around like a St. Bernard puppy, until she had dinner laid on the table and it was time for her to leave.

As a surprise for Jess when she got out of the hospital, Patty and I decided to do what Jess hasn't found time to do—fix up her apartment with the "little extras." So we spent last Tuesday taking the one-day-a-month-off that I am supposed always to take and haven't taken in the 11 months I have been with the Air Forces, and went shopping. The day Jess first returned home (for Sunday breakfast), the L.C. sent out some gorgeous flowers, which we placed on the table. Jess walked in, took one look around, said, "I can't stand for people to be so good to me," and came very close to weeping. Of course she is insisting on paying for the whole deal, but she thinks of it as a present, because Patty and I did it. Patty said, "I realize the home-making instinct is supposed to be strong, but when you take to nesting over an entire neighborhood, what will people think? This is the third apartment you have furnished." I must admit that the picture of me as an authority on where you put pictures and shove furniture leads me into mild cases of hysterics, quite often. And when I think what Maw and Dotty would think of me in that role, I collapse.

Bessie [Edna Floyd]—you remember her, don't you? The little, wide-eyed mouse from Tucson who entered basic when I entered O.C., and whom I enjoyed so much at Des Moines?—is now in my office, after a rather hard time of it recruiting on the west coast, and is, I think, beginning to enjoy the Air WAC office. I make it my one boast, and my one vanity, to have the people in my office *enjoy* that office and all that it means—the people they work with, the work they do, even the long hours and stop-press deadlines we have to meet, and the disappointments and impossibilities. It is so easy for people in government work to be more or less overcome by the immensity of the system, and to lose the joy which comes from individual effort and initiative *resulting* in some accomplishment. Our bunch has somehow kept that spirit of individual enterprise, throughout the 11 months—my two grand youngsters who are civilians, and my six officers. For one thing, I try to give them all an opportunity to go on to new things, whenever better opportunities open up. For another, no matter how tense the situation gets, we keep laughing. There is always some perfectly insane thing happening, and we all take time to clown about it.

Oh, Lord, I have received three requests for autographs in the last week! Doubtless from people wanting to forge checks.

Went to a dinner the L.C. gave last Friday night, for a visiting lady Elk from Canada. I sat next to the first woman scholar I have discovered in the British women's services—First Officer Alden, head of the WRNS here (British naval service). She taught (coached) Old English at Oxford, and I had a lovely time talking Chaucer and Alexander with her.[11] I asked her how she, as a university woman, happened to get in the service, and she said, "I kept that dark."

6.   *Betty Bandel to Mrs. Bandel*

1 April 1944

Thursday Gen. Arnold went out to Bolling Field to make a newsreel in the interests of the Air WAC program, & had me trail along, with some other Wacs. We had luncheon at the officers' club there, during all of which he kept trying to pin me down in a corner about Wac recruiting, & I kept side-stepping very fancily.[12] He is a perfect devil about loving to get you in front of sixteen people & then seeing if he can fuss you. Then he went out & reviewed the Wacs, & they did beautifully, & so did he, the old dear—complimenting them very handsomely, saluting them, & generally making them feel good. Then he was off in a flash for Walter Reed—most of the key men find some way to spend an afternoon a week there, talking to the officers & men who are laid up.

7.   *Betty Bandel to Mrs. Bandel*

Bandel encloses comments made by AAF officers about her lecture on WAC duties.

19 April I think

Staggered back to town last night, after five tiring but happy-flying days in the Deep South. In Montgomery I (me!) took a review of Air Cadets—nice young boys just finishing their pre-flight training—a whole wing of them, with their shining morning faces, white gloves, and sabres, all proudly playing soldier. And after the review I gave 70 Good Conduct ribbons to 70 good Wacs. I know they planned it knowing I had been in the Pentagon two years and couldn't salute any more—my arm was broken by the end of the ceremony. But was I proud! Like a mother hen.

In Orlando I was also royally entertained (cocktail party for me at the club, with nice little WAC officers hanging on my every word from Washington—gosh!). Boy, did I have fun!

I inclose, for your amusement and return, comments made by the students (officers in the AAF dragged unwillingly into Washington for a "staff course") at the last talk I gave before the AAF staff course.

[Enclosure: excerpts]
LECTURE: WAC
DELIVERED BY: Lt. Col. Betty Bandel

In an effort to constantly revise and improve the AAF Staff Course, the Director's office requests of each officer a daily critique of the lectures given that day. The remarks cited below are all actual quotations from the various individual critiques and are not to be construed as an expression of opinion by the Directors' office, but only as the reaction of the class as a whole.

1. This was a very enlightening discussion.

3. As no other lecture on the use of the WAC is included in the course, this lecture could well be expanded.

5. Very instructive lecture. I think I have gotten quite a bit out of it, as I have just returned from overseas and was not familiar with the WAC organization and employment.

6. Interesting lecture, well presented and illuminating as to the fine job our sister officers are doing.

9. A clear and able presentation of the WAC program. A subject which will become increasingly important as enlistment increases.

10. Excellent—perhaps a little more emphasis on the Air WAC might be good.

12. The lecturer provided a very informative discussion of a subject foreign to me.

14. The lecturer did much to strengthen confidence in WAC leadership, and to convince skeptics concerning the value of the WAC to the AAF and army generally.

16. The impression was definitely received that our WAC program is beyond reproach when handled by such an extremely competent officer as the lecturer.

8. Betty Bandel to Mrs. Bandel

25 April, 1944

Tonight Jess will leave for two weeks' sick leave with her mother, and I am moving back to my apartment. She is now able to comb her hair, etc., and can get along nicely for and by herself. I am glad, since I know Mrs. Rice has been terribly worried, and it will do her much good, even if Jess didn't need it.

Well, I may not go in for entertainment in Washington, but, boy, when I go to New York! I have always toyed lovingly with the thought of a week-end in New York devoted exclusively to amusing oneself, and I find I was right. [Jess Rice and I] went up Thursday night and took a room in the Sherry-Netherland—at $20 a night—a suite, actually, but positively the only room in New York that night. So we lived in splendor through breakfast Friday morning, and then moved to the Roosevelt. I have great faith in special little concessions for service people, so I found that the Roosevelt had recently taken care of an AAF meeting, got Caroline to call the manager, and he found space for us.

Friday morning we tried the officers' ticket service at the Commodore Hotel, but found that two things we particularly wanted to see—[Maureen] Sullivan in "Voice of the Turtle," and the Ringling Brothers-Barnum and Bailey circus—could only be gotten through scalpers. So they sent us to a nice scalper, and we got tickets, at something like $5 a ticket. Then we trotted down into the theatre district itself and picked up tickets for Cornell in *Lovers and Friends,* and ELIZABETH PATTERSON in *But Not Goodbye* for Sunday afternoon.[13] We *might* have wangled tickets for Lillian Hellman in her new play—said to be one of the few good war plays—but we decided to save [it] for another weekend.[14]

Sullivan was expert and entrancing in a perfectly lightweight bedroom farce about a young actress who falls in love with a soldier and is afraid to admit it for fear he will lose interest—she thinks men are interested only in passing affairs. The complete unmorality of the play has caused the Catholic church to ban it; it is therefore doing a land-office business; and Little Theatres all over the country will attempt it, to their sorrow, as a vehicle for the local Junior League starlet.

I thought Patsy's [Patterson's] play was grand fun, even though I believe its innocuous nature, etc., is going to close it shortly. After the play Jess and I went backstage—me dragging Jess practically with her feet braced—she gets shy at the oddest moments, for a completely successful, un-retiring person. I said, "Hello, Miss Patterson. I'm Betty Bandel." Her eyes got as big as saucers, and she yelped, "Betty Bandel! My Lord!" Then we were pumping hands, and I introduced Jess, and they liked each other because they come from the south, and we sat down and chatted while she took her make-up off. Boy, that greasepaint smelled good. I don't believe she quite understood who or what I was connected with—the Wacs probably are only a vague name to her, as they are to many people—but I'll bet she went out and found out who we are, after we left.

Good for Anne [Bandel's niece]! Tell her she is a better woman than I am, if she can make 100 in arithmetic.

9.   *Betty Bandel to Mrs. Bandel*

In these excerpts from 27 May and 5 June 1944 letters, Bandel comments on the promotion process in the WAC, and on the promotion of Emily Brown as an example of how the process brings the best Wacs to the top.

The papers are certainly giving the Wacs good coverage out there. Attick is in a part of the service in which promotes are slow. As a matter of fact, they are slow in most parts of the army today, as we level off toward the top of our building of new groups, etc. While the new regiments, divisions, posts, etc., were being built in tremendous numbers, officers were needed in increasingly responsible spots and were constantly promoted. Now we are filling up. In other words, I reached my present rank because I happened to be in on the ground floor.

I should love to see Emily in her new bars. Don't worry—she will end up doing a big job. Gradually, as we settle down into the army, the outstanding members of the Corps rise to the surface like cream to the top of a milk bottle. Of course there are outstanding cases of especially good people getting buried, but they usually show up after a time. In Emily's case, she could do so many things—company commander, public relations officer, radio specialist—that the difficulty will be to decide in which field she can contribute most. I think company commanders are about the most important people in the WAC.[15]

10. Betty Bandel to Mrs. Bandel

Bandel reveals her views on women in the military and in professions, asserting her belief in the progress that has been made in public attitudes.

25 June 1944

The evening with Frances [Rucks, of Tucson] was not dull, although it brought home to me, as my very occasional contacts with civilians so frequently do, how much I have changed—not they. It can all be summed up in Jess's answer when someone asked her why she joined the WAC: "So I would know what the conversation is about after the war." In that phrase is summed up not only Jess's instinctive insistence upon living the fullest, most earthy life that circumstances permit her—but also the basic urge to be a part of a great trend which, in my opinion, is the thing which drove us all into service.

Jess, Patty, and I took Major Margaret Craighill to dinner at the Raleigh last night. Maggie is head of the women doctors on the Medical Corps, and is, in civil life, dean of the women's division of an eminent medical school in Pennsylvania.[16] She and her husband practice medicine together, and she is one of the nicest and ablest people I have ever known. She tells me women doctors are in terrific demand today. A friend of hers is the senior brain surgeon on all the hospital staffs in Pittsburgh. Maggie told us about another woman doctor who is in the Medical Corps. She had a short leave with her children recently, and, as she left, said, "There's a lot of work still to be done, but perhaps I could arrange to get away and be with you again." The boy answered, "'Smatter, mom? War over?" In those four words—or are they five?—is summed up the progress

of women in the past quarter of a century. The boy expected his mother to devote her talent to the war, just as naturally as he would have expected the same
thing of his father. I am going to put them in a play, some day.

11. Betty Bandel to Mrs. Bandel

Upon Betty's return to Washington from the West and from home.

23 July 1944
Alexandria! Home! Huzzah!

[In response to a complaint from her mother about her lack of reaction to
home improvements.] I also thought the house was grand. What was I supposed
to do? Proclaim a national holiday? You will find everyone in the army equally
lacking in any great enthusiasm for anything at this point—we are all somewhat war weary and blasé, I fear. As a matter of fact, I don't expect to feel or
show any enthusiasm for anything again until I have spent a two-month holiday, at the close of this job, doing nothing. I never in my life felt such a great
desire to sit. And yet everyone here tells me I look better than I have in months,
and that my desert holiday certainly must have agreed with me.

My trip was hectic but fun. I will inclose the clippings of the press conference and of later interviews in Denver. I think you will be as amused as I was
over the L.A. Times—the reporter was a man, and was the only one present out
of at least 10 who had nerve enough to ask me how old I was and whether I was
married. I was a little apprehensive, because the press out on the west coast can
be anything but friendly if it finds you wanting in any particular, but Helen
Woods' headquarters has a grand public relations officer, and he briefed me be-
forehand and then fed me questions during the conference, so that it went along
swimmingly. The story of the Wacs overseas seems so oft-told to me that I had
no idea they would be so interested, but evidently the news hasn't trickled to
the west coast.

When I got back in the Biltmore I thought I was pretty well done, but Mildred had called me out at Riverside.[17] She has been working 24 hours a day
seven days a week for the Hollywood Guild Canteen, which runs a big hostelry
for service men and has recently opened one up for service women—the only
one for women in the L.A. area, and much needed, since all the women on
leave, pass, furlough, duty, etc., pass through L.A. from that end of the world,
and there is almost never adequate hotel space for them in town.[18] The Guild's
big old house gives them a nice clean bed, a place to press and wash their
clothes, and they can go down the street a block to the men's building for breakfast in the big, noisy, friendly cafeteria. It is all volunteer work, except for two
or three paid workers like Mildred. Before I left I sikked Mildred on Helen

Woods, so Helen, as the senior WAC officer in the area, could benefit from full knowledge of the Guild and its activities.

12. *Betty Bandel to Mrs. Bandel*

31st July 1944

[Bandel describes birthday celebrations and presents.] But that was only the beginning. Jess wanted to take me to dinner that night, but we couldn't go, so she settled for a trip to a FARM over the week-end. We went through Bull Run, and fought the First and Second battles of Manassas, as Jess calls them (these Southerners!) all over again, with Jess for impresario. We started out about 5 Saturday—Patty and Ann Danovsky and Jess and I. We had two double rooms with a bath between. Patty and Ann spent most of their time in sunsuits, sunbathing or walking in the woods. Jess and I, lazier, stayed in uniform, sat in the swing out front looking at the mountains and the fields, drove up the Skyline Drive to see the sunset. How's that for a birthday?

But I must tell you the big news. I am taking geopolitics at Georgetown! Jess said she had talked Father Walsh into letting me enter late, as an auditor, so I went with her, and for two hours heard the scholarly and brilliant Jesuit expound on the geographic influence on politics—a subject as new to me as theology.[19] The course is definitely for amateurs, and the good Father does not quote as many sources as I should like to have him do—I hate to hear opinion given, without also hearing the authority for the factual basis—but he is otherwise a delightful lecturer. He has the keen eyes and noble expression of your true student—"and gladly did he lerne, and gladly teche."[20] You cannot imagine what a thrill it was to me to see the young Jesuit students going into the chapel, and realize that that was the school Père went to.[21]

Then he did the most amazing thing. I hardly thought he had noticed me— of course he had seen Jess for three weeks—but he asked us if we could stay for a moment after class. When it broke up, he collected us, and a nice old lieutenant colonel (male) who is taking the course, and carried us upstairs to his study. He served coffee, we sat around and drank it while he told us a little of his school and his studies and his former students. It was a fascinating half-hour, and all the time Jess and I were trying to figure out why he had picked on us. But who were we to look a gift horse in the mouth?

13. *Betty Bandel to Mrs. Bandel*

25 September 1944

Jess is getting an exciting long trip, beginning in about a week, and is letting some other WAC officers have her apartment. She is sleeping on my sofa this week, until she goes. Then when she gets back (just before Christmas, or around then), we will either keep the two apartments or possibly try to get a larger apartment, and can in general live a riotous and luxurious life. Jess is walking on air—she is essentially a person of action and an executive, and the tour of duty here in Washington as a staff officer is harder on her even than on me, although she loves working for the Director. The inability to get anything done in a hurry on your own, without coordination with a thousand interested offices, is the thing that wears on one, and Jess chafes under it badly. So the trip, getting her out into the clear air of "the field," where people operate on a small enough scale to make up their minds on a course of action and then go ahead and carry it out, will do her a world of good. She is also needed where she will be visiting, with her remarkably wide knowledge of army procedure and plans.[22]

If I go to school after the war, it will probably not be at Arizona, so that I can have the prestige of an out-of-state advanced degree if I want to come back there and teach, later. I don't really have any idea what I will do. Teaching continues to intrigue me, partly so that I can have a little apartment and get a cat and sew a fine seam and otherwise enjoy my declining years.

14. *Betty Bandel to Mrs. Bandel*

[2 October 1944]

The last week has been busy but fun. We had General Marshall's national civilian advisory committee on WAC here Thursday through Saturday morning—about 20 prominent civilian women, ranging from leaders in professions, like Dr. Gilbreth, the noted engineer, to typical club women. Kate Goodwin, Emily Davis, and I (the three top officers in Service, Ground, and Air forces) acted as D-WAC's "staff," to answer questions throughout the three days. At least, that is the way it was supposed to work, but D-WAC got ahead of her schedule the first morning, and called on us to "discuss briefly the WAC program" in our respective components of the army. You try to make up a "brief" speech on a subject like that between the time you start from your chair and reach the speaker's stand, some day. Good mental exercise. Anyway, I at least had the advantage of knowing what I was talking about, as did the others, and I believe we didn't do too badly—but I told D-WAC the next time she called on me for a talk without giving me at least time to jot down an outline, I was going to get even. The generals who had been talking before us had been giving forth with platitudes, so I got down to the grass roots—what specific jobs women were doing, how Susy Jones reacted when she worked in a control tower, etc., etc.—and I believe the women appreciated it. Many of them have worked on WAC recruiting in their service commands, and knew too much about the WAC program to be handed anything in the line of generalities. The purpose of the meeting was to cover the history of the WAC program up to the present, outline the problems which still remain—and there are surprisingly few, of any importance—and see if the civilians, with a fresh outlook, could give us any ideas on how to tackle these remaining problems. They can assist greatly, of course, in all public relations matters—in disseminating information about the Corps to other women throughout the country—but they can also assist in things like giving pointers on how to assist in the re-absorption of women in civilian industry, as they leave the army at the end of the war, etc.

Gen. Marshall opened the meeting, and I think the women were tremendously impressed with his simple, forthright manner. D-WAC spoke—not up to her best, but she redeemed herself later, when she got over her nervousness, and by the second day had them eating out of her hand. Jess gave a magnificent talk on "Personnel," and there were some equally good talks by other WAC officers. At the end of the first day we in the Air Forces took over to give them a taste of WAC life. We had a trip to Bolling Field—we have two detachments on that field, and we had tea in the day room of one outfit, and then went and inspected the other outfit's area. I think the women were much impressed by the spirit of the women and the excellent place they have to live in. Mrs. Marshall came out, and we were terribly grateful to her for coming, since she has been accepting no social engagements since her son was killed in action last spring. She is very proud of "George"—told us a nice story about him. Some foreign dignitary said to her, "Do you know when I discovered your husband was a great man? It was when he was standing talking to President Roosevelt about a very important matter, with many people about, and you came up, remaining in the background so as not to interrupt. The General continued with the discussion, but, without seeming to lose his train of thought for a moment, turned briefly to his aide and said, 'Please get my wife a chair—she is standing over there.' Then I realized he was a great man, who could comprehend all important things, big and little." D-WAC asked her to speak to the Wacs, and she did say a word of greeting to them, but I think it almost killed her to say even so brief a message—she is very shy, indeed. D-WAC spoke to them, and, as always, they stood with their mouths open and worshipped her. I was terribly proud of the Wacs in both companies, and of the officers who had planned the party and inspection—they had said to me, "Ma'am, all you have to do is get them to the gate." The second day the group broke into sub-committees, and it fell to my lot to be "military advisor" to the group on, of all things, religion. I didn't realize, until after I had them all gathered, that I was inheriting all the minority groups—Mrs. Bethune, the great Negro leader; representatives of the Protestant, Catholic, and Jewish groups—a lovely Jewish woman named Mrs. Bachrach who is simply grand, by the way. It was she who had sense enough to object to any of them being made chairman, and insisted on a woman who was not an official representative of any religious group being chairman—Mrs. Bevis, Fifth Service Command representative and wife of the president of Ohio State. She is a grand, motherly woman, and we sailed along nicely, avoiding any possible shoals, thanks to her tactful leadership.[23]

Next week the new semester begins at Georgetown, and the advanced class in geopolitics meets Thursdays. D-WAC is going to take it with me.

15. Betty Bandel to Mrs. Bandel

She writes about why she would not choose the army as a career.

7 October 1944

There are things in the Army I'll miss, of course, as you say—the ease of never having to wear evening clothes, etc.—but my opinion of the Army today is what it was before I joined (we in the southwest knew the army pretty well—I went to school with it, for one thing):[24] I would NEVER want it for a peacetime career. It does not represent, by and large, the best thinkers of the land—it cannot, as I see it, since its whole peacetime job is to make ready for an eventuality which it hopes never will happen and which always represents a return to a less advanced era in the progress of mankind. Its regimentation, belief that officers must be able to do anything rather than a specialty, and other manifestations of a typically eighteenth-century type of organization are quite beyond me. Imagine having to wear a hat every time you stick your head out of doors!

The last week has been much as usual. Wednesday I took my three and rather lonely detachment commanders from Bolling Field, plus Bessie from my office and her roommate, to spaghetti at "Jene's." My party was quite a success, except that I arrived two minutes late, forgetting that respectful lieutenants and captains would undoubtedly arrive on time, and was embarrassed to death to find them all solemnly seated around a big table and have them rise like jumping jacks when I hove into view. Everybody in the place laid down his fork to watch me get seated. But we had a nice time, discussing Wacs and Marines and what not.

16. Betty Bandel to Mrs. Bandel

25 October 1944

Alack, alas, my social life gets in the way of my writing habits. Sunday passed without the usual letter, because I was serving after-dinner coffee out of your hot buttered rum cups, Maw, & the place was cluttered with polite Wacs. A nice captain named Brenda Boynton has just moved up here from Ft. Oglethorpe, into our little nest of apartment buildings, &, being filled with that wim, wigor, & witality which invariably lasts all of two weeks after you get to Washington, suggested getting the twelve WAC officers who live in this group of apartment buildings together—so we did. Patty had them to cocktails, Brenda had them for progress over to her house for fried chicken, and I had them for coffee, brandy, and fruit cake. They stayed until 10:30—part of the time two of them dancing Viennese waltzes with me—so I think they kind of liked it.

17. Betty Bandel to her family

6 December 1944

Off Thursday for Miami Beach and Greensboro, N.C.; back Sunday midnight. I feel much rested and refreshed from my week-end in Miami Beach. It was really lovely—beautiful turquoise sea, mild weather, pounding of the surf, a perfect beach—and they called it a business trip! Jess and I went down to see how the redistribution centers, which handle returnee personnel from overseas theatres, were set up to handle women. Capt. Kies, the WAC detachment commander there, took us around and arranged a luncheon for some of the base officers and a dinner for the WAC officers alone. We learned a lot, and then went to sleep both nights with the music of the surf pounding in our ears and with the moonlit sea just outside our windows.

D-WAC and we four lt. cols. hereabouts will entertain Sunday afternoon, Dec. 17, for the 500 WAC officers in Washington, at tea at the Sulgrave Club, of which the Director is a member. The little shindig will cost us a hundred dollars apiece, but none of us has entertained in a long time for the Wacs.

On our trip we had four hours in Atlanta between trains, so Jess told a long sad tale to the man in charge of cars there (she can argue absolutely anybody into anything), about how she hadn't been home in so long, and he hired her a car and drove us to her home in Griffin, 40 miles away. We had an hour with her Mother, and I saw over their big, plain, nice house, and ate fruitcake her Mother had just made and drank milk. Mrs. Rice was so overjoyed at seeing Jess it was almost sad. She is a wonderful woman—real "salt of the earth"—she sits there in her rocker and her plain little black dress, rocking and talking and watching her daughter, telling about the price of eggs at the store last week or something equally mundane, and all of a sudden she comes out with a penetrating comment on world affairs that shows a broad grasp, and an up-to-the-minute acquaintance with the latest broadcasts and periodical reports that would put youngsters to shame. And I got to see the red clay of the Georgia farms, between Griffin and Atlanta, and hear the driver tell all about hunting and bird dogs and horses in those parts.

18. Betty Bandel to Mrs. Bandel

6 January 1945

This week has been fun. New Year's Eve Jess and I spent quietly here at home. She went to sleep on my couch, and I woke her at midnight, and we had hot buttered rum. Then she went home, and the next day was a regular working day, except that I dropped in for a few minutes at the Statler that evening for eggnogs—the Air Surgeon always has an informal reception on New Year's.

Then Friday we did something we've been threatening to do for a long time—had the Little Colonel and Helen Gruber down for dinner. I spent most of the afternoon at home, cleaning silver and otherwise doing K.P., and Jess threw herself on the mercy of the butcher, with a long tale of her own helplessness, and he picked her out four of the nicest little T-bone steaks I ever saw. We won't have another red point for six months, but it was worth it.[25] Honestly, everything about that dinner just decided to go right. D-WAC sat and chortled at the sight of me puttering around fixing drinks and otherwise making a noise like a hostess. She and Helen both exclaimed over my apartment, and went from corner to corner ferreting out all the little things I consider rather special, like my framed parchment of music. Of course that pleased me very much, because I think they both have exquisite taste.

Just as we finished coffee, the phone rang and D-WAC and Jess had to go back to work—a sudden blitz—and worked all night. Or until 5 in the morning. Both were pretty well done in the next day.

19. *Betty Bandel to Mrs. Bandel*

21 January 1945

Well, I am off Tuesday morning at 8:45 for San Antonio, to attend a food conference which the Air Quartermaster is holding to educate all us ignorant personnel people as to the strides he has made in providing the right kind of diet for soldiers, male and female. I think it's very funny for me to be attending a food conference—it is primarily for the quartermasters and food experts of the various air commands, of course, but they are asking a few key personnel people from each air command and from headquarters— but, as I told the deputy air quartermaster, I didn't know anybody who needed more education about foods than I. Us non-experts are leaving after the first half of the meeting. The first day and a half are designed to give us a general picture of the overall food program of the Army Air Forces. I hope with samples.

The week has perked along as usual, with one or two nice little variations. We had an old beau of Jess's, a lieutenant commander in the navy who is now stationed here, out to dinner one night early in the week. I did most of the cooking (you may believe this or not, as you see fit), and it didn't turn out too badly. Then Thursday night Jess's old boss, a Georgia business man of some note, called up and wanted her to come to dinner at the Mayflower, and "bring a friend." So we went, and had a very nice dinner in his suite, with Mr. Verreen, Mr. Waldo DeLoach, a banker from down there, and Senator Dick Russell, the junior senator from Georgia. They are all nice Babbitts, simple and kindly, and they reminded me a bit of the west.[26]

20. Betty Bandel to Mrs. Bandel

29 January 1945

My trip was fun, because it was slightly silly. There I was surrounded by generals, experts from General Foods, etc., etc., about 200 strong, and we would all be standing around in the Swift Packing House watching them cut up a whole steer, and I would say, "Yes, but where is the tenderloin?" They all had a wonderful time educating me. They ran us all around town, out to the various army posts where demonstrations, lectures, and meals were held, in jeeps. We had helmets on, to make us think we were fighting the war, and I have no doubt looked as silly to the good townspeople of San Antonio as we felt. A wonderful crazyman named Col. Hinton, public relations officer for the Training Command and former Washington correspondent for the *New York Times* for many years, who rather took me under his wing, kept wondering if they were going to issue us picks after lunch to dig our own foxholes. I had a great time with this idiot—it is such fun to talk to a newspaperman again. He said something catty about somebody, and I, thus goaded, added something equally catty. He turned around and called the waiter: "Waiter! Bring the colonel a saucer of cream!"

Mary Freeman, now a lieutenant colonel, came down from Fort Worth to see me, and Wilma Hague, the WAC staff director in San Antonio, gave a lovely dinner for me at Randolph Field the second night. The rest of the time I ran around looking at WAC units (I will know how to say "How interesting!" in every known language and dialect and inflection including the Swahili by the time this war ends), and then went up and saw the Wacs at Indianapolis and at Dayton. And so ended my trip.

21. Betty Bandel to Mrs. Bandel

4 February 1945

I have been back since Monday night, and feel as if I had never been away. I am beginning to react like a travelling salesman: a trip is so routine a part of my life that I spend no more than 15 minutes the night before I leave throwing some clean shirts in a bag, and no more than 15 minutes the day I get back throwing the dirty shirts into my laundry sack—and that is the only way I know that I have altered the even temper of my days. I shall leave Tuesday week for Des Moines, to attend a meeting of the WAC staff directors of all the forces (air, ground, and service) and of the National Civilian Advisory Council on WAC. Jess and I plan to go out together, and all the WAC officers are going to be housed in Barracks 58—the same old barracks where I spent my O.C. days—remember it, Maw? You stood out on the porch and watched the girls march, when you visited there at graduation time. What a long time ago that seems! We have been nigh onto three years in the WAC, and it feels like ten! I, for one, will be glad when it is time to get off the uniform and go back—or ahead—to civilian ways.

22. *Betty Bandel to Mrs. Bandel*

Jess Rice's mother is visiting Jess, something that Bandel has been trying to get her own mother to do for nearly three years.

9 February 1945

We have spent the week very nicely, mostly on little special events for Mrs. Rice. Last night Bobby Bacchus, a WAC officer in charge of my outfit at Bolling Field, came out and got Mrs. Rice and took her all over the field and the WAC area. Then Jess, Patty, Kate Goodwin, Westray Boyce (who entertained D-WAC and me in Africa and Italy), and I all went out in Jess's car and joined them. Mrs. R. had been much impressed with the airfield, but was outraged that "all those girls have to live there in one room! The idea! Why, it's a wonder they don't take to throwing things at each other! Why can't they put up some beaverboard partitions?" Of course, it so happens that I agree with her. To put up partitions would cut down by one quarter the number of people who could be put in a barracks, but it is my opinion that the army will come to that eventually, for its permanent party personnel—the people who have to live on a post a long time and do the housekeeping while the trainees are shoaled through and go on out overseas.

Wednesday D-WAC and Jess and I went over to Air Transport Command's WAC outfit here to see the opening of a new Post Exchange. The kids, aided by the post itself, fixed themselves up with a lovely little refreshment room and store, decorating the refreshment room (where there are booths, a dance floor, and a bar from which to serve soft drinks and beer) with painted figures on the walls that would do credit to a New York interior decorator. The Wacs were *so* pleased with themselves and their new plaything.

Poor Mrs. Rice said to Jessie Pearl this morning, "We don't have to go out anymore, do we?" She declares she doesn't see how Jess and I even boil an egg, with the meagre supply of kitchen utensils we have. I was moaning to Kathie Johnson, a nice officer in D-WAC's office, that we were going to lose Mrs. R's cooking, and I thought we would have to get you up here for a visit, Maw. Kathie nodded approvingly, and said, "That's right. What you want to do is run a duty roster on 'em."

I spent Sunday in the public library, which is too durned far away. I didn't see the Inauguration—it didn't even occur to me to try to. I doubt if any war workers did.

23. Betty Bandel to Mrs. Bandel

23 February 1945

Well, it's been a busy two weeks. But now I am wrapped up in domesticity. Peggy dropped me a line to say she would pop in last Saturday for this two-week course.[27] Now if I could only cook. I haven't yet put anything together with flour in it, or wrestled with a potato, or satisfactorily fried anything, from a piece of bacon on up.

The meeting itself was great fun. It was like O.C. days again. As Helen Woods said, "The only difference is, I feel like Rip Van Winkle." The last night, I got up an impromptu chorus, and we sang barber shop harmony for three hours. Our National Civilian Advisory Council was in fine fettle, and I had a lot of fun with them—particularly with Geno Herrick, a crazy newspaperwoman from here, and Miss Ward, a dry New Englander who was formerly Commissioner of Internal Revenue for the New England states and went visiting down around Tucson to learn about our Border Patrol—evidently our boys really told the gray-ringletted little spinster some tall tales, and she matched 'em tale for tale.[28] Geno Herrick and her husband were out in Santa Fe with the Indian Service for a while. In making her report to the meeting, she dropped in things like this: "From Washington news goes out to every village and hamlet—to coin a phrase." Or, "If you know your politics, you will realize that the names on our Washington committee are balanced with a neat nicety."

The first and last days we met all together, with D-WAC presiding. The second, my Air Force bunch met separately, with me in the saddle. We got a lot of talking done, and came up with some good recommendations. I had the organization of a new AAF command to announce—Continental Air Forces, a command designed to preside over the four domestic air forces and the Troop Carrier Command, just as Mary Freeman's Training command presides over the five subordinate training commands. I also had the pleasure of announcing that Helen Woods will be WAC staff director for the new command. I had recommended her to those in charge, and was delighted when she was asked for—she is a swell old gal, with the best planning mind in the WAC, outside of Jess's. Now she is up here in Washington with me—the CAF headquarters will be here—and I am enjoying her immensely. She is a woman of surprises. Her partial deafness is keeping me shouting at her constantly, but otherwise everything is going along beautifully.

resignation of Hobby. Partly, it is a resentment that she can resign before the war has ended, an option few Wacs have. In reality, Hobby chooses to resign instead of obtaining a medical discharge, in order to transfer leadership of the WAC quickly to the next director.[2]

Throughout these last few months of Bandel's service, it is time to begin planning for the demobilization of the WAC troops. V-E Day (Victory in Europe, May 8, 1945) approaches, and the defeat of the Japanese in the Pacific is not far away. One of Bandel's "pet projects" is to utilize an AAF provision allowing for the discharge of women and men at equal rates to accelerate the rate of discharge of her division's Wacs.[3]

As the war nears its end, Bandel plans her life as a civilian. Her letters record her thoughts on the death of President Roosevelt and on the war's end.

1. Betty Bandel to Mrs. Bandel

The School for WAC Personnel Administration is born.

3 March 1945

Jess will be leaving Washington shortly for an indefinite time—perhaps 2 months, perhaps a year—to set up a new school for WAC officers who deal in the administration of WAC troops. It is a very important venture, at this stage in a long war, & Jess can do it better than anyone else. Naturally, I shall be lonely, but it will be such a relief to me to see Jess get out of the Washington tension & frustration for a while & genuinely get some rest that I am really glad she is going. The school will be at one of the big colleges—good for Jess's postwar contacts, although right now she swears she won't teach again—& I expect to attend an early class & then teach a class (each will last about 2 weeks).

2. Betty Bandel to Mrs. Bandel

10 March I think 1945

Another Sunday! And another spring! The sun is flooding in through the open windows on as perfect a spring day as Washington has ever produced—almost capable of being mentioned in the same breath with Arizona spring days. I have just seen Jess off on the plane—to Indiana, where she and Betty Smith, a WAC major in training, have gone to hunt a home for our new school for WAC administrators. I feel quite sure they will have made a deal with one of those middlewestern schools—they are all anxious to have us there. Then Jess will go to work on the curriculum, and she hopes to have the school ready to take its first class about 10 April. She plans to use a skeleton staff—not over three Wacs as permanent teachers, and three more on temporary duty, rotating each two and one-half weeks.

It seems a long, long time since all this began, and now, at last, the news is becoming so good that even the most cautious souls, like me, cannot help but begin to think about the new world that will begin "afterwards."[4] It will be a long time, I realize, before I can get out of uniform—but I am eagerly thinking about the time when that will be possible. I think now that I will go to school, get a master's degree in English and journalism (I believe I could get part of my expenses paid, under the G. I. Bill of Rights), and try to get a teaching position in that field on some small campus. Perhaps Arizona will have me. At any rate, I know I want to get back into the professions, and I believe I should prefer teaching to any other field. My third spring in Washington! Ye gods, it seems a lifetime! I don't know how I'll ever move my junk, when I finally pull out of here. Jess says it's getting positively dangerous to let me go to town on Saturdays to get my hair washed—I always end up with a taxi-full of stuff for the house. Louise, the girl who washes my hair at Guilbo's, found two gray hairs in my head yesterday! I was so entranced with them that she wanted to know if I wanted them curled separately, so they would stand up by themselves.

Thursday Jess and I went to a buffet supper at the Willard, given for Lana Turner, who was opening in "Keep Your Powder Dry," a WAC movie, that night at the Capitol Theatre.[5] D-WAC was also an honored guest, as was Admiral Halsey. We all trooped over to the Capitol, where Lana made a dutiful little innocuous speech, and D-WAC took a dutiful bow from a box. When the lights went down and the movie started, Jess and I sneaked out and went home, since we had seen the movie in a preview up at the Pentagon. It's a nice little play.

And so the week went. Neat but not gaudy. More anon, when there is more news.

3.   *Betty Bandel to Mrs. Bandel*

19 March 1945

We decided early in the week to have two suppers as a bit of a farewell for the people Jess has been saying for the past two years we ought to have out to the house—and whom we never have had out. She will be leaving in a little over a week now, and we are winding up loose ends. [Describes farewell parties.] Helen—a woman of constant surprises—disclosed that she once, in her youth, studied voice under De Reszke![6] I asked her why she gave it up, and she said she became possessed of a burning desire to sing Brunnhilde, and De Reszke said she would have to wait until she had had five children—and that discouraged her. Did I ever tell you the story she told me of gazing upon her firstborn son, as he lay helpless and infinitesimal on the bed before her? She was evidently looking at him with about the apprehension I would feel, and her mother said, "I think you would be helped if you remembered that they were meant to grow up."

Many thanks for the article on Otho. But the prize article to end all articles Emily Brown sent me—the story of Mr. Tenney's and Eleanor Cheney's marriage. She encloses one line: "Now it's up to you or me, keed."

4. Betty Bandel to Mrs. Bandel

Her thoughts upon the death of President Roosevelt.

13 April 1945

Just a brief note. I kept wishing, yesterday, that you were all near enough so that I could talk to you, and kept wondering what you in Tucson were doing, as the news of the President's death became known throughout the country. With Jess gone, there was no one in Washington with whom I particularly wanted to discuss it.

I thought, all through the afternoon and evening after I heard the news, of a line in the autobiography *And Gladly Teach,* by the great old Harvard and Princeton and Williams teacher Bliss Perry, which I recently sent to Alexander. Prof. Perry says that he never knew a man who was alive when Lincoln died, no matter how young a boy he was at the time, who did not remember precisely where he was and what he was doing at the time when he heard the news. I feel the same thing will be true, at least of me, this time. I know I shall remember all my life that I had just stepped into the little boat that goes across the Potomac from Gravelley Pt. to Bolling Field, and had sat down beside a soldier, when the soldier turned and said, "Did you know the president had died?" The newspaperman rose uppermost in me, during the moment's electric silence on the boat, and I said, "A radio report? Those things are often fragments of soap operas. Let's wait till we get to the other side and find out if it is an authentic report." But all across that quiet river, no one talked. The little boat put-putted along, and all of us carefully refrained from looking at each other, so that we wouldn't see how much each of us really believed it. I kept looking at the river and the sky and the green shores, thinking how strange it was that the boat's motor kept going, and we kept going, and the river kept going, when it really seemed to me that history should stop, for just a moment.

At the other side I was due to meet Helen Woods and drop in at a reception for her new general, Gen. St. Clair Street, and Mrs. Street.[7] We went into the Bolling Field Officers' Club, and obviously the [receiving] line had not been told the news. We didn't think it was up to us to tell the general, but obviously many people in the room knew what had happened. We hurried through the line, said a perfunctory "How d'ye do?" took a glass of ice water from the refreshment table, and left. Both Helen and I thought immediately of calling D-WAC, and were half-way to her house before we remembered it was the dinner hour. Then we turned and Helen took me to Virginia. I listened to the radio, cooked supper, took a bath, went to bed. And all the time I was thinking how different the world would have been, had Lincoln lived through the Reconstruction Period—and how different history's estimate of Lincoln might have been. Undoubtedly Franklin D. Roosevelt's curtain call at this time will serve to make his place in history more sharply defined than it would have been, had he lived longer—but undoubtedly, also, it may change the course of history. Later on, after rivalries and what not are forgotten, he will loom larger, in history's estimate, because of this; but the world may advance more slowly toward a world state, also because of this.

Ah, well, I suppose it is just up to us midgets to do a bigger job.
Love—Betty

5.   *Betty Bandel to Mrs. Bandel*

Bandel describes the School for WAC Personnel Administration.

15 April 1945

Purdue is in West Lafayette, Ind. Capt. Stratton, head of the SPARS, is dean of women there, and her friends are being wonderful to Jess in helping to set up the school.[8] Yes, the greatest need for the school will be in the first few months after the fall of Germany—while we will still be frightfully busy in this country, and yet everybody will be tired out and will need a little something to revive them and give them new interest. After the school has completed its mission, its staff will be available for reassignment. If there is no new job for them, they will be ready to go home—happy thought! The army has already discharged thousands and tens of thousands of people in this war, as their jobs have ended. Each of us looks forward, not to getting out all at once, but to finishing up whenever our job ends. I would say the school will last quite a long time, and, if there is much WAC activity when it closes, all its staff—being particularly able people—will be wanted for other jobs, until most of the WAC job ends.

6.   *Betty Bandel to Mrs. Bandel*

28 April 1945

Just a line before I pop into bed, because I must be up at the bust of dawn. I am catching the 7 a.m. train for New York, in company with Alice McNiff, a quite crazy and very nice New Englander, with a deceivingly precise manner and wild ideas, who is a WAC captain and a member of the AAF headquarters staff, in the training division. Caroline Essex is catching on quickly and shows every sign of being a jewel. I already feel safe about leaving Monday night for three days in Purdue, to see the end of the first class of the school and also to attend a meeting of WAC air inspectors out there. I shall fly back Friday in time to deliver a little talk at a meeting of the personnel heads of the various air commands. I am going to try to get out once during each of the first classes of the school, in order to see my air force company commanders, many of whom I have never seen.

Don't worry about spending money on the houses, Maw—we are building up quite a little nest egg. When you come east in the fall, we will spend some of it, just for fun. I am really having a very nice time vegetating just at present—spending my time as I did in the old newspaper days, mostly by myself and mostly writing or fooling around with studies and things. I don't mind at all not having anybody around for a while, after having people all over the lot for three years. Of course I would love to have Jess around, any time, but I used to get tired of flocks of the Wacs around.

Washington was stunned by the President's death, of course, Maw, but quickly got back into the routine, and now watches Mr. Truman approvingly. D-WAC did not go to the funeral, and none of us marched.[9] Most of us old gals couldn't, any more.

   Love, Betty

The School for WAC Personnel Administration begins to occupy Bandel's full energy and attention. In the following letters, Bandel describes how the school fosters both leadership and a spirit of cooperation and camaraderie among those officers attending.

7. Betty Bandel to Mrs. Bandel

5 May 1945

Back in Washington, after a wonderful 3 days in Purdue. Jess & her staff have really created a remarkable school, & have done an inspiring job in the 2 short weeks they have been there. The whole purpose of the school is to take WAC administrators—company commanders & staff officers in positions like mine—who went out in the field in the early days & have struggled along on their own as best they could, & draw them back together to permit them to learn what others doing the same job have learned regarding utilization & administration of women in the army framework. The first bunch—90 picked women— reported in with distinct mental reservations—they had gone out & made their own way, in the days when nobody had even seen a Wac, & nobody could tell *them* anything about how to run women in the army. Jess very wisely planned the course as a seminar, with 2 hours each day devoted to conference groups & forums. The women soon discovered that they themselves were making the course, & that their opinions & practices were what the group wanted to know. The ice began to melt on the second day. By the third day they discovered that nobody was trying to force his own opinion on them—nobody ever would, in anything Jess ran—& the ice fell away in sheets. Every afternoon they had 2 hours for their own kinds of recreation, & every night a member of the Purdue history faculty gave them an interesting hour on world history as it is being made today (one gets strangely out of touch with the world, in the army). This hour was followed by an hour of army films on various interesting subjects (this hour was optional). They had comfortable beds in single rooms, after GI cots in the little officers' quarters attached to WAC barracks, & 3 good meals a day. Purdue turned over 1 wing of the men's living quarters, part of which are occupied by the navy. The staff, of which Patty is one, did miracles to set up the first course, & Purdue was most cooperative. Its psychology faculty & other members are giving a number of the lectures. But the spirit of the place is Jess, whose peculiar gift is an unerring sense for how to deal with the people placed directly *under* one—the very quality which company commanders need most. Louise Smith, one of my AAF staff directors who was a temporary instructor during the first class, looked up from reading the critiques of the course which the bunch wrote as their final examination & said, "Can't you see all the little Jess's running around this country, after a couple more classes?" After they got over their first suspicion, the women began to relax, slept like logs every night, & let their tense nerves unwind for about a week. Then they began to bounce back up, & when I got there for the last 3 days they were working up to a climax of exuberance, renewed interest in their work, & gratitude to the staff. Capt. Stratton was out to make a talk while I was there, & I think was really astonished at the spirit of the women—Wacs always fly together, when they get a chance. Jess has made beautiful contacts with the university, & had invited a bunch of them to the final dinner that closed the first class. The kids had prepared a skit based on the recruiting officer accusing the co. commander & the co. commander accusing the staff director of all the ills in the army, & vice versa—it was really screamingly funny. The central character was one Penelope Snodgrass, a Wac who alleged that the recruiters had promised her she could be a rabbit fancier in "Africa, Texas." She wrote a letter to Congress when the C.O. wouldn't let her have carrots out of the mess hall for her rabbits—but by that time the C.O. was having her own troubles, because Penelope was raising rabbits in her own & everybody else's footlocker in the barracks. Capt. Kies, one of the finest AAF C.O.'s, played the co. commander, & did a beautiful job. In rehearsal they had built the thing around pigeons, instead of rabbits. Kies said "chickens," by mistake, & someone else, thinking to trip her, said, "I thought you said they were pigeons!" Kies, quick as a wink, ad-libbed, "Snodgrass just *thinks* they're pigeons." It was really awfully funny. Even the old Regular Army colonel who is in charge of the R.O.T.C. at Purdue laughed until I thought he was going to jounce out of his chair. Then they got serious & payed a lovely tribute to Jess, & gave her some red roses, & she ended the affair with Bernard de Voto's piece on what "old soldiers" can look forward to when they return from the wars—after the Revolution, only to build the United States; after the Civil War, only to make this nation first in the world in a single generation; etc.

After dinner some of Dorothy Stratton's Purdue friends—nice old maids & obviously good teachers—had Jess & me, two more nice old maids, I hope, over for sherry & conversation. Prof. Harriet O'Shea of the psychology department, the head of physical training for women, & others were there. They are a very nice bunch, & I argued with them violently on all the academic subjects about which I know nothing.

8. *Betty Bandel to Mrs. Bandel*

She describes community involvement in the welfare of the WAC in Dayton.

15 May 1945
Dayton, Ohio

Well, today is the 3rd anniversary of the founding of the WAC, & it has certainly been a gala day for the Wacs around Dayton. About 18 months ago Louise Kennedy Smith & Christine Moon, the two WAC Majors who head up the WAC program in Air Technical Service Command, with hq. here, began a campaign to get some kind of facilities for service women in downtown Dayton. They have over a thousand Wacs, some Waves, & some Canadian Air Force gals stationed here, with rather drab army surroundings. The townspeople were at first apathetic, but finally woke up to the real need, & got very, very busy. Mrs. Davidson, wife of a major general & daughter of the National Cash Register millions, gave her home (she is currently living in Washington), & the mayor, Chamber of Commerce, USO, WAC Mothers' Club, & others financed the taxes & a hostess for the house. They opened it on the WAC birthday, & had everybody & his brother here. I went out to Wright Field, & spoke to the WAC officers on the anniversary, the job ahead, etc. They were such a nice bunch— & I always feel as if there is so little of inspiration or real help that I can give them. Then Louise & Chris & I went down to this lovely house of Mrs. Davidson's. On the gate is a sign she just put up: "If you like, enter, walk around, enjoy the garden." The girls squealed particularly about the garden—two fish ponds, flowers, arbors, a place that can be made into an open dance pavilion, etc. There was a lovely, brief dedication ceremony. A few Wacs, Waves, &

Canadians raised the flag; the national anthem was played, & Gen. Adler said a few words—that was all, but it was most impressive. The kids were all on bleachers facing the house. In the usual pause while radio men scurried around putting up mikes, etc., the girls—all in high good humor—began to sing like angels. After 3 or 4 songs they burst into "Happy Birthday" for the Wacs, & chanted the line, "Stand up, stand up, stand up, Col. Bandel, stand up, stand up!"[10]—until I got up & waved, whereupon they all yelled in glee, & began calling for their own squadron commander, Capt. Johnson. Finally the thing started, & after the inevitable speeches by the dignitaries Mrs. Davidson got up & quite charmed them all with her informality. We all gave thanks for the women's services—I "on behalf of every woman in uniform who has gone to a strange new post & secretly gotten out a map & looked up the distance home." Then we all broke, & went into the garden for a show some of the soldiers put on. The treat of the day was to see the little Wacs stand around with their mouths open, try the easy chairs & bounce on the beds, & say, "Gee, it's ours!"

Sunday I had to go to Pittsburgh, suddenly, & give the first Air medal ever won by a WAC as a posthumous award to the father of the girl who won it. The little ceremony was very, very touching. Poor Mr. Babinetz, Austro-Hungarian miner from the Pennsylvanian hills, wore his best blue suit & white collar. His wife & son are in an Austrian concentration camp, the last he has heard (2 years ago), & his daughter, a charming girl who was recruiting & flying in an airplane making broadcasts urging women to join the service, was killed when her ship crashed last summer. The poor little man could speak little English, but his 2 married daughters explained things to him. The ceremony was in a little school an hour's drive from Pittsburgh, with the school band playing & the local Legion group present. A valiant WAC recruiting lieutenant acted as adjutant & read the citation, & I pinned the medal on. Mr. Babinetz was so little & so nice & old & manly that, when it was over, my little WAC lieutenant threw her arms around him & kissed him—& he took it very well.

9. *Betty Bandel to Mrs. Bandel*

Sunday—May 27 [1945], about
Purdue!

Ah! What a wonderful thing it is to get away from a city—& onto a campus! I have been here since Wednesday, & I feel like a new person. In fact, I expect to go back to Washington so full of good spirits that no one will be able to stand me. When I got here, the permanent staff descended on me in a body & informed me that my primary mission for the next three weeks would be to keep Jess from overworking & get her to take some recreation. She came to the school tired, of course & then had to devote the first few weeks to a perfect whirl of work to do the thousand & one things necessary in setting up a big new enterprise like this. Since the whole purpose of the course is to take tired company commanders & give them $2\frac{1}{2}$ weeks in which to refresh themselves & get their second wind, & since the students are largely people who have done a very good job in the early days when there was no one to instruct them & they had to work out their own problems on the basis of common sense rather than experience, the method of instruction is very important. It must not be wearisome or taxing; it must not seem dictatorial or "know-it-all;" it must take full advantage of the wealth of knowledge which the students themselves possess. Jess hit upon the idea of using conferences & forums to a large extent. During the $2\frac{1}{2}$ weeks about 5 general topics are covered, each having to do with the best practices that have been developed for using & administering women in an army set-up. When a new topic is begun, there are usually one or two lectures by the staff or visitors from the Purdue faculty. Then the 90 students break up in to groups of 15 to hash over the ideas that have been presented, criticize, add new thoughts, etc. Then they come together again for a forum in which a representative of each group presents that group's ideas, & there is a final round-up of the whole subject. Jess has to be at least in the background at most forums, etc., to do a little steering when necessary. She gets them to laughing, exclaiming, arguing, even cheering in an amazingly short time. I am slated to do a couple of lectures (Organization of the Air Forces; Disciplinary Procedures), conduct a conference group straight through, & preside at several forums. Well, the first 2 classes of the school were pretty strenuous, to the point that Jess spent two days in the hospital taking penicillin to stop a cold that threatened pneumonia. So we are taking as much of the routine work off her as we can, & I have been elected to see that she gets "recreation." She decided I needed recreation, too, so we are each busily seeing that the other takes some time out during the working day for play. Each goes docilely when the other suggests it, because each secretly believes she is doing something to help the other. Well, yesterday was my maiden effort at golf—& was I a sketch! I hit the ball on the average of 20 times to a hole, for 4 holes, when we were both exhausted & had to head for home. Jess couldn't hit it much, either, although she got a couple of good cracks in.

One of the things these people, who have for so long been living in barracks-type buildings, seem to appreciate most, is the very nice quarters they have to stay in—innerspring mattresses, comfortable chairs, etc.—& the totally unarmy atmosphere. Everything is very informal while they are here—they are students rather than soldiers, for the moment.

Emphasis is laid on recreation. Two hours are left free every afternoon for it. There seemed to be some holes in the recreation program—so I, the world's laziest white woman, am busily engaged in showing Patty how to run an archery tournament & in setting up a single stick [fencing] class. Shades of the people who wanted to make a phys. ed. instructor out of me! Every night after dinner there is a lecture on current history by one of the Purdue men, & then there are War Department films which students may attend or not, as they wish. In all, there is a full day's study, but it is spread out in a leisurely way.

10. Betty Bandel to Mrs. Bandel

Sunday, 3 June 1945
Purdue

It is Sunday morning, and I am "O.D." (officer of the day) until 1 o'clock. All that means, here, is that I arose in time to get downstairs by 9:30 o'clock and remain within sound of the telephones and sight of the front door, in case anybody wants to know anything. So I have plenty of time for a letter.

I find myself wishing constantly you could see this lovely place and share in the serene, restful calm. I am really having a wonderful time. I was about to say "rest," but I run around with my tongue hanging out, doing things. They are so different from what I would do in Washington, however, that doing them in it-self constitutes a rest.

Well, we got 90 student officers in last Monday by night, and began "school" Tuesday morning. Jess has planned this thing so that there is a factual lecture first thing in the morning, followed by group conferences with 15 in each group, followed by a forum in which the 90 come together again to put together the opinions that arose in the group conferences. Thus the students actively partici-pate in the schools by contributing their criticisms, suggestions, etc., in each group conference. It is a wonderful way to keep them from feeling that we are thrusting prepared opinions upon them. Since we're really discussing the per-sonnel management of women in the army throughout this course, and since the students are the people who have worked out the system for supervision of women in the army by doing it, they naturally feel that they have a good bit to say on the subject. We get into some lively discussions. Group conference lead-ers have to keep on their toes to see that no one monopolizes the conference, and to bring out of each conference a clear summary of opinions. The four tempo-rary duty instructors in each class (like me, drawn from various parts of the army to assist for three weeks) each take a group, and Patty and Jean Melin take the other two groups. We rotate each day, so the trick of placing each of the new names and faces as you face the group, drawing forth an animated but directed discussion, and selecting two or three people to represent the group in the forum—all in the space of one hour—is no mean task. It keeps you on your toes.

Then in addition I have lectured before the entire group, and have spoken in-formally, and taken questions, on various War Department directives which are sometimes misinterpreted in the field. These question periods on directives come at the close of each forum, every day. The day begins with breakfast at 7:15. After breakfast the staff gathers and plots the day (gets conference papers, etc.). At 9 we go over to the chemistry building for our lectures. Jess gave the first two, on history of the WAC and organization of the Army; I followed with Organization of the AAF; and Jean Melin and Maj. Helen Hart (she also of the temporary staff) followed with Organization of Ground and Service Forces. After the two hours of lectures, we break for conference discussions. Then we go back to Cary Hall for lunch, and before 1:30, when the forum is held, conference leaders and student representatives for that day give any pertinent information to the forum leader (one of the staff). She conducts the forum, calling on student representatives and encouraging free discussion from the floor. It is in the forum that Jess's magic touch is most apparent—she interrupts at just the right moments, to inject a positive approach to a problem rather than a negative, or some background information that tells the people in the field the "why" behind some of Washington's decisions, or to get a laugh when one is needed. She and I heckle each other a little in these sessions, whenever it seems that such heckling would add interest—and the kids seem to love it.

That ends the classroom part of the day, except when a special visitor is here, when Jess holds the group for one more hour (somebody like Col. Streeter, head of the women marines, or Capt. Stratton). One of the primary ideas of the school is to provide active recreation—take their minds away from the WAC and the army for a little while. The physical recreation program seemed to need a little prodding when I arrived, so I paraded all the temporary duty faculty and a couple of the regulars over to the gym to meet Helen Hazeltine (a grand woman in charge of physical training for women at Purdue) and her staff. Before we left we had gotten wonderful help from the physical education staff on the whole thing. Patty is conducting an archery tournament; Jean Melin is running bowling; one of the temporary duty people is taking badminton and another tennis: I am conducting a class in singlestick; there are fixed hours for using the pool in the gym, the golf course, bicycles, etc. To be sure they really got started on things, and also to get them to meet each other, Jess had Terry Bell of the physical education staff come over and hold a square dance in the lounge the first afternoon, partially to give them pointers on how they could run square dances in their groups. They were laughing and shouting by the end of the afternoon, and came to dinner that first night quite old friends, chattering among themselves at every table.

As you can see, this all adds up to a day which keeps you on your toes. There is never a moment when you aren't planning for the next thing. Jess had two training inspectors down from Service Command headquarters for two days, going over with her and the university the school contract. Thursday morning, one of the university men who was scheduled to lecture on Personnel Management failed to show up—mix-up on schedules. Jean Melin came back to where I was seated, with a stricken look, and I said, "Don't worry. I'll give my 'disciplinary procedure' lecture instead." So for 45 minutes I talked without notes or formal preparation on a subject I had expected to spend this week-end preparing for. They were kind enough to give me a round of applause when I finished.

Another little project that I am pursuing with enthusiasm is getting Jess out for some exercise. So yesterday and today, when I don't have my fencing bunch, I am taking her out for golf. Me and golf! Drag would have hysterics, if he could see me swing a club.[11] I carry the bag around faithfully, and yell at Jess across the fairway, "What do I hit it with now?" She yells back, "A mashie!" And then I have to yell back, "Which one is the mashie?" All we have been able to manage so far is five holes a day, but we may progress to nine before I leave. Yesterday for the first time I actually hit one ball that felt right—most of the time I could kick it as far as I hit it.

Jess has wisely planned a varied recreational program here. Beside the physical things, there are concerts, etc., and reservations are made for them so that they can go to Chicago or Indianapolis. Many of them have been stationed beyond reach of a good shop for more than two years. I think it is typical of the thoughtfulness that went into the planning for this school that the staff—Jess and the rest—realized how difficult it would be for 10 or 20 women to go up to Chicago, on their own, and get either a seat on the train or a decent hotel room. So they made arrangements for a group of rooms to be held at one hotel each week-end, and our gals can go in and claim them. The women who for so long have worked out every problem on their own seem particularly appreciative of this arrangement.

Friday we had Erica Morini![12] Of course when I heard Morini was to be here, I let out a loud scream for tickets, and Jess and I went. Helen Hazeltine, head of the phys. ed. dept., and the woman who shares her apartment, Prof. Harriet O'Shea of the psychology department, also went.[13] They are great good fun, and are Jess's particular friends on the campus—although she is actually friends with about every man and woman that we meet, so far as I can tell.

I promised to tell you more about Saturday of last week, when Col. and Mrs. Beere had Jess and me and Mr. and Mrs. Calinan of Purdue (some big business fella), out to the Country Club for dinner. It was one of the most hilarious evenings I have ever spent. Col. Beere is a grand old Regular Army guy, who likes Wacs because he doesn't have to worry about whether they know more about his job than he does. Mrs. Beere is in the finest tradition of the old army wife—the Helen Gruber type. Jess and I were kidding about the service and one thing and another, when Mr. Calinan, who had evidently had time for his cocktails to begin to warm him up, leaned back thoughtfully, looked at us both, and said, "You know, I wasn't expecting to enjoy this evening, but I'm having a hell of a good time." Well, I thought his wife was going to die, but the rest of us roared. He expressed so naively the typical middle western attitude toward women in the service, before they meet any. That set us off, and we got to having more and more fun. A woman who was seated at a nearby table with her husband kept looking at us, and when they rose to leave she stopped and leaned over Mrs. Calinan (who had obviously been hoping she wouldn't), gushing, "Do you remember me? I met you at the Episcopal Guild meeting last week."

She obviously wanted to see a Wac close up. Mr. Calinan, with a courtly bow, drew up a chair for her, and Col. Beere, who had been getting this gleam in his eye as he watched her, said, "Dear lady, for the first time I realize the full import of that old song, 'Capt. Cooke has come to town'." He began to sing it—some idiot jingle evidently written in the days when Cooke came back from the Arctic expeditions. Well, sir, this woman took him seriously, answering with a trilly little laugh and beginning to chatter about her sons in the service—only we discovered they were schoolboys in the service of the Episcopal church, as choir boys! Mr. Calinan, a vestryman of the Episcopal church, rose and called for donations. The four of us women tried to keep from exploding (Mrs. Beere had her head down in her hand, and her shoulders were shaking), and those two men began to play with that woman like a cat with a mouse. If you put it in a play, people would say, "How farfetched!" Then they got back to the sons in the "service," and asked if she had any daughters. She said one, older than the boys. "Ah!" says Col. Beere, "she can join the Wacs!" The woman says, "She's just about perfect—but not quite perfect," giggling a little modestly. Col. Beere, "Not quite perfect? Then she can't join the Wacs—she'll have to be a Wave." Mrs. W: "She's going to be a diplomat!" Col. Beere, "That's nice. How old is she?" Mrs. W.: "18." Mrs. Calinan: "Is she going to be an ambassador or a minister?" Mrs. W.: "A minister. As I say, she's not quite perfect, but her daddy and I—we love her." At this point Mrs. Calinan made the classic remark of the evening. With all the outrage of a woman whose hostess's party has been gummed up by some one of her own acquaintances, she looked Mrs. W. over and said, "Well, that's damned white of you!"

Finally Mrs. W. parted from us, but only when Mrs. Beere rose and broke the party up. I think otherwise she would have been with us yet. We parted with expressions of mutual esteem.

11. Betty Bandel to Mrs. Bandel

Ellipses here are in the text.

16 June I think [1945
Clarksburg, Virginia]

Dearest Family—

Well, my 3-weeks teaching idyll ended this morning at 6:30, when I pulled out for home. I really have had a grand time, & feel rested & relaxed—almost as if I had had a holiday. I wish Jess could get some rest—she went from one terribly fatiguing job to another, with no chance to rest between. She looks tired. I should love to have her get out & soak up some Arizona air & light for a while. Maybe "after the war" . . .

The last weeks went very fast. I conducted conferences, helped grade final "critiques," etc. Wednesday, the night before their exams & departure, the students gave a hilarious program during dinner. It was a variety show. They had been particularly impressed, I think, by the psychology lectures, so a lot of their characters were named "Skits—Farina" (It was the "Farina Breakfast Food Radio Program"), after schizophrenia, and "A. Social," after anti-social, etc. One helpless looking soul, with her shirt-tail sticking out, had a sign on her which read "The Revolving Chink." That is the name Jess gave, in classes, to the character that nobody will bother either to place in a job or discharge, & everybody tries to transfer to some other outfit. The girl who was playing "Chink" got up & stalked across the stage, to flop down in a chair on the opposite side, *all* through the program. She never allowed her face to show a thing—she just "revolved" throughout the show, always at a moment when someone else was talking or singing. Finally she reached into her pocket & drew forth a mammoth cigarette holder, & stuck it in her mouth. Everybody roared. That was a take-off on me, since I had smoked with a cigarette holder all through the course, & about a dozen holders had cropped up in the class as a result. The whole show was "younger" than those that the first two classes gave, but it was great fun.

The next day I went over & met nice old Dr. Creek, head of the English faculty here, & he & his staff gave me some pointers on good colleges for the type of studying I want to do after the war. He didn't seem to think I was all that crazy for wanting to switch to teaching—he grinned & said, "Don't let them make you a dean of women."

12. *Betty Bandel to Mrs. Bandel*

From Washington.

21 June 1945
[Washington]

A few minutes ago I was out at whiskbrooming the inside of my car, washing windows, and flecking off a few specks of dust. In the midst of my industrious polishing, I giggled to myself, remembering that Jess had said one of the principal reasons she wanted me to have a car was so she could think how happy I would be Sundays, out dusting it off and cleaning it up. Jess is, as I think I have told you, one of the people who can enter a room and by merely looking at it cause the various objects within to take up completely disorderly positions in all the wrong places. She doesn't have to touch a thing. It just happens that way. So my old maidish tendency to run around and set things straight, or clean up and polish up whatever I own, is almost more than she can bear.

Jess and I got a couple of Zippo cigarette lighters at the navy ship's store out at Purdue, and Jess hit on the bright idea of having our various insignia soldered on the things, so I took them to my friend, and he found a way to do it. He is putting the head of Pallas Athena (WAC insignia) on one side of each of them, and Jess's General Staff Corps insignia on hers, and my Air Corps insignia on mine. Then he is soldering the "U.S." insignia on one side and a miniature silver oak leaf (lt. col. insignia) on the other. They really look cute as anything.

We who are in the army are the last people in the world who could ask for anything for Col. Hobby—it would look as if we were asking for recognition for ourselves. The public will have to voice any such demand, if it is ever made.[14] I should like to see her finish her job as a general.

The inclosed pic of Jess and me is horrible of us both, but at least it shows the archway of Cary Hall, where the school is located. The "telegram" was "sung" to me by some idiot in the second class, the night I arrived to see the final party and program of the second class and to begin my work with the third class. During the program, they had this girl burst in, with a WAC cap of the old type serving as a "Western Union" hat, and sing telegrams to various people. It struck me as funny that they used "Tarara Bandalay" for mine, when the same song was Pere's favorite from his Georgetown days—of course, without the "Bandalay."[15]

I got back the day Eisenhower landed here, but was too busy to see any part of the celebration.[16] Planes buzzed overhead in tight formations, and evidently a large part of the town turned out to see him. The funniest Washington story that came out of the celebration was one Pat Chance (now a major!) told me today at lunch, about the wives of one of the generals just back with Eisenhower's party. This wife had managed to snare a ticket to the Capitol, to hear Eisenhower speak, and was about to sail out of her house when she saw a note from her husband on the mantel. He had left much earlier, to be in the official round of doings. It said, "Dear: Please send my suit out to be pressed, and have the boy at the corner polish my shoes, and get me a new shirt, and have them all ready by 3 this afternoon." She wrote back: "Dear: You'll just have to get used to the horrors of war. This is Washington in the year 1945, and those things take two weeks apiece nowadays. I'm going to the Capitol. Love."

13. Betty Bandel to Mrs. Bandel.

4 July 1945

There is some hope of moving back to the Pentagon, but I really don't expect to jar them into anything like action before fall. I have a series of new generals—my old ones are now all overseas—and I am just getting acquainted with them. Maj. Gen. Anderson, back from England after two years over there (I met him there) is our new Assistant Chief of Air Staff, Personnel. I have just talked to him twice since he took over, but he seemed very nice and easy to work with.[17] My work is so systematized now that I rarely need to see my generals—most of my work goes along smoothly with division heads, etc. When I was first setting up the WAC program in Air Forces, I was in the front office most of the time, proposing new plans, procedures, etc. But now that the system is established, that is rarely necessary.

The inclosed card is from Prof. Sears, the old nearsighted mid-Victorian history professor I told you about, who said he might come to Washington this summer. Well, he has, and look what I am invited to![18] I had no idea he would think to include other gentlemen. I called up Helen Hart, the dry Nebraskan who taught with me out at Purdue and whom he mentions in the note. (She is the one who said, one day at Purdue, that before the war she sat in the middle of Nebraska, teaching history and taking the Manchester Guardian and fighting the world's battles alone and unaided, undefeated even by Nebraska).[19] Anyway, all three of us are entranced by the idea of meeting the three old chaps, and really expect to have a very nice evening. Alice and Helen are going to wear their fancy white uniforms, and I shall wear my off-duty dress. I have never gotten a white uniform, because I don't approve of a uniform which may be worn by officers and not by enlisted women.

Last Thursday I took Betty Didcoct and Marion Lichty to dinner at the Mayflower and they suggested that I join them the following night on one of their favorite expeditions.[20] They took me on my first canoe voyage! I met them at "Reversia," the house in Georgetown that a lot of Wacs live in, including Marion. They had packed a picnic supper, and we went down to the river right above the house, and hired two canoes. We paddled down to Roosevelt Island, beached our craft, and had supper. Then we paddled on, in the sunset, to the Memorial Bridge, and tied up by "the barge" for the evening concert by the Watergate Symphony. It was an all-Wagner night, and the music across the water was quite lovely. It wasn't first rate music, but anything sounds good when you can lie on your back in a canoe and look at the stars. I had just settled lazily down on my back to listen, when the orchestra, after tuning up, burst into the National Anthem. I almost upset the canoe trying to figure out what to do, while Didcoct, practically in hysterics at my consternation, showed me what the others were doing—everybody merely raised his paddle over his head, in salute! There was a gray-haired woman Marine major in a rowboat near me, who was in uniform and therefore worse off than I. She was sitting on the rowing seat when the Anthem began, and after one frantic look around grabbed both oars, dragged them out of their oarlocks, and by a real feat of strength lifted *both* of them straight up on either side of her!

Jess and I were having fun planning a possible year's study in New York, if I decide to go to Columbia. As you know, she is half-way through her Ph.D. there. We were figuring out what our budget would be. We will get tuition free, under the GI Bill of Rights, and $50 a month apiece for expenses. It would be a game, to try to make that stretch, in New York. Our biggest problem is going to be getting a wardrobe, from the skin out! I think I will take my summer uniforms, which are much better material than anything I could get now, and have the tails of the coats cut off, the collars cut off, and the material dyed, so as to make a couple of standard winter suits. My dark green winter coat I expect to wear just as is, with insignia off, of course. That isn't exactly legal, but I don't think, after the war, anyone will recognize it for army stuff. Evening stuff and whatnot.

14. Betty Bandel to Mrs. Bandel

Hobby resigns as WAC director.

15 July 1945

Well, this week saw the end of an era. Little D-WAC had to do what Jess and I have feared she might have to do at any time for the last 12 months: go home. Her own health has been anything but good for long months, and now various family problems have arisen—business and things. Do not pass this on to anyone, as she does not wish to air her problems to the world. Some brief explanation will probably be made to the members of the Corps, and to the world, this next week. I have never felt so sorry for anyone. She fought through the battle of wondering whether she should leave, for her own health, six months ago, and had determined to stay on until the end, when suddenly about two or three weeks ago other things came up that made it imperative for her to leave the service. She told only four of us, before the press conference last Wednesday—Jess and Westray and Pat Chance and me. She would have told Helen Woods, but couldn't get hold of her in time, so I told Helen. Poor Westray, who has to take over her job, only knew it about three days before it all happened.

Strictly and completely off the record, I will tell you how they picked the new Director, WAC, but you must not pass this on to anyone, except, of course, Alexander, if you like. Little D-WAC sent up to the Chief of Staff five names— Jess's, mine, Westray's, Helen Woods', and one other—in alphabetical order, with no personal recommendation among the five.[21] Her immediate boss, and the person under whom the Director, WAC, has to work, added his recommendation—and very naturally, I think, gave it to the person who was serving as Deputy Director and whom he knew. The Chief of Staff approved that name, on that recommendation. Westray I think I have told you a good bit about, from time to time. She is the one who entertained the L.C. and me so royally in Africa and Italy. She is a North Carolinian, small, gray-haired, almost a professional Southerner. Her manners are perfect, her speech charming, her 18-year-old daughter well-brought-up. She is so soft and so sweet in manner that, at first, she appears almost too good to believe to us rough and tough customers whom they couldn't catch to put shoes on until we were ten. The manner is absolutely natural, however, and you soon learn that it is not at all an affectation. Westray has absolute personal integrity, great moral courage, and complete devotion to the WAC mission and the army mission. I don't have the slightest hesitancy to see her head the Corps, being confident that she will do a splendid job and will do her best to continue the program along the lines that the Director laid down. She does not have the keen planning mind that Helen Woods and Jess have, but you cannot wrap everything up in one package, and she possesses some good qualities which Helen and Jess don't have. My own personal choice for Director, WAC, would of course, have been Jess, since I think that she more than any of the rest of us possesses to a unique degree the quality of genuine and intelligent love for her fellow man, not as a mass abstraction but as a grass-roots, down-to-earth individual. For this reason she actually knows more about what should be done for every enlisted woman and officer in the WAC, and more about how to work with the people who can do these things, than any of us. But, selfishly, I should not have liked to have seen Jess made Director, because I think the strain would have been too much for her—she has already had to give more, physically and in every other way, than anyone else in the WAC, in the long months when she was deputy and the L.C. was sick. Besides, anyone who has had to fight the WAC battles—or any minority group's battles—in the War Department for long months is bound to have created considerable personal opposition, and that would be a hard thing to have to start bucking, from a new position of even greater responsibility.[22] Helen and I were, of course, automatically ruled out by being tarred with the Air Force brush—AAF and those who have worked with it for long are considered a thing apart. I, of course, would also have been counted out on the score of age. Those are only some of the considerations which would have come into anyone's selection of a new Director, WAC. All in all, I think the War Department did the perfectly logical and right thing, and I think we ended up with an excellent new director.

The thing I liked best about Westray's reaction to the whole business was her unfeigned humility. For several hours after she heard the news that the L.C. would have to leave, it didn't occur to her to wonder about a possible successor or her position in the business. She was genuinely Westray overcome by a sense of personal loss, and of the Corps' loss. Then when she woke up to the probable change in her own position, her reaction was one of deep uncertainty as to her own ability to do the job. We all bolstered her up, and she came through very well indeed. Both she and little D-WAC were under great emotional strain at the press conference Thursday. D-WAC got Jess up here from Purdue, for moral support, and Jess and Helen Woods and I clowned steadily for two days to keep everybody from coming apart at the seams. Helen, who has the most wonderful wit anyway, came up with the classic remark of the week when she turned to me, during the press conference, just after the L.C. and Westray had been held up for the twelfth time for "just one more picture," and whispered in a penetrating stage whisper, "They look like two figures from Mme. Tussaud's gallery, don't they?" Jess felt that D-WAC would feel at loose ends and pretty forlorn if she went off after the press conference and the rather harrowing "goodbyes" to everyone in the Pentagon, by herself, to her empty apartment. So she and Helen cooked up a plan to take the L.C., Westray, faithful Pat, and me to Helen's house in Georgetown for a drink and a little chitchat. D-WAC consented, and Helen, in her deft way, lengthened it out into a perfectly informal supper in the garden. She had us out there, anyway, for our drink, and then just had her maids bring plates of some delicious crab concoction out there, so that we eased on into supper almost without knowing we were doing it. I really think it bridged a hard gap for the little Boss. Every time we saw the tears quiver, one of us would start to clown, reminiscing about the "old days" in WAC. About 8:30 I drove them all home, dropping off Pat and Westray and finally the L.C. She was in actual tears when she left Jess and me at the Westchester, but she was o.k. again by the next day. Helen, who is deaf as a post sometimes, asked me what the Under Secretary of War had said when he announced to the press D-WAC's retirement. I said, "didn't you hear him?" She said, "So far as I was concerned, what Judge Patterson said was a secret between himself and the front row." They were all so wrought up that they were speaking practically in whispers—particularly D-WAC. There were about 25 Wacs there—key officers who have known her a long time—and it was, of course, a pretty big blow to all of them. They were sniffling, by the time they filed by her at the door, to say "goodbye." Her name has been linked with WAC as inextricably as [General "Hap"] Arnold's is with the AAF. She, like Arnold, began her outfit and worked with it throughout its period of growth. It will be quite something for the public to get used to anyone else as the Director, WAC. But it will mean the final integration of women in the military service.

The English people out at Purdue rather dissuaded me from going to Cornell—it seems the English faculty is having one of those departmental fights that sometimes develop in the best of faculties, and the calibre of teaching is not what it might be if they had their minds on their work. So I think maybe I will fix on Columbia. A year in New York mightn't be a bad way to polish off my life in the east.

15. Betty Bandel to Mrs. Bandel

She reflects on the reasons why Hobby resigned and why Boyce was chosen as her successor.

19 July 1945

Yes, Jess might well have been Director, WAC—but I honestly think the job would have broken her health. And as for me, it is true I would have been in

186 *An Officer and a Lady*

line, had I stayed in her office—but, had I stayed in that office as deputy for the past two years, I wouldn't have been equal to the job by now. I cannot tell you what the job of Deputy Director, WAC, under anyone as mercurial as the L.C., can mean, in the toll it takes on health and nerves. I had reached the point at which I would jump five feet if you said "hello" to me, when I left for the Air Forces—and Jess was worse by the time she pulled out. It is a job which has all the responsibility in the world, and no authority; and, if you are at all conscientious, it will break your heart. You have to fight all the battles of a minority group, in the frequent absences of the Director, and you have none of her authority—so everybody resents you. It is really a terrific spot—I think the hardest job in the army. I genuinely feel sorry for anyone who has to take over after the L.C., and I admire Westray tremendously for jumping into the breach.

[Note on envelope: "At least I mention VE day."]

16. *Betty Bandel to Mrs. Bandel*

News of the end of the war arrives.

14 August 1945

Good Lord, what a week! If they don't hurry up and have VJ-day, I am going to expire in a puff of atomic smoke, like the genii returning to their accustomed vase.[23] But I have had some fine days out of the mess, even so: Maggie Craighill from the Surgeon General's office was on the same train with me going out to Purdue Thursday night, and when we got into Lafayette Friday at 10:30 we knew absolutely nothing about the news, although the rest of the country had known it for hours. Big old, drawling, quiet Margaret Onion met us, got our bags into the carry-all, told us what was going on at the school, and then said, as she climbed into the car, "Oh, by the way, it isn't official yet." We said, "What isn't official?" She answered, "The peace." I thought Maggie and I were going to go through the pavement. Our tongues didn't stop wagging for hours. The school had gotten the news over the radio at 7:30 a.m., had gone tearing into Jess's room and wakened her from a sound sleep (she wakes slowly and reluctantly), and had yelled incoherently at her for ten minutes. When she finally figured out what they were saying, she muttered, "We'll have to have a prayer." They thought she was still asleep, but it developed that she was figuring the 90 Wacs wouldn't get a lick of work done, waiting for later developments, unless they had something to sober them and remind them of the tremendous job ahead. So Melin rose nobly to the occasion and volunteered to give the prayer, if somebody else wrote it; and Jess wrote it; and they gave it as the finale of a brief ceremony which followed breakfast and preceded the first class. We spent the rest of the day wondering and prophecying [*sic*] and waiting. I addressed my AAF Wacs in the afternoon, just before dinner, and was of course unable to

CHAPTER 7

"Don't Let Them Make You
Dean of Women"

By March 1945 the war effort is winding down, as is Bandel's frenetic work-
load. Nevertheless, the last months of her service see an important development: the School for WAC Personnel Administration at Purdue University.
Born of a need to revitalize WAC officers who have too long been in the field,
often isolated from other officers and less than enthusiastically supported by
their male counterparts, the idea is first broached to General Marshall by
Colonel Hobby in the summer of 1944. Although he supports it, Army Service
Forces opposes the idea, delaying the starting date until April of 1945.

Lieutenant Colonel Jess Rice, the school's creator and organizer, is an ideal
administrator. A born leader herself, Rice has the ability and vision to inspire
an esprit de corps and cooperation among the independent, strong-minded WAC
officers. They experience a renewal of energies, a give-and-take of ideas, that
sends them back to their units as better officers. The school's establishment
rather late in the war does not, in Bandel's point of view, reduce its impact on
WAC efficiency in the field: rather, it prepares the WAC to play an effective role
in the army of occupation and beyond. "It is, in my opinion," she says, "the last
big job we who have run the WAC can do for the army's program for use of
women in a military status during this war. When that is set and running, our
planning mission will be just about over; we will be purely an operating agency,
like any old, established part of the army."[1] As Bandel's letters make clear, the
school also fosters networking in the best sense: an informal camaraderie that
improves morale and work performance through the sharing of ideas and experiences among WAC officers.

In July, Oveta Culp Hobby resigns as director of the WAC, to be replaced by
Deputy Director Westray Battle Boyce, former staff director of the North Africa
Theater and of the Fourth Service Command. The rank and file of the WAC, as
well as some of the public and the families of Wacs, are in an uproar over the

answer all their questions as to "What next," but was glad to guess with them. After dinner we all went over to Harriet O'Shea's and Helen Hazeltine's, and had a nice visit. Patty left for a week's vacation in Uvalde. Saturday Jess and I, after school closed at noon, took off for McCormick's Creek, the state park 80 miles south of Purdue where we had visited when I was out there for the three-week stretch. Jess had made reservations, and we had grand accommodations. Sunday we went out and down to the stable and got the little buggy and white mule that the man rents out to drive through the park! I got to a corner and couldn't turn her, and Jess had hysterics. She said I might know how to ride, but I certainly didn't know how to drive a mule. After noon dinner, we drove to Indianapolis, and Jess put me on the plane at 4 o'clock before driving back to Purdue. It was a lovely week-end, and was leisurely and restful despite the driving.

[Discusses post-demobilization plans, trips to the Southwest, disposal of furniture, and college.] [Jess Rice and I] figure we could get a quite nice little apartment in New York, probably furnished, for not too much money, and have room for you and Mrs. Rice and anybody else who wanted to come visiting, in relays. This is all, as you can see, a glorious pipedream, and none of it may work out this way at all. Jess may decide not to return and complete her Ph.D. She is still wavering between the academic and the business fields, as she has all her life, and half the time she thinks she is too old to complete her Ph.D. and begin university teaching now. Then, too, now and again she gets the idea that she wants to write a political column, from Washington, for Georgia papers. Anyway, it's fun figuring.

The Little Colonel is quite well, I believe, and is resting at her house in Houston. I heard from her last week through Pat Chance, who was down there for a few days.[24] You are wrong on one thing—training does save lives. If you don't think so, ask some private who spent weeks learning to keep his head down when he crawled over open country. No, I wasn't surprised at Churchill's defeat, when you consider the British parliamentary system. If every man in England had had a chance to vote for Churchill, as we do for a president, I think they would have voted him in, because of his personal popularity, and voted in enough labor people to provide a balance. But if we in this country had to express our desire to have a certain man president by voting for some local pipsqueak whom we couldn't stand personally but who belonged to the same party that the prospective president did, I don't believe we would vote in half the men we have. That is what each Englishman must do. So the British people's choice of the Labor Party was not a renunciation of Churchill the man; they were simply, in typical British undramatic fashion, reaching "the time to study wars no more, and to be about the ways of Peace."[25]

And this, in an equally undramatic fashion, is what the women of the WAC proceed to do as well. Their vital work in the war effort accomplished, most, like Betty Bandel, leave the army to return home or to further their education and their careers—and be about the ways of Peace.

Postscript

In the final weeks before demobilization, Bandel made her plans for college, travel, and career. As she had said about her friend Jess Rice, Bandel, "like many other independent souls who have been in the army, doesn't want to work for anybody else but herself, for awhile."[1] In August 1945, at the third annual dinner of members of the first WAC officer candidate class, Bandel gave a speech in which she asserted that "the biggest job the Wacs have ever had is the one ahead: readjusting to peace smoothly and simply, with no attempt to hold back because there have been good jobs and good friends in the army." During the dessert, two Wacs "got a waiter to bring in, with a flourish, a hatbox which contained the *Cap, female, reconverted,* the funniest old stiff WAC hat you ever saw, with red and green festoons of gauze over it, designed, supposedly, to be given to each Wac as she leaves the service."[2] The cap was a symbol of the conversion to a new, less formal life, but it was also a reminder that the returning Wacs would be carrying with them, figuratively, the trappings of their life in the WAC, which had given them much of value to take with them into civilian life. In Bandel's postwar history of the Air-WAC, she reflects on how the WAC allowed women to leave sheltered environments at home and achieve self-confidence and a sense of self-worth.[3] From the rawest enlistee to the Director WAC, the vast majority went back to civilian life with finer skills, a new maturity, and a vision of themselves as worthy participants in a crucial part of the effort to win the war, which would bolster them in their future lives. As Jess Rice had suggested in an address at the School for WAC Personnel Administration, they, like other "old soldiers" returning from the wars, took skills acquired in the Women's Army Corps and helped forge a nation in which women would have greater opportunity to choose their futures—and to play a part in their country's future as well.[4]

In early September, WAC staff directors traveled to Des Moines to plan for the postwar Corps: Director Boyce outlined the demobilization procedures that the directors were responsible for implementing in the field. In Washington, Bandel now had time to relax with her fellow officers, as WAC headquarters was closing half days on Saturdays for the first time since its inception. Her own office was gradually reduced in size as she recommended staff for demobilization. In a late September letter, she noted that "I once had eight officers and two civilians in my immediate office, and I am very proud of the fact that I have personally recommended each reduction that has been made, as planning went along, before anybody had a chance to tell me I ought to reduce."

When asked why she had decided not to continue in the army, Bandel observed that, at the time, women were not permitted to go into combat and therefore could not have risen to the rank of chief of staff. "I never wanted to join an organization that I couldn't be the top of if I decided that I wanted it. If I want to be president of a university, I think I [could] be. And therefore [I went] into college teaching."[5] After being released from the army in November 1945, Bandel matriculated at Columbia University in January of 1946. She was awarded her M.A. degree in English shortly after having been recruited to teach English at the University of Vermont in 1947, and her Ph.D. degree in 1951. Bandel attributes her ability in teaching to the skills she learned in the WAC: discipline under pressure, and the art of leading and inspiring people.[6]

Emily Brown, after a slow start, became a successful officer during the war. Her experience in the China-Burma-India Theater led to her new postwar career teaching Far Eastern history and culture. Her life, like Betty Bandel's and those of many other women, was immeasurably enriched by her experience in the WAC. And in many ways, both within the army and later in civilian life, the women of the WAC paved the way for other women to follow. In her history of the Women's Army Corps in World War II, Mattie Treadwell closes with these words: "in a world where new frontiers had been hard to find, they had found one: in an age where pioneers and their problems were a memory, they were pioneers."[7]

NOTES

Introduction to the Letters

1. Lorry M. Fenner, "Ideology and Amnesia: The Public Debate on Women in the American Military, 1940–1973," Ph.D. dissertation, University of Michigan, 1995.
2. The *New York Times* published a number of articles between June 1940 and February 1941, and the *New Yorker* added one in October 1941 on these preparedness organizations and women wearing uniforms while participating in military support exercises.
3. Army women would transfer to the Women's Army Corps in 1943 when the auxiliary WAAC was integrated into the Corps structure to match the navy WAVES.
4. Between December 1941 and February 1942 the *New York Times* published a number of articles about women's rush to enlist even before the legislation was passed. These articles were carried by the Associated Press and United Press wire services.
5. The *New York Times* gave the congressional debate substantial coverage in the spring of 1942, particularly under Nona Baldwin's byline.
6. *Time,* "WAAC's First Muster," 8 June 1942, 71; *New York Times,* "10,000 Women Join in U.S. Rush to Join New Army Corps," by Lucy Greenbaum, 28 May 1942, 1; *Life,* "WAAC: U.S. Women Troop to Enlist in Army's First All-Female Force," 8 June 1942, 26–27; *Christian Science Monitor,* "Women Everywhere Answer 'Ready!' When Uncle Sam Calls the Waacs," 20 June 1942, 2–3.
7. *New York Times,* "Senate Sends Back New Bill for WAAC," 28 April 1942, 18; *Newsweek,* "Navy and Negroes," 20 April 1942, 32.
8. *New York Times,* "Mrs. Hobby Named Director of WAAC," 16 May 1942, 15, "Mrs. Hobby Sworn as WAAC Director," by Nona Baldwin, 17 May 1942, 32, "The WAACs" (editorial), 11 July 1942, 12, "Duty in England for Negro WAACs," 16 August 1942, 25, and "WAACs in Des Moines to Have 2 USO Clubs," 24 August 1942, 12. See also Charity Adams Earley, *One Woman's Army: A Black Officer Remembers the WAC* (College Station: Texas A&M University Press, 1989). Leisa Meyer, comments on draft, June 2003.
9. The *New York Times* and the *Times Magazine,* as well as *Life,* covered the training and commissioning of the first WAAC officers extensively from July through September 1942. They also reported on foreign women in militaries and in resistance forces.
10. *New York Times,* "Police Cautioned on Careless Talk," 23 March 1942, 6, "Bishop Assails the WAAC" (AP), 19 May 1942, 16, and "Catholic Women Oppose War 'Lure,'" 30 July 1942, 24; *Time,* "Catholics v. WAACs," 15 June 1942, 39.
11. *Newsweek,* "Wacks and Warns in Prospect for Petticoat Army and Navy," 30 March 1942, 33–34, "Mrs. Hobby's Wacks," 25 May 1942, 32, and "Army's Most Unusual Rookies Are 'Processed' into WAAC," 27 July 1942, 29–30; *Time,* "WAAC at Last," 18 May 1942, 62–63, and "WAAC's First Muster," 8 June 1942, 71; *New York*

Times, "Enter the WAACs" (editorial), 16 May 1942, 15. See also Mattie E. Treadwell's official army history of the WAAC/WAC: Mattie E. Treadwell, *The Women's
Army Corps,* vol. In *United States Army in World War II, Special Studies* (Washington, D.C.: Office of the Chief of Military History, Dept. Of the Army, 1954, c1953).
Hereafter referred to as Treadwell.

12. *Life,* "Yankee Girl," 7 September 1942, 82–91, and "Bataan Nurses," by Annalee Ja-
coby, 15 June 1942, 16; *New York Times Magazine,* "Our Nurses on the World's
Fronts," by Elizabeth R. Valentine, 13 September 1942, section 6, cover and 12; *New
York Times,* "First U.S. Nurses on African Front," 26 December 1942, 16, and
"Nurses in Africa Find Enjoyment," 30 December 1942, 5.

Chapter 1. Basic Training

1. Bandel interview, 1994, oral history of prominent women and people of color at the
University of Vermont. Folklore and Oral History Collection, Special Collections,
University of Vermont. Hereafter cited as Oral History.
2. Emily Brown commenced the officer training course at Fort Des Moines a few
months after Bandel. After the war, she returned to Arizona to earn her M.A. at Arizona State University and later a Ph.D. in history at the University of Arizona. She
taught at the American Institute for Foreign Trade (now the American Graduate
School of International Management at Thunderbird University in Glendale, Ariz.)
and later at the University of Northern Iowa, specializing in Far Eastern and Indian
history. *Directory of American Scholars,* 3rd ed., vol. 1, *History* (New York: R. R.
Bowker Co., 1974).
3. David Brinegar, letter of 10 December 1942, in Betty Bandel Papers, Special Collections, Bailey-Howe Library, University of Vermont, Burlington, Vermont. Hereafter cited as Bandel Papers.
4. Governor Sidney Osborn to Bandel, letter 18 August 1942, Bandel Papers.
5. American Legion Auxiliary.
6. Anne Dragonette, Bandel's young niece.
7. Bandel majored in music at the University of Arizona.
8. Frederick is referring to the belt and bars on his army uniform from World War I.
9. Bandel refers to the prospective assignments of each recruit in the WAAC, as con-
trasted with their occupations in civilian life.
10. Helen Harris was from Tucson.
11. An English round, "Southerly wind in a cloudy sky proclaim it a hunting morning."
Bessie (Edna Floyd) and Lillian Reilly were from Tucson. Floyd and Helen Harris,
unlike Bandel, were initially in training as auxiliaries rather than officers but were
transferred into a specialist training regiment in August. Reilly remained at Fort Des
Moines as a training officer after graduation.
12. Alice and Ruth Tildesley were friends of the Bandel family and writers in Hollywood.
13. The pay of enlisted men compared with that of enlisted Waacs of the same rank.
14. Charles Boyer was a well-known movie star.
15. Colonel Don C. Faith, first commandant of the WAAC training center. To avert crit-

icism from the army and the press, who were skeptical of bringing women into the military, he emphasized strict military training for the first Waacs. Promoted to brigadier general early in 1943, he continued to exert a strong positive influence on the quality of training for Waacs (Treadwell, 60, 102).

16. Jarman was the commander for Company 3, 1st WAAC Regiment (Bandel's company).

17. Dorothy Dragonette, Bandel's sister.

18. Susan Faherty was quite deaf, which demonstrates how relaxed the physical requirements were for WAAC officer training candidates. Age limits were also higher than for men, particularly for officers, due to the need to recruit a large contingent of women with leadership potential in a very short time. In comparison with male recruits, the educational level of Waacs was high; many were college graduates.

19. John Waddell, a family friend who was also in the army.

20. Oscar Colcaire was a singer at the University of Arizona, where Bandel majored in music.

21. Note that Bandel does not use "Colonel Hobby" but "Mrs. Hobby." In this and later letters, she reveals that, although she admired Hobby for her charisma and brilliance, Bandel did not view her as a soldier in the same sense as those who had come up through the ranks, because Hobby never went through basic training. Hobby very much desired to enter Officer Candidate School, but her superior officers in the army, including General Marshall, vetoed it, partly because of her rank (Treadwell, 59).

22. Bandel refers to "deans of women," meaning administrators, more than once in these letters, in instances both prior to her entering the WAAC and as she is planning to enter graduate school after leaving the army. Perhaps this reference characterizes her view of a dean as having merely supervisory duties, or perhaps she is using that word to indicate women like the WAVE officers, who were recruited directly from civilian life without going through basic training.

23. *Tillie the Toiler* by Russ Westover was a popular comic strip syndicated in William Randolph Hearst's newspapers. Tillie was an office worker; the strip was made into a film in 1941. From the Web site http://www.kingfeatures.com/history/historyeGeniusM.htm.

24. Bob Hope did give a plug for the WAAC on his radio show later in the war (Treadwell, 187).

25. A family friend who boarded with the Bandels in Tucson.

Chapter 2. Aide to the "Little Colonel"

1. Bandel, Oral History. Hobby was, like Bandel, in the news field, the copublisher with her husband of the *Houston (Tex.) Post.*

2. As related in Treadwell, 75.

3. Letter, 6 October 1942, Bandel Papers.

4. Bandel, Oral History, 12.

5. Letter, 6 October 1942, Bandel Papers.

6. Henry L. Stimson (1867–1950) played a major role in advocating increased re-

cruitment into the WAAC. In an interview at that time, he stated that the "need at the moment is for fighting men and capable Waacs." He believed that recruiting women for noncombatant military roles was preferable to using men not drafted for combat due to their 4-F classification: women often had the required skills already (Tread-well, 685). Secretary of state during Herbert Hoover's administration, Stimson was appointed secretary of war by Roosevelt in 1940. *Encyclopaedia Britannica Online,* "Stimson, Henry L.", http://www.search.eb.com/.

7. General Everett S. Hughes, at the time a major, had been appointed the army plan-ner for a women's corps in 1928. He advocated military training for women in such a corps, believing that basic training comparable to that of male recruits would be essential for the utilization of women in time of war. His plan, which recommended that women not be kept in a separate military organization from men but have sim-ilar privileges and responsibilities, was ignored when the WAAC was organized, until Hobby and Bandel met him while in London in November 1942 (Treadwell, 13–15).

8. Treadwell, 13–15, and as noted in Bandel's letters.

9. Treadwell, 75–76.

10. Treadwell, 100.

11. The *Citizen* is a Tucson newspaper. Binda Tuke, a refugee from England and a pro-fessional dancer, taught Bandel's niece Anne dancing lessons. Marie Padgett Ham-ilton, nicknamed "Alexander," was a professor of English and a Chaucer scholar, and Bandel's mentor at the University of Arizona. She also wrote *Race Conscious-ness in American Negro Poetry* in 1926.

12. At the time, Thorp and Bandel were both assigned to public relations in WAAC headquarters.

13. Colonel J. Noel Macy, one of the first army officers to be assigned to the WAAC na-tional headquarters, was on temporary loan from the Bureau of Public Relations. Colonel Hobby sent him to England, first to help her study the organization of the British women's services equivalent to the WAAC and later to assess whether the WAAC could reasonably be assigned to posts in England without overstretching its resources (Treadwell, 30, 32, 84).

14. Bandel refers to her mother's visit at Fort Des Moines for her graduation.

15. The WAAC chose as its emblem an image of Pallas Athena, the Greek goddess of wisdom and prudent warfare.

16. Jessie P. Rice, a Georgian who entered the WAAC at the same time as Bandel, was later assigned to be regional director with the Third Service Command. Described by Treadwell as the "chief author" of WAC policy along with Hobby, Rice was a deputy director, organizer of the WAC "All-States" Recruiting Campaign, and, in 1945, responsible for the organization of the School for WAC Personnel Adminis-tration at Purdue University (Treadwell, 88 and passim).

17. Hobby's husband, William P. Hobby, was former governor of Texas.

18. The army chief of staff's plane (Bandel, personal communication).

19. Bandel is referring to Colonel Hobby as the "Little Colonel," a nickname used in most of her subsequent letters in this collection.

20. Bandel's play was published in *Twenty Short Plays on a Royalty Holiday,* vol. 3 (1947–1950), ed. Margaret Mayorga (New York and Toronto: S. French, 1948).

21. Jere Knight was an adviser on public relations for the WAAC but not herself a Waac.

22. Martin was the official photographer of the WAAC, chosen for that one-year position in 1942 by the secretary of war. A press photographer in Washington, D.C., for many years, she was the first woman to be elected to the White House Photographers' Association, the first woman editor of art and photography of a major newspaper (the *Washington Times-Herald*), and the first woman sports editor in the country. In 1940, she became photo editor of the *Chicago Sun*'s Washington bureau and associate editor of the *Women's Home Companion,* one of the leading women's magazines of the day. *Current Biography Yearbook 1943* (New York: H. W. Wilson Co.).

23. Muni was an aide to Colonel Faith, liaison to the WAAC headquarters.

24. Drag (Fred) Dragonette, Bandel's brother-in-law, worked for the U.S. War Bond drive and perhaps met Ginger Rogers in a publicity drive. Anthony is Bandel's nephew.

25. Helen Gruber, wife of Brigadier General William R. Gruber, was hired by Hobby as an adviser on military protocol. She also managed Hobby's schedule. More than just a "personal secretary," her position was a complex one at that time, as the WAAC organizational structure was still struggling to establish itself and its position in the army (Treadwell, 50–52).

26. Lieutenant Colonel Harold P. Tasker was assigned in February 1942 to Colonel Hobby's office. Tasker had served in the Coast Artillery Corps and was an instructor in mathematics at West Point. He was assigned to visit army installations to prepare them for receiving WAAC units. At the time of this letter, he was about to be replaced as the executive officer by Colonel Thomas B. Catron, who had more direct experience in the War Department (Treadwell, 30, 42, 60, 86).

27. The WAAF (Women's Auxiliary Air Force) would actually have been the British counterpart to the Air-WAAC, which was not officially established until the spring of 1943.

28. Temporary M Building at the Pentagon was the first WAAC headquarters.

29. Chief Controller Jean Knox (Lady Swaythling), head of the British Auxiliary Territorial Service. The first woman major general in the British armed forces, Knox joined the ATS shortly after Prime Minister Neville Chamberlain went to Munich in 1939 to forestall war with Adolph Hitler. By October of that year, she became an officer and was given the task of solving the service's problems of poor leadership and lack of support for its members. She attained the rank of general in 1941, having transformed the ATS into a more professional and better-organized service. Knox was known for her stern discipline but also for her personal interaction with all levels of her service. At the time of this meeting, she was in North America to inspect Canadian ATS units (*Current Biography 1942,* 467).

30. Lieutenant Helen Hamilton Woods had served as a civilian adviser to Colonel Hobby earlier, dealing with legislative issues, recruiting, and administration. Widow of New York police commissioner Arthur Woods, she joined the WAAC and eventually rose to Lieutenant Colonel (Treadwell, 31, 111).

31. O.D.: olive drab, the original WAAC officer uniform color. "Pinks" were considered the dress uniform. Web site for the Army Women's Museum, Ms. Jerry G. Burgess, director and curator, U.S. Army Women's Museum, "The WAAC Uniform," http://www.awm.lee.army.mil/waac_uniform.htm.

32. That is, Helen Woods. "Shavetail" is army slang for second lieutenant.

33. Lady Dorothy Halifax was the wife of British ambassador Viscount Halifax. Mrs. Morganthau and Mrs. Wallace were the wives of Henry Morganthau, Jr., secretary of the treasury, and Henry A. Wallace, vice president from 1941 to 1945.

34. Edith Helm (1874–1962) was White House social secretary from 1915 to 1920 and 1933 to 1953. Felice Levy, comp., *Obituaries on File* (New York: Facts on File, 1979), 262.

35. Julia O. Flikke began her career in the Army Nurse Corps during World War I, retiring with the rank of colonel in 1943. She wrote the book *Nurses in Action* (Philadelphia: J. B. Co., 1943), about the Army Nurse Corps in World War II. *Who Was Who in America,* vol. 6 (1974–1976), 142. Sue Sophia Dauser entered the U.S. Navy in 1917 and was named superintendent of the Navy Nurse Corps in 1939. In that role, she was largely responsible for overseeing its expansion during World War II, advocating for navy nurses' gaining full military status. *Webster's American Military Biographies* (Springfield, Mass.: G. & C. Merriam Co., 1978), 93.

36. Although Bandel does not indicate what was talked about specifically at this conference, the participants were probably discussing the experiences of the British women's forces such as the ATS, which suffered in their early days from a too rapid expansion as well as from a "smear" campaign that accused military women of loose morals. This conference was convened in the hopes of learning from the British experiences, in order to avoid such problems with the WAAC (see Treadwell, 33, 34, 780).

37. L.C. ("Little Colonel") was the Waacs' affectionate nickname for Colonel Hobby.

38. Code name for Eleanor Roosevelt.

39. Hobby and Bandel were not allowed to wear uniforms while overseas on this trip, because they landed first in Ireland, which was neutral during World War II.

40. John Winant (1889–1947) was ambassador to Great Britain from 1941 to 1946. Although a Republican, he was an advocate for Roosevelt's Social Security program and a social reformer whom Roosevelt appointed to mediate textile strikes in the 1930s. He strongly lobbied for America's entrance into the war to aid Britain (*Current Biography 1941,* 928–930, and *1947,* 689).

41. Royal Air Force pilots also spread the myth that their accuracy in finding enemy planes was due to their consumption of carrots. In reality, they had acquired radar partway through the war but wished it kept secret.

42. Queen Elizabeth (1900–2002) and the rest of the royal family were enormously popular during the war, partly because they remained in London during the blitz. She and her husband, King George VI, helped bolster the morale of the British people by keeping a highly visible profile, touring bombed-out neighborhoods, and performing other public service.

43. The American invasion of North Africa, commanded by Eisenhower, began on November 7.

44. Elspeth Duncan, their driver in England.

45. Harris refers to Bandel's assignment to Hobby as her aide.

46. The mayor of Chicago at that time was Democrat Edward Kelly, elected in 1933.

47. Sister to the financier J. P. Morgan, Anne Morgan dedicated her life to volunteerism and philanthropy. Seventy years of age at the time of this writing, she had been a supporter of trade unions in the early part of the century and was active in such organizations as the American Women's Association, which supported working

women and advocated for better workplace conditions. She volunteered in both world wars in aid of refugees and displaced persons in France (*Current Biography 1946*, 412–414).

48. Hobby and Bandel had been ordered to Fort Leavenworth, Kansas, site of the Command and General Staff School, to lecture on modes of administration for WAAC troops (Treadwell, 100).

49. David Brinegar was a friend from Tucson and a fellow newspaperman.

50. A churchwarden pipe has a long, curved stem.

51. General George C. Marshall was the U.S. Army chief of staff from 1939 to 1944 and a strong supporter of the WAAC/WAC.

52. Brinegar refers to the insignia for a first lieutenant, one silver bar on each shoulder. At this point Bandel was third officer, the WAAC equivalent of second lieutenant. She did, in fact, skip a grade when she was promoted to captain (first officer) in late December and wrote Brinegar that his bars had brought her luck (letter, 28 December 1942, Bandel Papers).

53. "Franklin Pig" was a piglet named after the U. S. president by its owner, a farmer in Barham, England, not far from the site near the English Channel where Eleanor visited the widowed Duchess of Kent and her new baby. Rochelle Chadakoff, ed., *Eleanor Roosevelt's My Day: Her Acclaimed Columns, 1936–1945* (New York: Pharos Books, 1989), 264.

54. That is, attains the rank of general.

55. Hobby knew that some officers of the armed forces, as well as a certain proportion of the U.S. Congress, were adamantly opposed to women holding the rank of general. In fact, the congressional bill that officially brought the WAAC into full army status specifically forbade any WAC officer from attaining the rank of general (Treadwell, 220). No woman in the army achieved general officer status until 1970, when Elizabeth P. Hoisington and Army Nurse Corps Director Anna Mae Hays were promoted to brigadier general the same day; from "Military Women 'Firsts,'" http://userpages.aug.com/captbarb/firsts.html.

Chapter 3. Acting Deputy Director

1. Letter to the *Arizona Star and Citizen* colleagues, 26 December 1942, Bandel Papers.

2. Treadwell, 187.

3. Letter, 28 February 1943, Bandel Papers.

4. Letter to her mother, 23 January 1943, Bandel Papers.

5. Although Bandel calls herself captain here, the WAAC had its own equivalent officer grades. Her official rank was first officer.

6. At that time, Jess Rice was the deputy director and thus second in command. Services of Supply (SOS), later renamed the Army Service Forces, was one of the three army commands, along with the Army Ground Forces (AGF) and the Army Air Forces (AAF). The WAAC was initially assigned to the SOS command (Treadwell, 31–32). When the nine women were assigned as directors of the nine service com-

mands, they were only third officers (lieutenants), although their position was equivalent to that of army special staff officers who were colonels (Treadwell, 88–90).

7. Colonel Thomas R. Catron was called out of retirement by General George C. Marshall, replacing Colonel Tasker as the WAAC army executive officer in the fall of 1942. He reorganized WAAC headquarters, creating an Operating and a Planning Division. Treadwell considers this reorganization to have been as much of a failure as the previous system, with too much overlapping authority and little long-term planning. She notes that there was little communication between Director Hobby and the army administration: Hobby was not informed of the reorganization of the WAAC until some weeks after the decision was made by Catron (Treadwell, 86–88, 111).

8. Elk: a visiting person of authority.

9. L.C.: the "Little Colonel," Oveta Culp Hobby.

10. Lieutenant General Brehon B. Somervell was the commanding general of SOS's Personnel Division, to which the WAAC was assigned. He played a major role in the early administration of the WAAC (Treadwell, 53, 87–89, and *passim*). In the early days of the WAAC, there was considerable indecision about where it would fit into the military administrative structure: General George C. Marshall instructed Somervell to assign military advisers to WAAC headquarters.

11. Edith Helm, Eleanor Roosevelt's social secretary.

12. The Women's Overseas Service League was founded in 1921 by women who had served overseas in World War I.

13. General Everett S. Hughes was appointed the army planner for a women's corps in 1928. He advocated military training for women in such a corps, believing that it would be essential for the utilization of women in time of war. His plan, which recommended that women not be kept in a separate military organization from men but have similar privileges and responsibilities, was ignored when the WAAC was organized, until Hobby and Bandel met him while in London in November 1942 (Treadwell, 13–15). Bandel refers to the meeting in this letter.

14. See Bandel's letters of 11 to 19 November 1942. The radio broadcasts were used as part of a campaign to recruit more women into the WAAC (Treadwell, chap. 13 and passim).

15. Capra was, of course, the great film director, who produced this documentary on the WAAC for use in movie theaters—but ultimately without Bandel's assistance, as Hobby needed her more in headquarters.

16. Although Bandel does not elaborate here, issues concerning Waacs in the AAF included their use in the AAF Weather Service; prohibition of Wacs in the Military District of Washington, which included WAAC headquarters; and the question of whether Air-WAAC officers would administer WAAC enlisted personnel only or would be used in other jobs. Bandel, typescript, "The WAC Program in the Army Air Forces" (1946), 12–13, at the Center of Military History, Fort McNair, Washington, D.C.

17. B. Eugenia Leis, a civilian, was hired to oversee personnel planning and statistics. Treadwell notes that her hiring was the director's "first move to overcome the rigid channelization which prevented her contact with junior staff members, since Miss Leis was given authority to ignore all office channels in securing information for the Director" (Treadwell, 111).

18. "Safety pins": Bandel's first lieutenant's insignia, which she had sent to Helen Hamilton Woods.

19. Mrs. Bandel refers to her daughter's statement that she would serve her country by playing the bugle at Fort Des Moines, if asked to. Diplomats posted to Great Britain presented their credentials at the Court of St. James in London.

20. "Went over" to Europe: Waacs had been in Europe and North Africa since late November. Both Treadwell and Bandel recall that when Hobby, having cautioned a group of Waacs selected for service overseas that it might be a dangerous assignment, asked how many would still volunteer to go, all but two of three hundred stepped forward as one (Treadwell, 106; Bandel, personal communication).

21. In fact, Hobby became the first secretary of the Department of Health, Education, and Welfare in 1953 under President Eisenhower—and was on many boards of national organizations.

22. Alexander (Marie Padgett) Hamilton was alluding to the poem "Twilight, Tucson" by Sara Teasdale: "It was not long I lived there, But I became a woman Under those vehement stars." In John Farrar, ed., *Bookman's Anthology of Verse* (New York: George H. Doran Co., 1922).

23. Florence T. Newsome was assistant secretary to the General Staff. She was one of six WAC officers promoted to lieutenant colonel shortly after Bandel in early 1944 (Treadwell, 576, 701).

24. Wife of General George C. Marshall, U.S. Army chief of staff, from 1939 to 1945.

25. Mme. Chiang Kai-shek was the wife of the Chinese Nationalist president, later premier of present-day Taiwan after Mao Zedong conquered the Chinese mainland in 1949. At the time of these letters, she was in the United States to address a joint session of the U.S. Congress about conditions in China. She also wrote many articles on China for U.S. magazines and newspapers and was much admired, with her husband, because of her campaign against the threat of communism in China.

26. Senate Bill 495, which established the Women's Army Corps and granted women in the WAAC full military status, was passed on June 28 and signed by President Roosevelt on July 1. The regulations mentioned by Bandel here were designed to include safeguards for Wacs such as separate housing and messes, no assignments as entertainers or waitresses in army clubs, and assignment only to units commanded by WAC officers (Treadwell, 264).

27. Members of the Writers' War Board, as well as photographers, who had pledged to assist the WAAC in recruiting women to join, were being escorted to WAAC installations in order to learn about the Waacs' work preparatory to writing about them in newspapers and magazines (Treadwell, 187–188). The chairman of the board was Rex Stout, a popular writer of mysteries featuring fictional detective Nero Wolfe, among others. After the triumph of Nazism in Germany in 1938, he devoted his writing to exposing the evils of the Third Reich and its allies. In 1942, he became the "master of ceremonies" for the radio show *The Voice of Freedom,* sponsored by Freedom House, and appeared on the CBS program *Our Secret Weapon* later that year (*Current Biography 1946,* 575–577). Clifton Fadiman, editor in chief for the publishing company Simon and Schuster in the 1930s and book reviewer for the *New Yorker* magazine, was the radio emcee for the enormously popular *Information, Please,* a program that brought the ideas of leading authors, intellectuals, and actors to the public at large. He also sponsored the Reader's Club in 1940, which by 1941 already had a membership of eighty thousand (*Current Biography 1941,* 266–267).

Margaret Leech won the Pulitzer prize in history twice, in 1942 for *Reveille in Washington* and in 1960 for *The Days of McKinley*. At the time of these letters, she was the widow of the late Ralph Pulitzer (*Who Was Who in America,* vol. 6, 242). Franklin P. Adams, journalist and poet, worked for a number of newspapers during his career, including the *Chicago Journal* and several New York papers. At this time, he was writing for the *New York Post.* W. J. Burke and Will D. Howe, 3rd rev. ed. by Irving R. Weiss, *American Authors and Books, 1640 to the Present Day* (New York: Crown Publishers, 1962, 1972), 4. Paul Gallico was a popular author of short stories and books, including *The Snow Goose* and *The Secret Front* (both 1940), as well as a noted sportswriter. He was also a screenplay writer during the war years (*Current Biography 1946,* 201). Russel Crouse, with Howard Lindsay, adapted to the stage the hugely popular *Life with Father* by Clarence Day. Lindsay and Crouse had produced a number of plays and musicals, including Cole Porter's *Anything Goes* in 1934 (*Current Biography 1941,* 187–189). Later, they would write the script for Rodgers and Hammerstein's *The Sound of Music* (1960).

28. Hobby's husband William, former governor of Texas.

29. Major General Miller G. White was assistant chief of staff for personnel. It was his recommendation, in November 1942, that the WAAC increase its recruits to 150,000 by July of 1943. He was a strong advocate for transferring the WAAC to full military status and testified on its behalf in Congress when S495 was being considered (see Bandel's letter of 4 March, describing the issue). Later in 1943, when recruiting was flagging, he personally took part in recruitment conferences to try to devise solutions to the problem (Treadwell, 98, 120, 231).

30. General Karl Truesdell, Sr., was their host in Fort Leavenworth. He was commandant of the Command and General Staff School there.

31. *Lavender and Old Lace* (1902) by Myrtle Reed was a sentimental love story with genteel, old-fashioned characters.

32. Duncan was driver for Hobby and Bandel on their trip to England in November 1942.

33. Fannie Hurst wrote *Stardust* (1919), *Lummox* (1923), *A President Is Born* (1927), and her autobiography, *Anatomy of Me* (1958). She has been grouped with Willa Cather and Edith Wharton as one of the influential woman authors of the early to mid–twentieth century. See Stephanie Lewis Thompson, *Influencing America's Tastes: Realism in the Works of Wharton, Cather, and Hurst* (Gainesville: University Press of Florida, 2002).

34. That is, her new lieutenant's bars.

35. Author of many books, including *Ariel: The Life of Shelley* (1924) and biographies of several other English and French literary and political notables.

36. There are a number of "Native Sons" organizations, including the Native Sons of the Golden West and other groups with ancestors who were westward immigrants.

37. Colwell was sufficiently impressed with Bandel to send her a letter of congratulation upon her promotion to major in May, saying he was "proud to know" her (letter, Colwell, 6 May 1943, Bandel Papers).

38. Goodman published a group of articles written by correspondents during the war: *While You Were Gone: A Report on Wartime Life in the United States,* by Allan Nevins, Paul Gallico, Anna W. M. Wolf, and others (New York: Simon and Schuster, 1946).

39. Toni Frissell was from New York City, a well-known photographer whose works had appeared in *Life, Look,* and *Vogue* magazines; see Jules Heller and Nancy G. Heller, *North American Women Artists of the Twentieth Century: A Biographical Dictionary,* Garland Reference Library of the Humanities, vol. 1219 (New York: Garland Publishing, 1995). She volunteered to serve as a Red Cross photographer in Europe in 1941, documenting the ravages of war on the people of England and Scotland, and served as the official photographer of the WAC, making photographs used by the Office of War Information to publicize the WAC (*Current Biography 1947,* 220–221).

40. Runbeck was a writer of both fiction and nonfiction, publishing in the leading popular magazines of the day (*Current Biography 1952,* 508).

41. Bandel reveals in a later letter that President Roosevelt and General Marshall were both at the review.

42. That is, a colonel's insignia.

43. Annie V. Gardner was assigned to the U.S. Army Services of Supply (USASOS) in the Southwest Pacific in 1944 (Treadwell, 424).

44. Bandel, personal communication.

45. Fort Oglethorpe, Georgia, was the site of the then newly activated Third WAAC Training Center.

46. The WAAC was about to select auxiliaries who had received specialist training to go to OCS, to head WAAC specialist units.

47. Brown worked at the *Arizona Daily Star,* in the clippings "morgue."

48. The incident to which she refers took place off the coast of North Africa; see Bandel's letter of 4 April.

Chapter 4. Chief Air-WAAC Officer

1. See chapter 1, letter of 14 August 1942.

2. Letters and telegrams in Bandel Papers, May 1943. The Green Guards are mentioned in Treadwell, 15–16.

3. General Arnold was chief of the Army Air Corps, and Army Air Forces from 1938 to 1946. He was commanding general of the Allied Air Forces during the war (Treadwell, 132, 228, 250, 282).

4. Bandel, Oral History, 14. The AAF had four commands that formed units for service overseas as well as six others: Flying Training, Service, Troop Carrier, etc., some of which are mentioned in this chapter. They were all countrywide in scope, which is one reason why Bandel traveled so widely as the Air-WAC officer. General Brehon Summervell, commanding general of the SOS, under which the WAAC was subsumed initially, was particularly unreceptive to policy proposals from WAAC headquarters. After many frustrating obstructions and mutual disagreements on policy, Sommervell recommended that the WAAC be transferred to the Office of the General Staff, stating that policy issues with the WAAC were wider in scope than the SOS. Hobby concurred (Treadwell, 53, 270, 272).

5. Treadwell, 283.

6. *New York Daily News,* June 1943, as cited in the 10 June article in the *New York Times* that condemned the outright misinformation in the article.

7. Treadwell, 198–199, 216.

8. Bandel comments on this problem in her interview, Oral History, 59–60, and in Treadwell, 207.

9. Treadwell, chap. 11, "The Slander Campaign." Stimson's position and a denunciation of O'Donnell's article was published in the *New York Times*, 10 June 1943.

10. Treadwell, 221, 224–228.

11. Copy of a letter, Colonel Branch to Oveta Culp Hobby, 10 May 1943, in Bandel Papers.

12. Bernice Cosulich of the *Arizona Daily Star* to Mrs. Bandel, 24 March 1944, Bandel Papers.

13. Captain Mary Priscilla Spangenberg, 11 May 1943, Bandel Papers.

14. The president's famous dog.

15. Laura Zametkin Hobson (1900–1986) wrote fiction for many popular magazines of the day before publication of her first novel, *The Trespassers* (1943), which spoke against the quota system of immigration that barred many Jewish refugees entry to the United States. Her 1947 novel *Gentleman's Agreement,* a story of anti-Semitism in America, is perhaps her best known; 20th Century Fox made it into a film the same year.

16. Sons of Lena Burges of the *Arizona Star* and *Citizen.* The graduation was from radio school, so Bandel's exclamation here may be a comment on the frequent placement of trained Waacs in positions where their skills were not used.

17. That is, what insignia Bandel would be wearing as head of Air-WAAC.

18. Major Florence Jepson was assistant to Major General Joseph N. Dalton, head of ASF, in the Military Personnel Division (Treadwell, 260).

19. Mrs. Bandel, a former actress, refers to William Shakespeare.

20. Bandel's father had died in 1931.

21. Mrs. Bandel alludes to Bandel's birth thirty years earlier.

22. Dorothy Muni was one of the first attendees of the Command and General Staff School, and first in the OCS class of which Bandel was second.

23. Possibly Captain Hazel Miller, WAAC director for the Ninth Service Command.

24. The commandant of the Command and General Staff School from 1942 to 1945 was Major General Karl Truesdell, Sr. Boyd L. Dastrup, *The US Army Command and General Staff College: A Centennial History* (Manhattan, Kans.: Sunflower University Press, 1982), 149–150.

25. The G-3 Division of the army was Operations and Training; G-3 was also an abbreviation for the assistant chief of staff for that division.

26. Test of Operations and Medical Evaluation?

27. C.G.: commanding general.

28. Colonel Robert L. Branch was head of the WAAC Planning Service, one of the two new organizational divisions at WAAC headquarters, the other being Operations. The reorganization of which this letter writes had been accomplished earlier in the year, abolishing a previous setup of General Somervell's, which was an administrative failure (Treadwell, 111, 175).

29. Major Elizabeth Smith was transferred to the Military Training Division of ASF from WAAC headquarters at the time of integration into the army, and the administration of WAC training centers was transferred to the service commands, part of a move to decentralize WAC administration generally. Mostly, this was approved by

Hobby and her officers, as they had advocated it much earlier. Although Smith's specific reasons for opposing the move aren't clear, she did note in a postwar history of WAC training that various special recruiting plans at this time made planning for training and assignment of Wacs difficult (Treadwell 260, 655).

30. Treadwell was referring to St. Elizabeth's Hospital for the Insane, a federal facility in Washington, D.C.

31. General Whitten was director of base services at Air Forces headquarters at that time. As assistant chief of M, M, and D., General Echols was indeed occupied with other things: he was one of the chief directors of the production of airplanes and other materials for the air war (air force biography Web site, http://www.af.mil/lib/bio/).

32. *The Army Hour* was carried by NBC radio during the war for the U.S. Army: it brought news of the war to the home front, as well as airing interviews of both officers and enlisted men. "Col. Edward M. Kirby," in *Transmitter,* vol. 2 (2000), online magazine of the Library of American Broadcasting, http://www.lib.umd.edu/LAB/TRANSMITTER/.

33. Anna Wilson was eventually in charge of more than eight thousand Wacs and was promoted to lieutenant colonel shortly after Bandel, in January 1944 (Treadwell, 135, 380).

34. Wilson was to note in the European Theater of Operations (ETO) board report after the war that too much of her time was spent at social and public relations work, and not enough at directing the WAC (Treadwell, 381).

35. Jessica Dragonette, Bandel's sister-in-law and a prominent concert soprano.

36. Although it is uncertain to what letter Brown is referring, General Miller G. White played a major role in persuading Congress to enact the bill to integrate the WAAC into the army, as well as personally participating in the WAC recruitment campaign later in 1943 (Treadwell, 98, 118, 231).

37. Treadwell was one of Bandel's Air-WAAC officers.

38. Bandel's birthday was in July.

39. Betty Clague was the WAAC/WAC staff director (Treadwell, 165).

40. Treadwell, 203–204. The journalist responsible for the smear was John O'Donnell of the *New York Post* (rebuked in an article in the *New York Times,* 10 June 1943).

41. Mitchel Air Force Base was in Hempstead, Long Island. It was the site of the First Air Force, responsible for air defense planning and organization along the eastern seaboard. It also trained personnel for air defense tactical units overseas (cited from the Web site for the base, http://www.hempsteadplains.com/mfhst00.htm).

42. That is, Anne's brother Anthony.

43. Operations, Commitments, and Requirements, Army Air Forces.

44. According to Bandel, the script was never produced.

45. Brown later reapplied and was accepted. She went on to work in public relations and was sent to India during the war (Brown obituary, *Arizona Daily Star,* 9 July 2001).

46. Brown is referring to those Waacs who chose to resign during conversion to army status rather than reenlist.

47. PRO: Public Relations Office.

48. OTI: Office of Technical Information. A small OTI within WAAC headquarters was responsible for publicizing the WAAC in the news media and for aiding in recruiting (Treadwell, 194, 262).

Chapter 5. Lieutenant Colonel, Regular Army

1. Letter, Colonel Hobby to all WAC recruiters, 20 September 1943, as quoted in Treadwell, 237.
2. Treadwell, 235.
3. Treadwell, 258–263.
4. Bandel interview, Oral History, 8; Bandel, "The WAC Program in the Army Air Forces," 30.
5. Bandel, Oral History, 9.
6. Bandel, Oral History, 16.
7. Letter, General Giles to Bandel, 3 March 1944, Bandel Papers.
8. Westray Battle Boyce, WAAC staff director for the Fourth Service Command.
9. That is, staying out in the field visiting WAC units under her supervision. At the time, Clapham was Boyce's commanding officer.
10. Captain Bernice Keplinger of Tucson.
11. Hoffman was a subordinate in Rice's office.
12. The Holabird Signal Depot near Baltimore deployed over one hundred Waacs. Edgewood Arsenal in Maryland was part of the Chemical Warfare Service (CWS) of the army. At Edgewood and other CWS installations, Wacs played a considerable role in the development of chemical and biological warfare weapons and decontamination techniques (Treadwell, 316, 322, 325).
13. Captain Mildred McAfee, head of the WAVES.
14. Gretchen Thorpe was director of public relations for the WAAC; Hammick was in the English equivalent of the WAAC, the ATS.
15. Brigadier General Madison Pearson, deputy chief of Administrative Services, Services of Supply (SOS), was the immediate superior army officer at WAAC headquarters. He was part of the February 6 conference, which included representatives from the G-3 Division, WAAC director Hobby, and SOS, which planned for expansion of the WAAC (Treadwell, 86, 122, 155).
16. "Safety pins:" her third officer/second lieutenant insignia, which her mother pinned on at her officer school graduation ceremony.
17. Freeman was WAAC staff director in the Flying Training Command. She eventually attained the rank of lieutenant colonel (Treadwell, 735n).
18. It is unclear if she is quoting from a literary work. It may be Josiah Gilbert Holland's poem "Wanted": "God give us men. The time demands strong minds, great hearts. . . . Tall men, sun-crowned, who live above the fog in public duty and in private thinking" (*Bartlett's Familiar Quotations,* 1919 ed., 730).
19. Hobby had recommended this initiative for some time. It was not until the following year that her report to General Marshall, citing the need for this education, was put into operation (Treadwell, 272–275).
20. Imperfect Latin, but Bandel probably meant "consultant for good taste, or elegance."
21. An upscale department store in downtown Washington, closed in 1996.
22. Materiel, Maintenance, and Distribution, the division under which Bandel's office was placed in the AAF.
23. Bandel is referring to her swearing in to the army.
24. Visavee: vis-à-vis, her opposite at table.

25. From Geoffrey Chaucer's *Canterbury Tales*. "Wost tu why": Middle English for "do you know why?"

26. Finney had worked at the *Arizona Daily Star* with Bandel.

27. The 2 AF: the Second Air Force Command.

28. Bernie was apparently connected with the Tucson Chamber of Commerce.

29. Mr. White was a journalist with the *Arizona Daily Star.*

30. The Midland Army Air Force Base in Midland, Texas, was the largest bombardier training base during World War II (The American Airpower Heritage Museum Web site, http://www.airpowermuseum.org/index.html).

31. Mrs. Bandel had written of Emily Brown's view that WAC officers at the Fort Des Moines Officer School were not as able as the male officers they had replaced (letter, Mrs. Bandel, 11 October 1943, Bandel Papers).

32. General Carl B. McDaniel was then wing commander of the Seventy-sixth Flying Training Wing at Smyrma (Tenn.) Army Air Field. Lieutenant General Robert W. Harper was the assistant chief of air staff for training at Army Air Corps headquarters in Washington, D.C., at that time, having served there since July 1942 in the office of the assistant chief of Air Staff for Operations (from his biography, http://www.af.mil/news/biographies/harper_rw.html).

33. Major Mary Freeman, WAC staff director, AAF Flying Training Command.

34. Lieutenant Stryker was attached to the WAC; see letter of 16 January 1943. She became an air command director later in the war (Treadwell, 735n). It is not clear what the issues were between her and Freeman. Bandel notes that they were both strong personalities, often at odds with one another (personal communication, 2003).

35. Helen Hamilton Woods, at that time at the AAF Western Flying Training Command in Santa Ana, California.

36. Patty [Mattie] Treadwell and other members of Bandel's Air-WAC staff. "L & L" are either Lillian Smoak and Libby Wooden or the two civilian office workers, Miss Lenz and Miss Lottman.

37. Pierce was one of Bandel's administrative officers.

38. This is likely to have been a bet on who would be the first lieutenant colonel in the WAC.

39. Pinks: the WAC officers' uniform.

40. Bandel must have been mistaken: Edsel Ford (1893–1943), the only son of Henry Ford, the auto manufacturer, had died in May of that year.

41. Major General James M. Bevans was chief of Air Staff for Personnel, A-1 Division. He also served on the planning board for WAC recruiting (Treadwell, 283, 688).

42. Mrs. Flaccus was probably a Tucson socialite and charitable volunteer.

43. In fact, the trip was worldwide. She is writing about AAF General Barney Giles, who had been made chief of the Air Staff in July 1943 (from "Lieutenant General Barney M. Giles" at the Web site of the USAF biography, http://www.af.mil/bios.html).

44. Bandel was the first WAC major to be promoted to lieutenant colonel. She mentions, in addition to Rice and Brown: Florence T. Newsome, assistant secretary to the General Staff; Elizabeth H. Strayhorn, senior WAC officer at Fort Oglethorpe; Army Ground Forces WAC officer Emily E. Davis; and Westray Battle Boyce of the North African Theater.

45. At this time, London was not experiencing any heavy air raids, but Wacs were serving as part of the network of air raid wardens and fire spotters. In June, the first V-1 rockets would fall in England.

46. Mount Vesuvius was in eruption in 1944.

47. Bandel alludes to Virgil's *Aeneid,* in which Aeneas of Troy, being shipwrecked off the coast of Africa, is rescued by Dido, queen of Carthage, who falls in love with him. She throws herself on a funeral pyre after Aeneas leaves her to continue on to Italy.

Chapter 6. Fighting for Wacs, Caring for Colonels

1. Letter, 27 May 1944, Bandel Papers.

2. Bandel, "The WAC Program in the Army Air Forces," 68. Arnold's letter also affirmed that there should be no conflict between soldiers, Wacs, or civilians in the Air Forces, since all were needed.

3. Treadwell, 458, 484–485, 693–694.

4. Treadwell, 458. Kenworthy (1891–1980) was a psychiatrist who taught at the Columbia University School of Social Work from 1921 to 1957. Her specialty was the field of psychiatric social work. In 1958, she would become the first woman to be elected president of the American Psychiatric Association. Phyllis J. Read and Bernard L. Witlieb, *The Book of Women's Firsts: Break-through Achievements of Almost 1000 American Women* (New York: Random House, 1992), 240.

5. Treadwell, 718.

6. Bandel is referring in part to the letter that Arnold wrote to the commanding generals, mentioned above.

7. According to Bandel, "the boys in the South Pacific ran a story [in *Guinea Gold* (New Guinea)] entitled 'Col. Oveta Culp, head of the hobbies section of the WACs, is overseas inspecting Wacs. She is accompanied by Major Betty Bandel.'" the *New Yorker* magazine quoted the headline and added, "You mean Major Betty, leader of the Bandel?" (Bandel, personal communication, and the *New Yorker,* 19 February 1944, 43).

8. Rice had breast cancer; she died shortly after her term of service in the WAC.

9. One of these "irons" was the Air-WAC recruiting campaign.

10. Rice had just been promoted to lieutenant colonel.

11. Alexander (Marie Padgett) Hamilton, Bandel's mentor, was a noted Chaucer scholar.

12. The issue may have had to do with the recruitment of Wacs for overseas theaters: there were issues with the other branches of the army about filling quotas and thus possibly depleting domestic units of skilled Wacs (Bandel, "The WAC Program in the Army Air Forces," 76–77).

13. Katherine Cornell (1898–1984) and Elizabeth Patterson (1875–1966) were distinguished American actresses. Cornell was also the manager of this play. *Who's Who in the East* (Chicago: A. N. Marquis Co., 1951), 249. Bandel highlights Patterson's name because she was in the theater with Bandel's mother, Emma Frederick Bandel.

14. *Watch on the Rhine.*

15. In fact, Brown remained in public relations and was promoted to major before she left the WAC in 1945 (Women in Military Service for America Memorial Foundation, Washington, D.C.—Brown was a charter member of this organization).

16. Margaret Craighill was the first women's doctor in the Army Medical Corps, appointed in 1943 to plan for the medical care of the WAAC and army nurses. She was dean of the Women's Medical College in Philadelphia at the time. She improved both the initial physical examination of and medical care for Waacs. "Craighill, Margaret," in *Women and the Military: An Encyclopedia* (Santa Barbara, Calif.: ABC-CLIO, 1996), 84.

17. Mildred Leven, a family friend formerly of Tucson.

18. The Hollywood Guild Canteen was famous for its entertainment for servicemen, performed by film stars.

19. The Reverend Edmund A. Walsh founded the Georgetown University School of Foreign Service in 1919 (*Encyclopaedia Britannica Online,* link to Georgetown University Web page).

20. From Geoffrey Chaucer, *Canterbury Tales.* "And gladly wolde he lerne, and gladly teche." Prologue, line 310.

21. Père: Bandel's father.

22. Rice was probably visiting WAC installations in her capacity as deputy director, before Hobby returned from medical leave.

23. Frank and Lillian Gilbreth were reknowned for the development of motion study as an engineering and management technique. Their work was popularized in the book by two of their twelve children, Frank G. Gilbreth, Jr., and Ernestine Gilbreth Carey, *Cheaper by the Dozen* (New York: T. Y. Crowell Co., 1948). Mary McCleod Bethune (1875–1955) was an educator and founder of Daytona (Florida) Normal and Industrial School for Negro Girls, which later merged with Cookman Institute to form Cookman College (named Bethune-Cookman College in her honor later). President of the college from 1904 to 1942, she also founded the National Council of Negro Women in 1935, was a special adviser to President Roosevelt on minority affairs from 1936 to 1944, and vice president of the National Association of Colored People (NAACP) in 1940. From http://library.thinkquest.org/10320/Bethune.htm, and from Rackham Holt, *Mary McLeod Bethune: A Biography* (Garden City, N.Y.: Doubleday, 1964).

24. Growing up in Tucson, Bandel undoubtedly went to school with children of military personnel.

25. Red points were part of the rationing system. During the war, many items were rationed, including tires, automobiles, sugar, gasoline, fuel oil, coffee, meats, and processed foods. "Office of Price Administration," *The Columbia Encyclopedia,* 6th edition (New York: Columbia University Press, 2001).

26. A long-time and influential U.S. senator from Georgia, Richard B. Russell, Jr. (1897–1971), a New Deal Democrat in most respects, had led a filibuster campaign against the antilynching bill in Congress in the 1930s. Returning from a tour of war areas in 1943, he vociferously criticized the lack of postwar planning he said he had found in the U.S. military there. He supported America's participation in the early United Nations (*Current Biography 1949,* 536–539). Presumably, Bandel refers to Sinclair's *Babbitt,* in which the protagonist is a nice but provincial person.

27. Peggy Waddell of Tucson, and at the time of this letter working in the Red Cross.

28. Genevieve Forbes Herrick (1894–1962) was a prominent newspaperwoman who had served as Hobby's public relations adviser in the early days of the WAAC (Treadwell, 30, 48). A well-known "front-page" reporter in the 1920s and 1930s for the *Chicago Tribune,* she covered the Leopold-Loeb murder trial in 1924. One of her biographies notes that she came to specialize in political reporting, attending Eleanor Roosevelt's women-only news conferences regularly. During the war, she also did public relations work for the War Department, becoming chief of the magazine and book division of the Office of War Information. Joseph P. McKerns, ed., *Biographical Dictionary of American Journalism* (New York: Greenwood Press, 1989), 334–336.

Chapter 7. *"Don't Let Them Make You Dean of Women"*

1. Letter, Bandel to family, 13 April 1945, Bandel Papers.
2. Treadwell, 722–723.
3. Treadwell, 732.
4. At this time, the Allies had just captured Cologne and established a bridge across the Rhine River at Remagen, important advances in the invasion of Germany.
5. This 1945 film dramatized a rivalry in WAC Officer Candidate School between a "wealthy playgirl and an Army brat" (from Web site at http://www.eonline.com/ Facts/Movies/).
6. Jean De Reszke (1850–1935) was a renowned opera singer. David Hamilton, ed., *The Metropolitan Opera Encyclopedia: A Comprehensive Guide to the World of Opera* (New York: Simon and Schuster, 1987).
7. Major General St. Clair Street (1893–1970) was the first commander of the Continental Air Force, having served as commanding general of the Second and Third Air Force and the Thirteenth Air Force Task Force (U.S. Air Force Historical Research Agency Web site at http://www.maxwell.af.mil/au/afhra/wwwroot/personal_papers/).
8. SPARS were the women serving with the U.S. Coast Guard.
9. Wacs did march in the procession of Roosevelt's casket, from the train that brought it to Washington to where it would lie in state at the Capitol. Apparently the most senior WAC officers were not part of that. The funeral, however, took place in Hyde Park, New York, which probably explains why Hobby did not attend.
10. To the tune of "My Bonnie Lies over the Ocean" (Bandel, personal communication).
11. Fred Dragonette, Bandel's brother-in-law.
12. Erica Morini was an Austrian-born violinist who left Austria during the Nazi Anschluss, having already become a successful concert artist. *Baker's Biographical Dictionary of Musicians,* 8th ed. (New York: Macmillan, 1992), 1250, 1904.
13. Harriet Easterbrooks O'Shea (1895–1986) was a noted psychologist who taught at Purdue University from 1931 to 1964. She established the psychological clinic and a children's nursery there and was prominent in the training program for clinical psychologists. *American Psychologist* 43 (1988), obituary, 71.
14. The question was whether Hobby would be made a general.
15. Père: Bandel's father. The song: "Tarara Bandalay, Here's what we have to say: We hope you're here to stay, Tarara Bandalay," to the tune of "Tarara Boom-de-ay," a

song popular since Edwardian times and originally sung, according to its composer, Henry Sayers, in one of the St. Louis brothels (http://members.tripod.com/~snow19/flor/flor4.html).

16. Eisenhower was in Washington on June 18 to be honored for the Allied victory in Europe against Germany, culminating in the German surrender on May 8, 1945.

17. Probably General Samuel E. Anderson, who was chief of staff, Continental Air Force, Bolling Field, Washington, D.C., at that time (from the air force biography Web site, http://www.af.mil/news/biographies/anderson_se.html).

18. Probably Louis Martin Sears, a historian of U.S. foreign relations, who taught at Purdue.

19. The *Manchester Guardian* is a British weekly newspaper leaning toward a liberal/socialist view.

20. Didcoct is mentioned in earlier letters. A former Tucsonan, she was working at the State Department at the time of this letter.

21. Lieutenant Colonels Jessie Rice, assistant director and formerly regional director of the Third Service Command; Westray Battle Boyce, deputy director and formerly staff director of the Fourth Service Command; and Helen Hamilton Woods, Control Division, WAC headquarters. Lieutenant Colonel Anna Wilson may have been the fifth candidate, or Pat Chance, executive officer in the WAC Washington office.

22. Rice had been outspoken during addresses at the Personnel Administration School in Purdue, for example, in her criticism of the WAAC Table of Organization, which assigned women to relatively menial duties even if they were highly educated professionals (Treadwell, 146 and 146n).

23. V-J Day: the day that Japan surrendered. The United States had dropped atomic bombs on Hiroshima and Nagasaki on August 6 and 9, respectively.

24. In addition to other duties, Pat Chance wrote the monthly *WAC Newsletter* (Treadwell, 481, 483).

25. Bandel is referring, of course, to the British Conservative Party's defeat in the general election in July. In her final quote, she is probably paraphrasing the biblical passage in Isaiah 2:4: "Nation shall not lift sword against nation; neither shall they learn war any more," or perhaps the African-American spiritual, "Ain't gonna study war no more." Also, having majored in music in college, Bandel may be recalling the libretto from Felix Mendelssohn's *Elijah,* chorus 9: "Blessed are the men who fear Him: they ever walk in the ways of peace," from the Old Testament Psalm 128:1).

Postscript

1. Letter, Bandel to Mrs. Bandel, 30 August 1945, Bandel Papers.
2. Letter, 30 August 1945, Bandel Papers.
3. Bandel, "The WAC Program in the Army Air Forces," 51–52n.
4. Rice's statement is mentioned in Bandel's letter of 5 May 1945.
5. Bandel, Oral History, 10.
6. Bandel, Oral History, 13.
7. Treadwell, 764.

SUGGESTED READING

Anderson, Karen. *Wartime Women: Sex Roles, Family Relations, and the Status of Women During World War II.* Westport, Conn.: Greenwood Press, 1981.

Earley, Charity Adams. *One Woman's Army: A Black Officer Remembers the WAC.* College Station: Texas A&M University Press, 1989.

Fenner, Lorry M. "Ideology and Amnesia: The Public Debate on Women in the American Military, 1940–1973." Ph.D. dissertation, University of Michigan, 1995.

Grahn, Elna Hilliard. *In the Company of Wacs.* Manhattan, Kans.: Sunflower University Press, 1993.

Green, Blanche. *Growing Up in the WAC: Letters to My Sister, 1944–1946.* New York: Vantage Press, 1987.

Hartmann, Susan M. *The Home Front and Beyond: American Women in the 1940s.* Boston: Twayne Publishers, 1982.

Henderson, Aileen Kilgore. *Stateside Soldier: Life in the Women's Army Corps, 1944–1945.* Columbia: University of South Carolina Press, 2001.

Holm, Jeanne M. *Women in the Military: An Unfinished Revolution.* Rev. ed. Novato, Calif.: Presidio Press, 1992.

Litoff, Judy Barrett, and David C. Smith, eds. *We're in This War, Too: World War II Letters from American Women in Uniform.* New York: Oxford University Press, 1994.

Mayer, Leisa D. *Creating GI Jane: Sexuality and Power in the Women's Army Corps during World War II.* New York: Columbia University Press, 1996.

Moore, Brenda L. *To Serve My Country, to Serve My Race: The Story of the Only African American WACS Stationed Overseas during World War II.* New York: New York University Press, 1996.

Morden, Bettie. *The Women's Army Corps, 1945–1978.* Washington, D.C.: Center of Military History, U.S. Army, 1990. Available online through the Center of Military History, U.S. Army, http://www.army.mil/cmh-pg/books/wac/index.htm.

Randolph, Margaret, et al. *Behind the Lines: Gender and the Two World Wars.* New Haven, Conn.: Yale University Press, 1987.

Treadwell, Mattie E. *The Women's Army Corps.* In *United States Army in World War II, Special Studies.* Washington, D.C.: Office of the Chief of Military History, Department of the Army, 1954, c1953.

Bibliographies and Reference Works

Friedl, Vicki L. *Women in the United States Military, 1901–1995: A Research Guide and Annotated Bibliography.* Research Guides in Military Studies, no. 9. Westport, Conn.: Greenwood Press, 1996.

Huls, Mary Ellen. "Women in the Armed Forces." In *United States Government Documents on Women, 1800–1990: A Comprehensive Bibliography.* Vol. 2, *Labor.* Westport, Conn.: Greenwood Press, 1993.

Sherrow, Victoria. *Women and the Military: An Encyclopedia.* Santa Barbara, Calif.: ABC-CLIO, 1996.

INDEX

Adams, Franklin P. (Writers' War Board), 73, 200n

African-Americans: in the WAC and other military services, xxi–xxii; at White House, 38. *See also* Bethune, Mary McLeod; Racial and ethnic attitudes

Air-WAAC/WAC: Air-WAC companies, 164 (*see also* Headquarters companies); early organization of, 103–104, 106; esprit de corps in, 151–152; first Air-WAAC officers (March 1943), 74; officers, in air commands, 97, 104, 110, 125, 173; problems in the field, 134–135; WAAC specialists, 74; WAAC specialists, problems of, 108; women pilots in, World War II, xvii

Air-WAAC/WAC headquarters staff, 109–111, 119, 137, 170–171; AAF Military Personnel office, 106; Bandel assigned as Air-WAAC officer, 97 (*see also* Bandel, Betty); Elizabeth Wooden, officer in Bandel's office, 133. *See also* Elrod, Mary; Treadwell, Mattie; Varn, Caroline

Air-WAAC/WAC planning and administration, 114, 189; conferences, with AAF officers, 126–127, 162, 163; conferences, recruiting, 128; conferences, WAC staff directors, 106; demobilization, 167, 189; issues and problems, 198n; recruiting planning, 128, 130, 152

All-States Recruiting Campaign: Emily Brown writes articles on WAC for, 131; Jessie Rice creates, 120, 123–124; success of, xx, 120, 135–136

American Legion Auxiliary: recruiting and publicity for WAAC, 30–31

American Women's Association: supports WAAC/WAC, 49

Arizona Daily Star: publicizes WAAC, 54; staff sends Christmas gifts to Bandel, 56

Armored Replacement Training Center (AGF): Waacs at, 82

Army Air Forces (AAF): air commands described, 201n; airbases, 203n, 205n; Air-WAAC/WAC officers, in air commands, 97, 110, 165; Alliance Airbase (Nebr.), 115–117, 131–132; general officers, 135, 203n, 205n, 208n; Maj. Gen. Anderson, 181; Gen. James M. Bevans, 137, 205n (*see also* Arnold, Henry H.; Giles, Maj. Gen. Barney M.); problems of WAAC/WAC administration, 198n; and problems with Air-WAAC, 65, 198n; staff courses, on Air-WAC, 152–153. *See also* Air-WAAC/WAC

Army Medical Corps: Maj. Margaret Craighill, head of women doctors in, 155, 207n

Army Nurse Corps, xxiii, 39; Col. Julia O. Flikke, 39, 196n; founded (1901), xiv; and military status, xiv, 59

Army Recruiting Service: WAAC recruiting and publicity, 68

Army Service Forces (ASF): Control Division, 78; Finance Department, 48; Special Services Division, and WAAC/WAC publicity, 63; and Writers' War Board, 73

Arnold, Henry H. (commanding general, Army Air Force): Bandel on collaboration with, 146, 152, 185; support for Air-WAAC/WAC, 95, 106–107, 121, 145

Ashby, Hannah: first WAAC officer training class, 18

Assignments, auxiliaries and noncommissioned officers: clerical, typists, 21, 24, 58; communications, 21; field companies, 81, 82, 117; food preparation, 4, 23, 54, 68, 141; and foreign language abilities, 68, 132–133; Headquarters companies, 48, 74, 159; motor transport, truck drivers, 4, 21, 47; musicians, 83; photo laboratory technicians, 132; problems with, 74–75, 108, 121, 132, 199n; radio operators, 61–62, 74–75, 116–118, 132; radio operators, in AAF, 108; Signal Corps, 21, 25–26; statisticians, 24; supply sergeants, 46; telephone operators, 121

Assignments, officers: as company commanders, 20–21; as company commanders,

Training Centers: planning conferences, commandants, 76; supply shortages at, 28. *See also* First WAAC/WAC Training Center; Second WAAC/WAC Training Center; Third WAAC/WAC Training Center

Travel, official, 30–31, 33–34, 54; inspection tours, worldwide, 139–144; per diem for, 48; priority, 54

Treadwell, Mattie ("Pattie"): on Bandel's Air-WAAC/WAC staff, 105, 109, 119, 139; first CGS School class, 104; instructor, School for WAC Personnel Administration, 172; joins WAC headquarters staff, 148, 149; writes and produces play, 112–114

Truesdell, Brig. Gen. Karl, Sr.: commandant, Command and General Staff School, 49, 75, 202n

Tuke, Binda: family friend in Tucson, 194n

Tyndall, Maj. Gen. Robert, 75

Uniforms and dress, WAAC/WAC, 9, 195n, 196n; Bandel on officers' wearing uniforms not worn by enlisted, 182; first Officer Training School, 10; "pinks," 37, 46; satires about, by Wacs, 83, 189; specialist variations, Armored Forces, 82; supplies of, at Ft. Des Moines, 47; use of, post war, 183

U.S. Army General Staff: G-1 (Assistant Chief, Personnel), and WAAC organization, 67, 145; G-3 (Assistant Chief, Operations), 202n; G-3, and WAAC organization, 67; Florence ("Bessie") Newsome, secretary to, 69, 199n

U.S. Army service commands: WAAC command problems at, 84; WAAC/WAC directors, 58, 84–85, 197n

Van Dalsem, Arthyeta: officer on Hobby's staff, 32, 36, 55, 74; transferred to Air-WAAC (March 1943), 74

Varn, Caroline (officer, Air-WAC staff), 104, 105, 110, 114–115, 119, 149; inspects Air-WAC recruitment in field, 134–135; on problems in Air-WAC installations, 134–135

Waacs/Wacs, attitudes and morale: esprit de corps, 9, 11, 13, 14, 20, 59; in Headquarters companies, 159; reasons for joining Corps, 1, 150, 155; at School for WAC Personnel Administration, 170–179 (*see also* Camaraderie and teamwork); songs and singing, 5, 13, 15. *See also* Attitudes of Waacs/Wacs, toward service in the military; Auxiliaries; Officers

Waacs/Wacs, injuries and deaths, 123; first WAAC contingent, torpedoed at sea, 76, 86; posthumous award, 174

Waacs/Wacs, prewar occupations of, 7, 8, 22, 24, 80; lawyers, 71; newspaperwomen, 141 (*see also* Bandel, Betty; Brown, Emily); religious orders, 83; teachers, 3, 182

WAAC/WAC: anniversary celebrations, first officer training class, 104, 125, 189; director (*see* Directors, WAAC/WAC); Headquarters companies, 48; lack of authority within army command structure, 105; lack of authority, Bandel on, 145, 148; lack of authority, circumvention of by WAC administration, 146, 148, 198n; lack of authority, effect on morale, 148, 186; married women in, 15, 141 (*see also* Hobby, Col. Oveta Culp; Reilly, Lillian)

WAAC/WAC, organization and planning: conferences, National Civilian Advisory Committee, 158, 163, 165; conferences, of staff directors, 106, 163, 165; conferences, planning for expansion of WAAC, 204n; conferences, planning of training centers, 76 (*see also* Air-WAAC/WAC planning and administration, conferences); postwar planning, 166; reorganization (1943), Planning Division, 102, 202n; reorganization (1944), and move to ASF G-1 Division, 146; successes, administrative and planning, xx. *See also* WAAC/WAC Headquarters; Women's Army Auxiliary Corps

WAAC/WAC Headquarters (Washington, D.C.), 27, 29, 57; administrative problems at, 198n; Bandel on problems with army, 99; conversion from WAAC to WAC, planning and policy for, 71; moves to Army General Staff (1944), 146, 149; moves to Pentagon, 40; reorganization (1943), and Army Planning Division, 102; teamwork of staff at, 58, 69, 72; work schedule, 36, 53, 64, 162

WAAC/WAC Headquarters staff, 30, 35, 69; Brown, Mary-Agnes, WAC executive director, 140; Col. Thomas B. Catron, executive officer, 195n; Helen Gruber, administrative aide, 35, 39, 195n; Col. J. Noel Macy,